Appalachian Trail Guide to Tennessee-North Carolina

D1280723

Appalachian Trail Guide to Tennessee-North Carolina

Kevin Edgar
Field Editor

Tenth Edition

Appalachian Trail Conference
Harpers Ferry

942570

Published by the Appalachian Trail Conference
P.O. Box 807
Harpers Ferry, West Virginia 25425

Tenth edition
Printed in the United States of America

ISBN 0-917953-52-5

Preface

The *Appalachian Trail Guide to Tennessee-North Carolina* contains a generalized description and detailed Trail data in both directions for the Appalachian Trail from Damascus, Virginia, just north of the Virginia-Tennessee boundary, to the southern end of Great Smoky Mountains National Park. It includes information on the Unaka and Pisgah mountain ranges and side trails in the Great Smokies.

The Trail is described in three major sections: the Trail from Damascus to Sams Gap, Tennessee-North Carolina; the Trail from Sams Gap to Davenport Gap, Tennessee-North Carolina; and Trail in the Great Smoky Mountains National Park, from Davenport Gap to Fontana Dam, North Carolina.

Special thanks to field editor Kevin Edgar of Kingsport, Tennessee, for over-all coordination of this guidebook. The Trail data for the segment from Damascus to Spivey Gap were reviewed by Darrol S. Nickels of the Tennessee Eastman Hiking Club, and the segment from Spivey Gap to the Pigeon River was reviewed by Lewis Blodgett of the Carolina Mountain Club. Richard Ketelle of the Smoky Mountains Hiking Club reviewed the data for the A.T. and side trails in the Great Smoky Mountains National Park. Supportive material was added to the basic Trail data by Raymond F. Hunt, Jr., and Collins Chew, both of the Tennessee Eastman Hiking Club.

Constant changes occur along the Trail route. Those who observe changes in approaches, accommodations, new trails, or anything affecting the data in the guide are asked to report such findings to: Editor, *Appalachian Trail Guide to Tennessee-North Carolina*, Appalachian Trail Conference, P.O. Box 807, Harpers Ferry, W.Va. 25425-0807.

Contents

Preface v
Notice to All Trail Users ix
Safety and Security x
How to Use This Guide xi

The Appalachian Trail 1
    Trail History 1
    Maintaining Clubs 4

General Information 5
    Trail Marking 5
    Trail Relocations 5
    Water 6
    Equipment 6
    Getting Lost 6
    Distress Signals 7
    Pests 8
    Parking 8
    Hunting 8
    Trail Ethics 9
    Shelters 10
    Campfires 11
    Group Hikes and Special Events 11
    Publications 12

First Aid Along the Trail 13
    General Emergencies 13
    Chilling and Freezing Emergencies 15
    Heat Emergencies 17
    Artificial Respiration 18
    Lyme Disease 19
    Lightning Strikes 19
    Snakebites 20
    First-Aid Kit 22
    References 22

The Southern Appalachians 23
    Geography 24
    Geologic History 25
    Geology Along the Trail 28
    Plants and Animals 30
    Spruce-Fir Forest 30
    Balds 31
    Hardwood Forest 31
    Social History 33

Trail Route 37
    National Forests 38
    Great Smoky Mountains National Park 38
    Game Preserves 38
    Maps of the Trail Route 39
    Shelters 39
    Suggestions for Extended Trips 39
    Services for Hikers 40

Damascus, Virginia, to Sams Gap, Tennessee-North Carolina 41
    Section One: Damascus to U.S. 421 (Low Gap) 43
    Section Two: U.S. 421 (Low Gap) to Tenn. 91 52
    Holston Mountain Side Trail 57
    Section Three: Tenn. 91 to Watauga Dam Road 60
    Section Four: Watauga Dam Road to Dennis Cove Road 68
    Section Five: Dennis Cove Road to U.S. 19E 81
    Section Six: U.S. 19E to Carvers Gap 96
    Section Seven: Carvers Gap to Hughes Gap 109
    Section Eight: Hughes Gap to Iron Mountain Gap 115
    Section Nine: Iron Mountain Gap to Nolichucky River 122
    Section Ten: Nolichucky River to Spivey Gap 134
    Section Eleven: Spivey Gap to Sams Gap 142

Sams Gap to Davenport Gap 153
    Section Twelve: Sams Gap to Devil Fork Gap 155
    Section Thirteen: Devil Fork Gap to Allen Gap 161
    Section Fourteen: Allen Gap to Hot Springs 172
    Section Fifteen: Hot Springs to Max Patch Road 182
    Section Sixteen: Max Patch Road to Davenport Gap 192

Great Smoky Mountains National Park 200
    Geology of the Appalachian Trail in the Great
        Smoky Mountains National Park 205
    Section Seventeen: Davenport Gap to Newfound Gap 209
    Section Eighteen: Newfound Gap to Little Tennessee River 222
    Side Trails of the Great Smoky Mountains National Park 238

Important Addresses 245
Summary of Distances 247
Index 252

Notice To All Trail Users

The information contained in this publication is the result of the best effort of the publisher, using information available to it at the time of printing. Changes resulting from maintenance work and relocations are constantly occurring, and, therefore, no published route can be regarded as precisely accurate at the time you read this notice.

Notices of pending relocations are indicated. Maintenance of the Trail is conducted by volunteers and maintaining clubs listed in the guidebooks, and questions about the exact route of the Trail should be addressed to the maintaining clubs or to the Appalachian Trail Conference, Washington and Jackson Streets, P.O. Box 807, Harpers Ferry, West Virginia 25425-0807; telephone, (304) 535-6331. On the Trail, please pay close attention to—and follow—the white blazes and any directional signs.

Responsibility for Safety

It is extremely important to plan your hike, especially in places where water is scarce. Purify drinking water drawn from any source. Water purity cannot be guaranteed. The Appalachian Trail Conference and the various maintaining clubs attempt to locate good sources of water along the Trail but have no control over these sources and cannot, in any sense, be responsible for the quality of the water at any given time. You must determine the safety of all water you consume.

Certain risks are inherent in any Appalachian Trail hike. Each A.T. user must accept personal responsibility for his or her safety while on the Trail. The Appalachian Trail Conference and its member maintaining clubs cannot ensure the safety of any hiker on the Trail, and, when undertaking a hike on the Trail, each user thereby assumes the risk for any accident, illness, or injury that might occur on the Trail.

Enjoy your hike, but please take all appropriate precautions for your safety and well-being.

Safety and Security

Although criminal acts are probably less common on the Appalachian Trail than in most other human environments, they do occur. Crimes of violence, up to and including murder and rape, have taken place over the years. It should be noted, however, that such serious crimes on the A.T. have a frequency rate on the order of perhaps one per year or less. Even if such events are less common on the Trail than elsewhere, they can be more difficult to deal with because of the remoteness of most of the Trail. When hiking, you must assume the need for at least the same level of prudence as you would exercise if walking the streets of a strange city or an unknown neighborhood.

A few elementary suggestions can be noted. Above all, it is best not to hike alone. Be cautious of strangers. Be sure that family and/or friends know your planned itinerary and timetable. If you customarily use a "Trail name," your home contacts should know what it is. Although telephones are rarely handy along the Trail, if you can reach one, ask the operator to connect you to the state police if you are the victim of, or a witness to, a crime.

The carrying of firearms is **not** recommended. The risks of accidental injury or death far outweigh any self-defense value that might result from arming oneself. In any case, guns are illegal on national parklands and in certain other jurisdictions as well.

The Appalachian Trail Conference, with the cooperation of Trail clubs, has embarked on a program of developing a more formal emergency information network. When complete, it will result in the posting of emergency information at shelters and other key points along the Trail. Pertinent information will be included in future editions of this and other guidebooks and will be publicized in other ways as well.

In the meantime, be prudent and cautious, without allowing common sense to slip into paranoia.

How to Use This Guide

The Trail data in this guide have been divided into 16 Tennessee-North Carolina sections: from Damascus, Virginia, to Davenport Gap, and then through the Great Smoky Mountains National Park. These sections are separated by highway crossings or other geographical features.

The chapters for each Trail section are divided into three parts. The first part includes general information needed primarily for planning. This material is arranged under individual headings in the following order:

Brief Description of Section
Road Approaches
Public Transportation
Maps
Shelters and Campsites
Supplies and Services
Public Accommodations

The detailed "Trail Description," the actual guide to the footpath, follows in two parts. Data are given first for walking south on the Trail and then for walking north. Trail data are presented in both directions of travel so hikers do not have to mentally reverse Trail descriptions. A column of distances on the left gives the mileage from the start of the section to important points along the Trail. Each point (such as stream crossings, shelters, summits, or important turns) is briefly described, followed by directions to the next point.

The Appalachian Trail

The Appalachian Trail (A.T.) is a continuous, marked footpath extending 2,143 miles from Katahdin, a granite monolith in the central Maine wilderness, south to Springer Mountain in Georgia, along the crest of the Appalachian mountain range.

The Trail traverses mostly public land in 14 states. Virginia has the longest section, with 545 miles, while West Virginia has the shortest, almost 26 miles along the Virginia-West Virginia boundary and a short swing into Harpers Ferry at the Maryland border. The highest elevation along the Trail is in this section; 6,643 feet at Clingmans Dome in the Great Smoky Mountains. The Trail is only slightly above sea level near its crossing of the Hudson River in New York.

Trail History

Credit for establishing the Trail belongs to three leaders and countless volunteers. The first proposal for the Trail to appear in print was an article by regional planner Benton MacKaye of Shirley, Massachusetts, entitled, "An Appalachian Trail, a Project in Regional Planning," in the October 1921 issue of the *Journal of the American Institute of Architects*. He envisioned a footpath along the Appalachian ridge line where urban people could retreat to nature.

MacKaye's challenge kindled considerable interest, but, at the time, most of the outdoor organizations that could participate in constructing such a trail were east of the Hudson River. Four existing trail systems could be incorporated into an A.T. The Appalachian Mountain Club (AMC) maintained an excellent series of trails in New England, but most ran north-south; the Trail could not cross New Hampshire until the chain of huts built and operated by the AMC permitted an east-west alignment. In Vermont, the southern 100 miles of the Long Trail, then being developed in the Green Mountains, were connected to the White Mountains by the trails of the Dartmouth Outing Club.

In 1923, a number of area hiking clubs that had formed the New York-New Jersey Trail Conference opened the first new section of the A.T., in the Harriman-Bear Mountain section of Palisades Interstate Park.

The Appalachian Trail Conference (ATC) was formed in 1925 to stimulate greater interest in MacKaye's idea and coordinate the clubs' work in choosing and building the route. The Conference remains a nonprofit educational organization of individuals and clubs of volunteers dedicated to maintaining, managing, and protecting the Appalachian Trail.

Although interest in the Trail spread to Pennsylvania and New England, little further work was done until 1926, when retired Judge Arthur Perkins of Hartford, Connecticut, began persuading groups to locate and cut the footpath through the wilderness. His enthusiasm provided the momentum that carried the Trail idea forward.

The southern states had few trails and even fewer clubs. The "skyline" route followed by the A.T. in the South was developed largely within the new national forests. A number of clubs were formed in various parts of the southern Appalachians to take responsibility for the Trail there.

Perkins interested Myron H. Avery in the Trail. Avery, chairman of the Conference from 1931 to 1952, enlisted the aid and coordinated the work of hundreds of volunteers who completed the Trail by August 14, 1937, when a Civilian Conservation Corps crew opened the last section (on the ridge between Spaulding and Sugarloaf mountains in Maine).

At the eighth meeting of the ATC, in June 1937, Conference member Edward B. Ballard successfully proposed a plan for an "Appalachian Trailway" that would set apart an area on each side of the Trail, dedicated to the interests of those who travel on foot.

Steps taken to effect this long-range protection program culminated first in an October 15, 1938, agreement between the National Park Service and the U.S. Forest Service for the promotion of an Appalachian Trailway, through the relevant national parks and forests, extending one mile on each side of the Trail. Within this zone, no new parallel roads would be built or any other incompatible development allowed. Timber cutting would not be permitted within 200 feet of the Trail. Similar agreements, creating a zone one-quarter mile in width, were signed with most states through which the Trail passes.

After World War II, the encroachments of highways, housing developments, and summer resorts caused many relocations, and the problem of maintaining the Trail's wilderness character became more severe.

In 1968, Congress established a national system of trails and designated the Appalachian Trail and the Pacific Crest Trail as the initial scenic-trail components. The National Trails System Act directs the secretary of the interior, in consultation with the secretary of agriculture, to administer the Appalachian Trail primarily as a footpath and protect the Trail against incompatible activities and the use of motorized vehicles. Provision was also made for acquiring rights-of-way for the Trail, both inside and outside the boundaries of federally administered areas.

In 1970, supplemental agreements under the act—among the National Park Service, the U.S. Forest Service, and the Appalachian Trail Conference—established the specific responsibilities of these organizations for initial mapping, selection of rights-of-way, relocations, maintenance, development, acquisition of land, and protection of a permanent Trail. Agreements also were signed between the park service and the various states, encouraging them to acquire and protect a right-of-way for the Trail outside federal land.

Slow progress of federal efforts and lack of initiative by some states led Congress to strengthen the National Trails System Act. President Jimmy Carter signed the amendment, known as The Appalachian Trail Bill, on March 21, 1978.

The new legislation emphasized the need for protecting the Trail, including acquiring a corridor, and authorized $90 million for that purpose. With less than 60 miles unprotected by mid-1992, this project is expected to be completed by the end of the decade.

In 1984, the Interior Department formally delegated the responsibility of managing the A.T. corridor lands outside established parks and forests to the Appalachian Trail Conference. The Conference and its clubs retain primary responsibility for maintaining the footpath, too.

The Conference publishes information on constructing and maintaining hiking trails, official A.T. guides, and general information on hiking and trail use.

The Conference is governed by a volunteer Board of Managers, consisting of a chair, three vice chairs, a treasurer, a secretary, a corresponding secretary, and 18 members, six from each of the three regions of ATC: New England, mid-Atlantic, and southern.

The Conference membership consists of organizations that maintain the Trail or contribute to the Trail project and individuals. ATC membership provides a subscription to *Appalachian Trailway News*, published five times a year, and 15-percent discounts on publications. The Conference also issues two newsletters, *The Register*, for Trail maintainers, and *Trail Lands*, for contributors to its land-trust program, the Trust for Appalachian Trail Lands. Annual membership dues range from $18 to $30, with life memberships available for $500 (individual) or $750 (couple).

Membership forms and a complete list of publications are available from the Appalachian Trail Conference, P.O. Box 807, Harpers Ferry, W. Va. 25425, (304) 535-6331. The office is open nine a.m. to five p.m. (Eastern Time), Monday through Friday, year-round and nine to four on weekends from mid-May through October.

Maintaining Clubs

Three clubs maintain and manage the Appalachian Trail in the area described by this book.

The Tennessee Eastman Hiking Club of Kingsport, Tennessee, has volunteer responsibilities for the A.T. from Damascus, Virginia, to Spivey Gap, North Carolina. The club, founded in 1946, is sponsored by the Tennessee Eastman Recreation Club. Membership is open only to employees, although others are welcome to participate in all activities. The club has diverse interests, such as canoeing, backpacking, and day-hiking, with a strong program for maintaining and managing the Appalachian Trail.

The Carolina Mountain Club of Asheville, North Carolina, has volunteer responsibilities from Spivey Gap, North Carolina, to the Great Smoky Mountains National Park. This club, founded in 1923, also has diverse interests but devotes its major effort to protecting and maintaining the Appalachian Trail.

The Smoky Mountains Hiking Club of Knoxville, Tennessee, maintains the A.T. in the Great Smoky Mountains National Park in cooperation with the park staff.

General Information

Hikers who use the Appalachian Trail for more than day-hiking need a thorough understanding of the Trail and should study the introductory parts of this guide carefully. Hikers planning an extended trip should write or call the Appalachian Trail Conference (ATC), P.O. Box 807, Harpers Ferry, W. Va. 25425-0807, (304) 535-6331, for advice and suggestions on long-distance hiking.

Trail Marking

The Appalachian Trail is marked for travel in both directions. The marks are white-paint blazes about two inches wide and six inches high on trees, posts, and rocks. Occasionally, in open, treeless areas, stone cairns identify the route. In some areas, diamond-shaped A.T. metal markers mark the Trail. Two blazes, one above the other, signal an obscure turn, change in route, or a warning to check blazes carefully.

When the route is not obvious, normal marking procedure is to position the blazes so that anyone standing at one blaze will always be able to see the next. When the footway is unmistakable, blazes frequently are farther apart. If you have gone a quarter-mile without seeing a blaze, retrace your steps until you locate one and then check to ensure that you did not miss a turn. Since the Trail is marked for both directions, a glance back may locate blazes for travel in the opposite direction.

Side trails from the A.T. to water, viewpoints, and shelters usually are blazed in blue paint. Intersecting trails not part of the A.T. system are blazed in a variety of colors.

At trail junctions or near important features, the Trail route is often marked by signs. Some list mileages and detailed information.

Trail Relocations

Always follow the marked Trail. If it differs from the guidebook's Trail description, it is because the Trail was recently relocated in the area, probably to avoid a hazard or undesirable feature or to remove it from private property. If you use the old Trail, you may be trespassing and generating ill will toward the Trail community.

Information on Trail relocations between guidebook revisions is reported in ATC's magazine, *Appalachian Trailway News*, issued five times annually. Every effort has been made in this guide to alert you to relocations that may occur. Do not follow new trails that are not blazed, because they may not yet be open to the public.

Water

Although the A.T. may have sources of clean, potable water, any water source can become polluted. Most water sources along the Trail are unprotected and consequently very susceptible to contamination. All water should be purified by boiling, chemical treatment, or portable water filters before using. Take particular care to protect the purity of all water sources. Never wash dishes, clothes, or hands in the water source. Make sure food and human wastes are buried well away from any water source.

Equipment

The basic equipment rule is, never carry more than you need. Some items should be with you on every hike: the *A.T. Data Book*; guidebook and maps; canteen; flashlight, even on day trips; whistle; emergency food; tissues; matches and fire starter; multipurpose knife; compass; rain gear; proper shoes and socks; warm, dry spare clothes; and a first-aid kit (see page 22).

Take the time to consult periodicals, books, employees of outfitter stores, and other hikers before choosing the equipment that is best for you.

Getting Lost

Stop, if you have walked more than a quarter-mile (1,320 feet or roughly five minutes of hiking) without noticing a blaze or other Trail indicator (see page 5). If you find no indication of the Trail, retrace your course until one appears. The cardinal mistake behind unfortunate experiences is insisting on continuing when the route seems obscure or dubious. Haste, even in a desire to reach camp before dark, only compounds the difficulty. When in doubt, remain where you are to avoid straying farther from the route.

Hiking long distances alone should be avoided. If undertaken, it requires extra precautions. A lone hiker who suffers a serious accident or illness might be risking death if he has not planned for the remote chance of isolation. Your destinations and estimated times of arrival should be known to someone who will initiate inquiries or a search if you do not appear when expected. On long trips, reporting your plans and progress every few days is a wise precaution.

A lone hiker who loses his way and chooses to bushwhack toward town runs considerable risks if an accident occurs. If he falls helpless away from a used trail, he might not be discovered for days or even weeks. Lone hikers are advised to stay on the Trail (or at least on a trail), even if it means spending an unplanned night in the woods in sight of a distant electric light. Your pack should always contain enough food and water to sustain you until daylight, when a careful retracing of your steps might lead you back to a safe route.

Distress Signals

An emergency call for distress consists of three short calls, audible or visible, repeated at regular intervals. A whistle is particularly good for audible signals. Visible signals may include, in daytime, light flashed with a mirror or smoke puffs; at night, a flashlight or three small bright fires.

Anyone recognizing such a signal should acknowledge it with two calls—if possible, by the same method—then go to the distressed person and determine the nature of the emergency. Arrange for more aid, if necessary.

Most of the A.T. is used enough that, if you are injured, you can expect to be found. However, if an area is remote and the weather bad, fewer hikers will be on the Trail. In this case, it might be best to study the guide for the nearest place people are likely to be and attempt to move in that direction. If it is necessary to leave a heavy pack behind, be sure to take essentials, in case rescue is delayed. In bad weather, a night in the open without proper covering could be dangerous.

Pests

Rattlesnakes and copperheads are found in Tennessee and North Carolina. See page 20 for the recommended treatment of snakebites.

Ticks, chiggers, no-see-ums, mosquitoes, and other insects could also be encountered. Carry repellent.

Poison ivy, stinging nettle, and briars grow along many sections of the Trail in Tennessee and North Carolina. Long pants are recommended. Trailside plants grow rapidly in spring and summer, and, although volunteers try to keep the Trail cleared, some places may be filled by midsummer with dense growth, especially where clearings have been created by fallen trees or insect infestations.

Parking

Park in designated areas. If you leave your car parked overnight unattended, you may be risking theft or vandalism. Please do not ask Trail neighbors for permission to park your car near their homes.

Hunting

Hunting is prohibited in many state parks and on National Park Service lands—whether acquired specifically for protection of the Appalachian Trail or as part of another unit of the national park system. However, most of the boundary lines that identify these lands have yet to be surveyed. It may be very difficult for hunters to know when they are on NPS Trail lands. Hunters who approach the A.T. from the side, and who do not know that they are on Trail lands, may have no idea that the Trail is nearby. The Trail traverses several other types of landownership, on which hunting is allowed as part of a multiple-use management plan (national forests) or specifically for game (state gamelands).

Some hunting areas are marked by permanent or temporary signs, but any sign is subject to vandalism and removal. The prudent hiker, especially in the fall, makes himself aware of local hunting seasons and wears blaze orange during them.

Trail Ethics

In Tennessee and North Carolina, the A.T. crosses private property as well as public lands. In all cases, treat the land with care to preserve the beauty of the Trail environment and ensure the Trail's integrity.

Improper use can endanger the continuity of the Trail. Private landowners may order hikers off their property and close the route. Vandalism, camping and fires where prohibited, and other abuse can result in Trail closure. Please follow a few basic guidelines:

Do not cut, deface, or destroy trees, flowers, or any other natural or constructed feature.

Do not damage fences or leave gates open.

Do not litter. Carry out all trash. Do not bury it for animals or others to uncover.

Do not carry firearms.

Be careful with fire. Extinguish all burning material; a forest fire can start more easily than many realize.

In short: Take nothing but pictures, leave nothing but footprints, kill nothing but time.

Dogs are often a nuisance to other hikers and to property owners. Landowners complain of dogs running loose and soiling yards. The territorial instincts of dogs often result in fights with other dogs. Dogs also frighten some hikers and chase wildlife. If a pet cannot be controlled, it should be left at home; otherwise, it will generate ill-will toward the Appalachian Trail and its users. Also, many at-home pets, muscles, foot pads, and sleeping habits are not adaptable to the rigors of A.T. hiking.

Ask for water and seek directions and information from homes along the Trail only in an emergency. Some residents receive more hiker-visitors than they enjoy. Respect the privacy of people living near the Trail.

Keep to the defined Trail. Cutting across switchbacks, particularly on graded trails, disfigures the Trail, complicates route-finding, and causes erosion. The savings in time or distance are minimal; the damage is great. In areas where log walkways, steps, or rock treadway indicate special trail construction, take pains to use them. These have been installed to reduce trail-widening and erosion. In areas above treeline, it is of utmost importance to stay on the Trail. Plants and soil in these areas are extremely sensitive.

Shelters

Shelters are generally three-sided, with open fronts. They may be fitted with bunks or have a wooden floor serving as a sleeping platform. Water, a fireplace, and, in some cases, a privy, a table and benches are usually nearby. Hikers should bring their own sleeping equipment, cooking utensils, and a stove.

Shelters along the Trail are provided primarily for the long-distance hiker who may have no other shelter. People planning overnight hikes are asked to consider this and carry tents. This is good insurance in any case, since the Trail is heavily used and shelters are usually crowded during the summer. Organizations—such as Scouts—should keep their groups small (eight to ten people, including leaders), carry tents, and not monopolize the shelters (see page 11). Although shelter use is on a first-come, first-served basis, please cooperate and consider the needs of others. If a shelter has a register, please sign it.

Shelters are for overnight stays only, and, except for bad weather, injury, or other emergency, hikers should not stay more than one or two nights. Hunters, fishermen, and other non-Trail hikers should not use the shelters as bases of operation.

Use facilities with care and respect. Do not carve initials or write on shelter walls. Do not use an ax on any part of the shelter or use benches or tables as chopping blocks. The roofing material, especially if it is corrugated aluminum, is easily damaged; do not climb on it. Avoid putting excess weight or strain on wire bunks; the breaking of one wire endangers air mattresses and sleeping bags.

Be considerate of the rights of others, especially during meal times. Keep noise to a minimum between nine p.m. and seven a.m. for the sake of those attempting to sleep.

Preserve the surroundings and the ecological integrity of the site. Vandalism and carelessness mar the site's pristine nature and cause maintenance problems. Never cut live trees. Keep to trodden paths. Be conservative and careful with the environment.

Leave the shelter in good condition. Do not leave food in the shelter; this may cause damage by animals. Remove unburned trash from the fireplace, including aluminum foil, and pack out food and refuse.

Campfires

All travelers should be extremely careful with campfires or smoking materials (cigars, matches, pipes). Individuals responsible for fire damage to a national or state forest or park are liable for the cost of the damage. Because of the decreasing availability of firewood, it is wise to carry a camping stove.

Fires at shelters should be built in the fireplaces provided. If building a fire elsewhere, kindle it only in a cleared, open area, keeping the burning area minimal, and, upon leaving, remove traces of the campfire. Fires should be attended at all times.

No matter how many people use a fire, all share in responsibility for it. Be especially alert for sparks blowing from fires during periods of high wind.

Use wood economically. Use dead or downed wood only, even if this requires searching some distance away. Many campsites have suffered visible deterioration from hikers cutting wood from trees within the site. The effective cooking fire is small. Do not build bonfires. If you use wood stored in a shelter, replenish the supply.

Upon leaving the campsite, even temporarily, ensure that your fire—to the last spark—is out. Douse it with water and overturn the ashes until all underlying coals have been thoroughly extinguished.

Group Hikes and Special Events

Special events, group hikes, or other group activities that could degrade the Appalachian Trail's natural or cultural resources or social values should be avoided. Examples of such activities include publicized spectator events, commercial or competitive activities, or programs involving large groups.

The policy of the Appalachian Trail Conference is that groups planning to spend one or more nights on the Trail should not exceed ten people, and day-use groups should not exceed 25 people, unless the local maintaining organization has made special arrangements to both accommodate the group and protect Trail values.

Publications

The Appalachian Trail Conference, as part of its charter to serve as a clearinghouse of information on the Trail, publishes a number of books other than guides and also sells books from other publishers. ATC members receive a 15-percent discount on publications sold through the Conference. Proceeds from sales help underwrite the costs of A.T. maintenance and Trail-corridor management.

A complete list of the publications and merchandise available from ATC can be obtained by writing ATC at P.O. Box 807, Harpers Ferry, W. Va. 25425, or calling (304) 535-6331.

Those seeking basic information about hiking and equipment might consider joining one of the hiking clubs connected with ATC or consult the following books:

The Complete Walker III, by Colin Fletcher, Alfred A. Knopf, New York, 1987.

Backpacking: One Step at a Time, by Harvey Manning, Vintage Books, New York, 1986.

Starting Small in the Wilderness: The Sierra Club Outdoors Guide for Families, by Marilyn Doan, Sierra Club Books, San Francisco, 1979.

Mountaineering First Aid, A Guide to Accident Response and First Aid Care, The Mountaineers, Seattle, 1985.

Maps and Compasses, A User's Handbook, by Percy W. Blandford, TAB Books, Inc., Blue Ridge Summit, Pa., 1984.

First Aid Along the Trail

By Robert Ohler, M.D., and the
Appalachian Trail Conference

Hikers encounter a wide variety of terrain and climatic conditions along the Appalachian Trail. Prepare for the possibility of injuries. Some of the more common Trail-related medical problems are briefly discussed below.

Preparation is key to a safe trip. If possible, every hiker should take the free courses in advanced first-aid and cardiopulmonary-resuscitation (CPR) techniques offered in most communities by the American Red Cross.

Even without this training, you can be prepared for accidents. Emergency situations can develop. Analyses of serious accidents have shown that a substantial number originate at home, in the planning stage of the trip. Think about communications. Have you informed your relatives and friends about your expedition: locations, schedule, and time of return? Has all of your equipment been carefully checked? Considering the season and altitude, have you provided for water, food, and shelter?

While hiking, set your own comfortable pace. If you are injured or lost or a storm strikes, stop. Remember, your brain is your most important survival tool. Inattention can start a chain of events leading to disaster.

If an accident occurs, treat the injury first. If outside help is needed, at least one person should stay with the injured hiker. Two people should go for help and carry with them notes on the exact location of the accident, what has been done to aid the injured hiker, and what help is needed.

The injured will need encouragement, assurances of help, and confidence in your competence. Treat him gently. Keep him supine, warm, and quiet. Protect him from the weather with insulation below and above him. Examine him carefully, noting all possible injuries.

General Emergencies

Back or neck injuries: Immobilize the victim's entire body, where he lies. Protect head and neck from movement if the neck is injured, and

13

treat as a fracture. Transportation must be on a rigid frame, such as a litter or a door. The spinal cord could be severed by inexpert handling. This type of injury must be handled by a large group of experienced personnel. Obtain outside help.

Bleeding: Stop the flow of blood by using a method appropriate to the amount and type of bleeding. Exerting pressure over the wound with the fingers, with or without a dressing, may be sufficient. Minor arterial bleeding can be controlled with local pressure and bandaging. Major arterial bleeding might require compressing an artery against a bone to stop the flow of blood. Elevate the arm or legs above the heart. To stop bleeding from an artery in the leg, place a hand in the groin, and press toward the inside of the leg. Stop arterial bleeding from an arm by placing a hand between the armpit and elbow and pressing toward the inside of the arm.

Apply a tourniquet only if you are unable to control severe bleeding by pressure and elevation. Warning: This method should be used only when the limb will be lost anyway. Once applied, a tourniquet should only be removed by medical personnel equipped to stop the bleeding by other means and to restore lost blood. The tourniquet should be located between the wound and the heart. If there is a traumatic amputation (loss of hand, leg, or foot), place the tourniquet two inches above the amputation.

Blisters: Good boot fit, without points of irritation or pressure, should be proven before a hike. Always keep feet dry while hiking. Prevent blisters by responding early to any discomfort. Place adhesive tape or moleskin over areas of developing redness or soreness. If irritation can be relieved, allow blister fluid to be reabsorbed. If a blister forms and continued irritation makes draining it necessary, wash the area with soap and water and prick the edge of the blister with a needle that has been sterilized by the flame of a match. Bandage with a sterile gauze pad and moleskin.

Dislocation of a leg or arm joint is extremely painful. Do not try to put it back in place. Immobilize the entire limb with splints in the position it is found.

Exhaustion is caused by inadequate food consumption, dehydration and salt deficiency, overexertion, or all three. The victim may lose motivation, slow down, gasp for air, complain of weakness, dizziness, nausea, or headache. Treat by feeding, especially carbohydrates. Slowly replace lost water (normal fluid intake should be two to four quarts per day). Give salt dissolved in water (one teaspoon per cup). In the case of overexertion, rest is essential.

Fractures of legs, ankles, or arms must be splinted before moving the victim. After treating wounds, use any available material that will offer firm support, such as tree branches or boards. Pad each side of the arm or leg with soft material, supporting and immobilizing the joints above and below the injury. Bind the splints together with strips of cloth.

Shock should be expected after all injuries. It is a potentially fatal depression of bodily functions that is made more critical with improper handling, cold, fatigue, and anxiety. Relieve the pain as quickly as possible. Do not administer aspirin if severe bleeding is present; Tylenol or other nonaspirin pain relievers are safe to give.

Look for nausea, paleness, trembling, sweating, or thirst. Lay the hiker flat on his back, and raise his feet slightly, or position him, if he can be safely moved, so his head is down the slope. Protect him from the wind, and keep him as warm as possible. A campfire will help.

Sprains: Look or feel for soreness or swelling. Bandage and treat as a fracture. Cool and raise joint.

Wounds (except eye wounds) should be cleaned with soap and water. If possible, apply a clean dressing to protect the wound from further contamination.

Chilling and Freezing Emergencies

Every hiker should be familiar with the symptoms, treatment, and methods of preventing the common and sometimes fatal condition of *hypothermia*. Wind chill and/or body wetness, particularly aggravated by fatigue and hunger, can rapidly drain body heat to dangerously low levels. This often occurs at temperatures well above freezing. Shivering, lethargy, mental slowing, and confusion are early symptoms of hypothermia, which can begin without the victim's realizing it and, if untreated, can lead to death.

Always keep dry, spare clothing and a water-repellent windbreaker in your pack, and wear a hat in chilling weather. Wet clothing loses much of its insulating value, although polypropylene, synthetic pile, and wet wool are warmer than other fabrics when wet. Always, when in chilling conditions, suspect the onset of hypothermia.

To treat this potentially fatal condition, immediately seek shelter and warm the entire body, preferably by placing it in a sleeping bag

Wind Chill Chart

Actual Temperature (°F)

	50	40	30	20	10	0	-10	-20	-30	-40	-50
	Equivalent Temperature (°F)										
0	50	40	30	20	10	0	-10	-20	-30	-40	-50
5	48	37	27	16	6	-5	-15	-26	-36	-47	-57
10	40	28	16	4	-9	-21	-33	-46	-58	-70	-83
15	36	22	9	-5	-18	-36	-45	-58	-72	-85	-99
20	32	18	4	-10	-25	-39	-53	-67	-82	-96	-110
25	30	16	0	-15	29	-44	-59	-74	-88	-104	-118
30	28	13	-2	-18	-33	-48	-63	-79	-94	-109	-125
35	27	11	-4	-20	-35	-49	-67	-82	-98	-113	-129
40	26	10	-6	-21	-37	-53	-69	-85	-100	-116	-132

Wind Speed (mph) (row labels at left)

This chart illustrates the important relationship between wind and temperature.

and administering warm liquids. The addition of another person's body heat may aid in warming.

A sign of *frostbite* is grayish or waxy, yellow-white spots on the skin. The frozen area will be numb. To thaw, warm the frozen part by direct contact with bare flesh. When first frozen, a cheek, nose, or chin can often be thawed by covering with a hand taken from a warm glove. Superficially frostbitten hands sometimes can be thawed by placing them under armpits, on the stomach, or between the thighs. With a partner, feet can be treated similarly. Do not rub frozen flesh.

Frozen layers of deeper tissue beneath the skin are characterized by a solid, "woody" feeling and an inability to move the flesh over bony prominences. Tissue loss is minimized by rapid rewarming of the area in water slightly below 105 degrees Fahrenheit (measure accurately with a thermometer).

Thawing of a frozen foot should not be attempted until the patient has been evacuated to a place where rapid, controlled thawing can take place. Walking on a frozen foot is entirely possible and does not cause increased damage. Walking after thawing is impossible.

Never rewarm over a stove or fire. This "cooks" flesh and results in extensive loss of tissue.

Treatment of a deep freezing injury after rewarming must be done in a hospital.

Heat Emergencies

Exposure to extremely high temperatures, high humidity, and direct sunlight can cause health problems.

Heat cramps are usually caused by strenuous activity in high heat and humidity, when sweating depletes salt levels in blood and tissues. Symptoms are intermittent cramps in legs and the abdominal wall and painful spasms of muscles. Pupils of eyes may dilate with each spasm. The skin becomes cold and clammy. Treat with rest and salt dissolved in water (one teaspoon of salt per glass).

Heat exhaustion, caused by physical exercise during prolonged exposure to heat, is a breakdown of the body's heat-regulating system. The circulatory system is disrupted, reducing the supply of blood to vital organs such as the brain, heart, and lungs. The victim can have heat cramps and sweat heavily. Skin is moist and cold with face flushed, then pale. The pulse can be unsteady, and blood pressure low. He may vomit and be delirious. Place the victim in shade, flat on his back, with feet 8-12 inches higher than his head. Give him sips of salt water—half a glass every 15 minutes—for about an hour. Loosen his clothes. Apply cold cloths.

Heat stroke and *sun stroke* are caused by the failure of the heat-regulating system to cool the body by sweating. These are emergency, life-threatening conditions. Body temperature can rise to 106 degrees or higher. Symptoms include weakness, nausea, headache, heat cramps, exhaustion, body temperature rising rapidly, pounding pulse, and high blood pressure. The victim may be delirious or comatose. Sweating will stop before heat stroke becomes apparent. Armpits may be dry and skin flushed and pink, then turning ashen or purple in later stages. Move victim to cool place immediately. Cool the body in any way possible (*e.g.*, sponging). Body temperature must be regulated artificially from outside of the body until the heat-regulating system can be rebalanced. Be careful not to overchill once temperature goes below 102 degrees.

Heat weakness: Symptoms are fatigue, headache, mental and physical inefficiency, heavy sweating, high pulse rate, and general weakness. Drink plenty of water, find as cool a spot as possible, keep quiet, and replenish salt loss.

Sunburn causes redness of the skin, discoloration, swelling, and pain. It occurs rapidly and can be severe at higher elevations. It can be prevented by applying a commercial sun screen; zinc oxide is the most effective. Treat by protecting from further exposure and covering the area with ointment and a dressing. Give the victim large amounts of fluids.

Artificial Respiration

Artificial respiration might be required when an obstruction constricts the air passages or after respiratory failure caused by air being depleted of oxygen, such as after electrocution, by drowning, or because of toxic gases in the air. Quick action is necessary if the victim's lips, fingernail beds, or tongue have become blue, if he is unconscious, or if the pupils of his eyes become enlarged.

If food or a foreign body is lodged in the air passage and coughing is ineffective, try to remove it with the fingers. If the foreign body is inaccessible, grasp the victim from behind, and with one hand hold the opposite wrist just below the breastbone. Squeeze rapidly and firmly, expelling air forcibly from the lungs to expel the foreign body. Repeat this maneuver two to three times, if necessary.

If breathing stops, administer artificial respiration, as air can be forced around the obstruction into the lungs. The mouth-to-mouth, or mouth-to-nose, method of forcing air into the victim's lungs should be used. The preferred method is:

1. Clear the victim's mouth of any obstructions.
2. Place one hand under the victim's neck and lift.
3. Place heel of the other hand on the forehead, and tilt head backwards. (Maintain this position during procedure.) Use thumb and index finger to pinch nostrils.
4. Open your mouth, and make a seal with it over the victim's mouth. If the victim is a small child, cover both the nose and the mouth.

5. Breathe deeply, and blow out about every five seconds, or 12 breaths a minute.
6. Watch victim's chest for expansion.
7. Listen for exhalation.

Lyme Disease

Lyme disease is contracted from bites of certain infected ticks. Hikers should be aware of the symptoms and monitor themselves and their partners for signs of the disease. When treated early, Lyme disease can usually be cured with antibiotics.

Inspect yourself for ticks and tick bites at the end of each day. The four types of ticks known to spread Lyme disease are smaller than the dog tick, about the size of a pin head, and not easily seen. They are often called "deer ticks" because they feed during one stage of their life cycle on deer, a host for the disease.

The early signs of a tick bite infected with Lyme disease are a red spot with a white center that enlarges and spreads, severe fatigue, chills, headaches, muscle aches, fever, malaise, and a stiff neck. However, one-quarter of all people with an infected tick bite show none of the early symptoms.

Later effects of the disease, which may not appear for months or years, are severe fatigue, dizziness, shortness of breath, cardiac irregularities, memory and concentration problems, facial paralysis, meningitis, shooting pains in the arms and legs, and other symptoms resembling multiple sclerosis, brain tumors, stroke, alcoholism, mental depression, Alzheimer's disease, and *anorexia nervosa*.

It may be necessary to contact a university medical center or other research center if you suspect you have been bitten by an infected tick. It is not believed people can build a lasting immunity to Lyme disease. For that reason, a hiker who has contracted and been treated for the disease should still take precautions.

Lightning Strikes

Although the odds of being struck by lightning are low, 200 to 400 people a year are killed by lightning in the United States. Respect the force of lightning, and seek shelter during a storm.

Do not start a hike if thunderstorms are likely. If caught in a storm, immediately find shelter. Hard-roofed automobiles or large buildings are best; tents and convertible automobiles offer no protection. When indoors, stay away from windows, open doors, fireplaces, and large metal objects. Do not hold a potential lightning rod, such as a fishing pole. Avoid tall structures, such as ski lifts, flagpoles, powerline towers, and the tallest trees or hilltops. If you cannot enter a building or car, take shelter in a stand of smaller trees. Avoid clearings. If caught in the open, crouch down, or roll into a ball. If you are in water, get out. Spread out groups, so that everyone is not struck by a single bolt.

If a person is struck by lightning or splashed by a charge hitting a nearby object, the victim will probably be thrown, perhaps a great distance. Clothes can be burned or torn. Metal objects (such as belt buckles) may be hot, and shoes knocked off. The victim often has severe muscle contractions (which can cause breathing difficulties), confusion, and temporary blindness or deafness. In more severe cases, the victim may have feathered or sunburst patterns of burns over the skin or ruptured eardrums. He may lose consciousness or breathe irregularly. Occasionally, victims stop breathing and suffer cardiac arrest.

If someone is struck by lightning, perform artificial respiration (see page 18) and CPR until emergency technicians arrive or you can transport the injured to a hospital. Lightning victims may be unable to breathe independently for 15 to 30 minutes but can recover quickly once they can breathe on their own. Do not give up early; a seemingly lifeless individual can be saved if you breathe for him promptly after the strike.

Assume that the victim was thrown a great distance; protect the spine, treat other injuries, then transport him to the hospital.

Snakebites

Hikers on the Appalachian Trail may encounter copperheads and rattlesnakes on their journeys. These are pit vipers, characterized by triangular heads, vertical elliptical pupils, two or less hinged fangs on the front part of the jaw (fangs are replaced every six to ten weeks), heat-sensory facial pits on the sides of the head, and a single row of scales on the underbelly by the tail.

The best way to avoid being bitten by poisonous snakes is to avoid their known habitats and reaching into dark areas (use a walking stick to move suspicious objects). Wear protective clothing, especially on feet and lower legs. Do not hike alone or at night in snake territory; always have a flashlight and walking stick. Do not handle snakes. A dead snake can bite and envenomate you with a reflex action for 20 to 60 minutes after its death.

Not all snakebites result in envenomation, even if the snake is poisonous. The signs of envenomation are one or more fang marks in addition to rows of teeth marks, burning pain, and swelling at the bite (swelling usually begins within five to ten minutes of envenomation and can become very severe). Lips, face, and scalp may tingle and become numb 30 to 60 minutes after the bite. (If these symptoms are immediate and the victim is frightened and excited, then they are most likely due to hyperventilation.) Thirty to 90 minutes after the bite, the victim's eyes and mouth may twitch, and he may have a rubbery or metallic taste in his mouth. He may sweat, experience weakness, nausea and vomiting, or faint one to two hours after the bite. Bruising at the bite usually begins within two to three hours, and large blood blisters may develop within six to ten hours. The victim may have difficulty breathing, have bloody urine, vomit blood, and collapse six to 12 hours after the bite.

If someone you are with has been bitten by a snake, act quickly. *The definitive treatment for snake-venom poisoning is the proper administration of antivenom. Get the victim to a hospital immediately.*

Keep the victim calm. Increased activity can spread the venom and the illness. Retreat out of snake's striking range, but try to identify it. If you cannot do this easily, kill the snake with a blow to the head, and take it to the medical facility so the authorities can identify it and estimate the amount of antivenom necessary. (Remember to carry the snake in a container so that the jaws' reflex action cannot harm someone else.) Check for signs of envenomation.

Immediately transport the victim to the nearest hospital. If possible, splint the body part that was bitten, to avoid unnecessary motion. If a limb was bitten, keep it at a level below the heart. *Do not apply ice directly to the wound.* If it will take longer than two hours to reach medical help, and the bite is on an arm or leg, place a 2"x2", 1/4"-thick cloth pad over the bite and firmly wrap the limb (ideally, with an elastic wrap) directly over the bite and six inches on either side, taking care to check for adequate circulation to the fingers and toes. This wrap may slow the spread of venom.

First-Aid Kit

The following kit is suggested for those who have had no first-aid or other medical training. It costs about $15, weighs about a pound, and occupies about a 3" x 6" x 9" space.

Eight 4" x 4" gauze pads
Four 3" x 4" gauze pads
Five 2" bandages
Ten 1" bandages
Six alcohol prep pads
Ten large butterfly closures
One triangular bandage (40")
Two 3" rolls of gauze
Twenty tablets of aspirin-free pain killer
One 15' roll of 2" adhesive tape
One 3" Ace bandage
Twenty salt tablets
One 3" x 4" moleskin
Three safety pins
One small scissors
One tweezers
Personal medications as necessary

References

Red Cross first-aid manuals.
Mountaineering First Aid: A Guide to Accident Response and First Aid, The Mountaineers, Seattle, 1985.
Emergency Survival Handbook, by the American Safety League, 1985. A pocket-sized book and survival kit with easy instructions.
Medicine For the Outdoors: A Guide to Emergency Medical Procedures and First Aid, by Paul S. Auerbach, M.D., Little Brown & Co., Boston, 1986.

The Southern Appalachians

The southern Appalachian Mountains, described in this guide and in the *Appalachian Trail Guide to North Carolina-Georgia*, are the highest and among the most rugged of the entire Appalachian chain. Except perhaps for those in Maine, they represent the superlative in the "wilderness" and the "primitive" areas made accessible by the A.T. Much of the route is virtually ridgecrest travel and above the 5,000-foot elevation for long distances. The outlook is generally a vast, bewildering sea of lofty mountain ranges in all directions.

Travelers from the other sections of the A.T. will find considerable contrast here. With increasing elevation, particularly in the Great Smokies, the flora become similar to that found farther north. Southern Appalachian "balds," great unforested summits comparable to the glaciated heights of New England, have magnificent outlooks.

Apart from the endless ridges, perhaps the most impressive feature of Trail travel in the southern Appalachians is the profusion of flowering shrubs—rhododendron, azalea, and laurel. In full bloom, their dense masses and "thickets" make the traveler's path one of indescribable beauty. The floral display reaches its height in late June and early July. Elevation influences the blooming season, and on the summits the display occurs much later than in the valleys. The probability of heavy rains characteristic of the region during this season may offset the advantage of travel to witness the floral display, however.

The Trail hiker will encounter an unusual variety of trees here. The Great Smoky Mountains National Park alone contains more species of trees than all of Europe. *The Appalachians*, a book by Maurice Brooks (Houghton Mifflin Co., Boston, 1965), vividly describes the Trail and its environment. Much of the route in this region lies in two national forests, the Cherokee (in Tennessee) and the Pisgah (in North Carolina), and in the Great Smoky Mountains National Park. Such public ownership results in protection of the footpath and ensures the preservation of the primitive aspects of the Trail environment. Recent purchases of land by the National Park Service (NPS) and U.S. Forest Service (USFS) for the Trail corridor have increased the publicly owned areas. The completion of this acquisition program will result in a continuous public domain for those who walk and camp. Most of the Trail footway covered by this guide lies inside national forest boundaries. Within the national forests, much of the Trail is graded and avoids steep ascents and descents. It bypasses many minor summits that have no views in the summertime. As a rule, this type of trail allows easier walking than that which more closely follows the ridgeline. The graded trail built by NPS in the eastern Smokies from Davenport Gap to Clingmans Dome (38 miles) is wider, has easier grades, and is more obviously constructed than the USFS trails. Contrasting with the graded Trail in the eastern Smokies, the 26-mile stretch of Trail from Clingmans Dome to Shuckstack Mountain above the Little Tennessee River has an unworked footway for most of the distance.

The Trail in the southern Appalachians provides mostly off-road travel, except for short stretches on country roads. It is constructed and intended for foot use only, except for short parts of the Trail in the Great Smokies where horses are permitted by special exception. In general, riding is unsuitable and is discouraged. Use of motorized vehicles is expressly prohibited on the A.T. under the National Trails System Act.

Geography

The southern Appalachians stretch as one ridge from the Susquehanna River across southern Pennsylvania, Maryland, and Virginia to the point where the Roanoke River cuts across the Blue Ridge, a narrow crestline trending south-southwest. Where the range rises again, south of the Roanoke River, it forks. The two forks, sometimes 50 miles apart, form an immense oval and join again at Springer Mountain in northern Georgia. Parallel, lofty, transverse ranges, enclosing beautiful elevated valleys, connect the eastern and western forks.

The eastern fork or rim preserves the name Blue Ridge and forms the watershed. Although higher than the eastern fork, the western range is broken into segments by rivers that rise on the western slope of the Blue Ridge. All these segments are part of the western range, yet, unlike its eastern counterpart, it is unnamed as a whole. The nomenclature of the segments has been extremely confused. The name "Unaka" or "Unicoi," in particular, has been applied to segments on each side of the Great Smokies. The conflicting usages have, to some extent, been settled by decisions of the U.S. Board on Geographic Names.

The rivers cut across the range through sheer canyons. The transverse ridges, dividing each river valley from its neighbor to the north and south, contain ranges, such as the Blacks, some of which are loftier and more impressive than either the western or eastern rims.

In the Black Mountains, 34 miles northeast of Asheville, N.C., are Mt. Mitchell (6,684 feet) and Mt. Craig (6,663 feet), the two highest peaks in the United States east of the Mississippi. Richland Balsam, in the transverse range of the same name, is 6,540 feet high.

The first recorded climbs of many of the peaks in the Unaka and Pisgah are those made by Arnold Guyot just before the Civil War. Guyot established a system of measuring elevations by barometer and developed a systematic geographic outline of the mountain system of the eastern United States, spending some ten summers climbing the peaks of the Appalachian chain. The summers of 1856, 1858, 1859, and 1860 were devoted to the southern Appalachians.

Unaka, as used here, applies to the western fork of the mountains from below Roanoke, to the Pisgah in North Carolina. Unaka is the white man's corruption of the Cherokee name for a section of the southern Appalachians. It means "land of the white mountains," which refers to the white quartzite cliffs so characteristic of these mountains.

The Unaka region and the adjoining Pisgah National Forest to the south provide much of the route of the A.T. in Tennessee and North Carolina. The southern boundary of this segment at Davenport Gap is the eastern terminus of the Great Smokies, the best known and most frequented region of the southern Appalachians.

Geologic History

More than one billion years ago, the land on which the Appalachian Mountains now stand was the interior of a great continent. Many details of this distant time are unknown. Rocks were heated and changed to form large crystals of many minerals, mostly quartz (silica), feldspar (a white or pink silicate mineral), and several dark minerals. The rocks flowed like plastic, as curving bands of light and dark minerals show. Although some of these patterns were made during later movements and heating events, the rocks were basically formed a billion years ago. The Appalachian Trail lies on those rocks most of the way (north to south) from U.S. 19E over Roan Mountain to Unaka Mountain, Big Bald, and the area of Devil Fork Gap. The Trail crosses another section of it at Brown Gap, south of Max Patch Mountain.

The next period of rock formation came between 800 and 600 million years ago. The earth's crust developed splits and cracks as the land masses began to separate to form an ocean somewhat like the Atlantic Ocean and roughly in the same location in relation to North America (although North America was in a different location—far to the south and turned about 90 degrees clockwise). The first small cracks filled with molten material, which cooled to black basalt. A few of the narrow, straight bands are visible on the A.T. near Jane Bald, Tennessee/North Carolina. As the stretching continued, some land sections dropped down and the low places filled with mud, sand, grit, and pebbles. Some of the material lay in flat, even beds, but some was also deposited in great undersea slumps or avalanches. Mud became dark slate, and beds of sand and silt were turned to sandstone and siltstone. The slumps, found primarily in the western Great Smokies, turned into a massive gray rock containing pebbles of blue quartz, small feldspar crystals, and slivers of slate. This series of rocks lies under the A.T. just south of Devil Fork Gap, around Rich Mountain, and south of Max Patch through the Smokies to Fontana Dam. Other rock formed at that time was greatly heated and altered and came to visually resemble the billion-year-old rock. This altered rock lies south of the Smokies in North Carolina.

Some rock was melted deep in the earth and later cooled to another generally light-colored, coarse-grained rock. This rock is under the A.T. at White Rocks Mountain, Tennessee, and at Max Patch Mountain, North Carolina/Tennessee.

About 600 million years ago, the Appalachian area was generally above sea level with a deep ocean where the Atlantic is now. But, the land began to sink, and a shallow sea spread across the area. A layer of sand with some mud collected along the advancing shoreline and eventually covered the area. The sand turned into very hard sandstone or even harder quartzite, while the mud turned to shale. Both rocks show their original form and bedding, usually flat for shale, but some of the sand shows diagonal bands (called crossbedding) where sand flowed over the edge of sandbars. The quartzite and sandstone are very resistant to erosion and their upturned ledges form the long ridges just northwest of the older rocks described earlier. The sandstone and quartzite lie under the A.T. from the Virginia state line along Holston Mountain, Cross Mountain, Iron Mountain, and Pond Mountain to Laurel Fork Gorge, also at the Nolichucky River Gorge and at Big Butt, Camp Creek Bald, and the ridge between the two. At Hot

Springs, N.C., the A.T. is on this rock in the valley at the Lovers Leap overlook.

Five hundred seventy million years ago, animals first developed hard shells. Their fossilized remains are common in many rocks of that age and younger.

A clear sea lay over the area for most of the next 100 million years while great layers of lime (much from various types of seashells) formed and turned into thick beds of limestone. The rocks sank as the deposits built up, so the sea stayed shallow throughout the time. On occasion, some mud and sand washed from North America into the sea and left some beds of shale and sandstone in the limestone. This rock lies mostly northeast of the A.T., although there is a very small section of limestone near Watauga Dam. It primarily underlies the broad low farms and wooded areas in Tennessee seen from A.T. overlooks.

Roughly 450 million years ago, the ocean began to narrow, and the dense crust of the ocean bottom was drawn down below the surface. Islands, which are less dense, were pushed into North America, and the old rocks (called the Blue Ridge) began to be pushed up and over the limestone beds. By 300 million years ago, swamps grew behind sandbars, and organic material was covered and gradually turned to coal. Rivers washed sand and mud from the Blue Ridge and highlands out across the limestone to the northwest, where it was deposited in thick, nearly flat sheets. Throughout this period, volcanos were active in offshore islands, and many rocks were heated and altered. Uneven compressive action continued for perhaps 200 million years until the ocean was completely closed and a continent, probably Africa, collided with North America.

During the collision with Africa, the area was compressed so that its width was reduced by perhaps 60 miles, with a total northwest movement of perhaps 150 miles. Rock layers broke and slid up and over other, younger beds for miles. Beds of formerly flat sediments were folded into long wrinkles like a crumpled rug. Great uplift occurred, but it is unknown how high the mountains became because rivers were eroding the area as it rose. In a similar collision today, the Himalayan Mountains are forming as India pushes into Asia.

Somewhat less than 200 million years ago, the crust began to split apart. The continents of North America and Africa (and others) separated while the Atlantic Ocean formed between them. New ocean crust continues to form as dark lava (basalt) erupts through a long crack along the mid-Atlantic ridge, which now runs through Iceland. The crack lies in a ridge because the underlying rock is very hot, which makes it less dense, causing it to "float" higher in the earth's crust. Rock that is farther from a ridge cools and sinks and the ocean is deeper there.

Rock that had eroded from the mountains was washed into the Atlantic Ocean, the present Mississippi Valley, and the Gulf of Mexico. The coastal plain is underlaid by sediments deposited when the sea level was higher on the continent. Land rises slowly at about the same rate that erosion lowers the surface. Topography, mountains, and valleys develop as resistant or nonresistant beds of rock appear at the surface, creating over time the scenes of today's Appalachians.

Geology Along the Trail

Since hiking south-to-north is more common, the rock formations along the Trail will be reviewed in that direction. Hiking north from Fontana Dam, the rock formation crossed is the Great Smoky conglomerate, which is mostly graywacke. You will also see slate, which breaks into flat sheets. At Doe Knob, turning east along the crest of the Smokies, the Great Valley of Tennessee can be seen on a clear day to the left in the distance. The valley is a lower area of long, straight ridges and valleys, and the rock is the limestone and shale laid down in the ancient, shallow sea. The rock is often turned up on edge by folds and faults. The resistant beds form ridges; the softer beds form valleys. This type of rock is found along the Trail all the way to New York. Views to the east consist of the jumble of disorganized peaks and valleys of North Carolina. These rocks are termed crystalline because the minerals in them are generally in crystals large enough to be visible.

The nearest valley to the north in Tennessee is Cades Cove. It is a broad, open valley of fields and farms, underlaid by limestone that formed in a shallow sea. It is completely surrounded by older rock similar to that on the Trail. The older rock slid over the limestone long ago along a fault. A creek cut down to the limestone and carved out the valley. This is called a "window" through the flat-lying fault. Many of these windows are found on the Tennessee side of the mountain, and a few on the North Carolina side. Echo-sounding techniques have shown that the limestone underlies the older rock as far east as the Piedmont plateau and possibly the coastal plain.

The old sediments called the Ocoee Series continue well past the Smokies to Brown Gap, where the A.T. first reaches billion-year-old rock. One mile farther north, the A.T. reaches the coarsely crystalline granite of the Max Patch area. This mass was a deeply buried molten mass about 600 million years ago. Slow cooling during crystallization allowed time for large crystals to grow. Here, one crosses an area of rock of the old islands. It is a light gray or red granite gneiss. That means it is coarsely crystalline and shows evidence of very thick flow patterns left from a time when it was quite hot. This type of rock sometimes looks like a partly stirred chocolate sundae, the dark and light minerals in streaks that bend and swirl. The Trail crosses shales and sandstones as it passes through Hot Springs and then reenters the Ocoee Series. Camp Creek Bald and Big Butt are on younger sandstone.

Approaching Devil Fork Gap is a long stretch of rock that is mostly granite gneiss. This section is about 100 miles long, ending in Laurel Fork Gorge, north of U.S. 19E. These are billion-year-old rocks like those found at Brown Gap. The individual crystals are large enough for easy mineral identification. From Roan Mountain to Carvers Gap, the gneiss is 1.8 billion years old, the oldest rock along the A.T. On Jane Bald, north of Roan Mountain, dikes of dark rock formed when molten rock forced its way into the rock along long, straight cracks as the land stretched. The straight black dikes are from six inches to many feet wide, and the ends are not visible.

Just before U.S. 19E are the remains of Wilder Mine. Magnetic iron ore was shipped from this mine by rail for several years around 1900. A very large similar mine was at Cranberry, N.C., several miles to the east along U.S. 19E. Near Wilder Mine are rocks of red, white, and green minerals (feldspar, quartz, and epidote).

In Laurel Fork Gorge, along the old railroad grade, the Trail crosses from the gneiss into the Unicoi formation of sandstone. This was laid down as sediment directly on the gneiss when the gneiss was on the surface, 600 million years ago. Several beds of sandstone, shale, and limestone are found between Laurel Fork Gorge and Watauga Dam. Low grades of manganese ore have been mined from clays weathered from the limestone.

At Watauga Dam is a rare sight. The great fault, where the old sediments slid up and over the limestone, has been bent down from its original slope and is seen as a great diagonal slash in the cliff. It reaches lake-level behind the vertical, round emergency spillway.

From Watauga Dam to Damascus, the Trail remains on the sandstone that was laid down as beach sand over 550 million years ago. The Trail crosses from Iron Mountain to Holston Mountain on Cross Mountain, where a large fault displaced these sandstones to connect the mountains.

For further information, consult *Underfoot: A Geologic Guide to the Appalachian Trail*, (published and sold by ATC), from which the preceding sections were drawn.

Plants and Animals

The great variety of plant life in the Appalachians is perhaps the mountains' most distinguishing feature. The southern forest of broad-leafed trees, which drop their leaves in autumn, is unsurpassed in the world. Other distinctive areas are the high grassy "balds" and, at high elevations, the northern spruce-fir forest.

Spruce-Fir Forest

Although glaciers never reached the southern mountains, the ice ages greatly influenced plant life. The great ice sheet to the north so cooled the southern Appalachians that a spruce-fir forest covered much of the area. As the climate warmed, the forest of broad-leafed trees moved into the mountains from the south. The spruce-fir forest moved north and upslope to the mountaintops. On the high, cool, moist places, this forest of red spruce and Fraser fir is well adapted and dominant. In the forest are plants and animals that would be expected in more northern regions.

Canada mayflower, Clinton's lily, and wood oxalis are typical of plants found far south of their usual range. Ravens, juncos, and various warblers are the northern birds in these southern mountains.

The lungless salamander breeds in decaying spruce logs, moving up the mountain slopes with the spruce trees. Each mountain range was isolated as the broad-leafed trees replaced the spruce and filled the valleys and lower passes between the ranges. On each separate range, the salamanders developed differently, and each range has separate and unique species, bringing biologists flocking to the area in search of new ones.

Balds

The high, treeless grasslands, or "balds," are one of the outstanding scenic features of the southern Appalachians. Situated on mountaintops and ridgeline gaps, they provide fine views and floral displays. This far south, the mountains do not approach the elevation required for a true timberline and the origin of the balds is subject to much debate.

Cherokee legends called the balds "udawagunda," and the Cherokee believed that, in ancient days, the balds were occupied by an "ulagu," a monster that swooped down and carried off their children. After the Indians had killed the monster, the Great Spirit decreed that the summits should remain unforested so the people could station sentinels there to watch for other ulagus.

The balds were maintained and expanded by local farmers who used the grassy highlands for summer pastures. Never a static life zone, the grassy balds are perhaps the most beautiful a few years after grazing has ceased and flame azalea is established along the edges in the grass. In late spring, the balds are ablaze with yellow, gold, and red flowers. Other areas, called heath balds, are solid with purple rhododendron blossoms. Grazing has ceased on most balds, and natural succession is turning them to forest.

Great Smoky Mountains National Park personnel have decided to maintain Gregory Bald and Andrews Bald as open, grassy areas. These balds may be reached by short hikes from the Trail. Other balds in the park have already been lost. Balds in the northern areas of this guide were grazed by cattle until quite recently and many are still in excellent shape. The U.S. Forest Service, working with ATC and the Southern Appalachian Highlands Conservancy, intends to maintain them as grassland.

Hardwood Forest

The majority of the Trail is in the great hardwood forest. Here, the scenery changes each season. Winter is stark among the bare trees with brown leaves or white snow underfoot. Winter is also the time for distant views of the valley farms and other mountains. Rhododendron and occasionally pines add a touch of green. When a series of side ridges are oriented just right, pines will make a series of green stripes on the drier, southward-facing sides of the ridges.

Spring is a time of beauty, as many small wildflowers bloom before being shaded by tall trees. A small tree, serviceberry (pronounced "sarvice"), proclaims spring on the mountain and the white apple-like blossoms can be observed from great distances. The small trailing arbutus blooms early, followed by bloodroot, violets, hepatica, and anemone. Later, the ground beneath the bare trees may become white with masses of flowers—spring beauties or fringed phacelia—interspersed with delicate yellow trout lilies. Showy trilliums of white, yellow, and burgundy dot the bare hillsides while flowering trees bloom just before the leaves. The new tree leaves appear in many shades of chartreuse or light green before becoming the uniform chlorophyll green of summer.

Summer also brings many flowers, but in the deep woods they are often small and inconspicuous. Red and yellow flowers, such as mints and coneflowers, line the edge of the woods, where they can get light. The woodland Trail becomes a green tunnel. Stinging nettle becomes a problem in the woods, and blackberry vines try to fill the open areas. A small comfort is the fact that blackberries have few or only small thorns above 5,000 feet elevation.

In fall, the daisy family of flowers (yellow goldenrod, pink Joe Pye Weed, asters of many colors, white boneset snakeroot, and purple ironweed) line the openings.

Perhaps the animal best known to the backpacker is the Trail-shelter mouse. This mouse is adept at climbing, chewing through bags, and hiding things.

Black bears are native along much of the Trail but are rarely seen, except in the Smokies, where they often steal food. Common turkey, deer, and grouse are observed fairly often. The sudden noise of the large grouse taking wing is one of the most startling sounds heard on the Trail.

Poisonous snakes are rarely seen but are native to most of the area. They commonly hunt at night but are inactive in cold weather. Skunk sightings occur often. The native raccoon, bobcat, red fox, mole, bat, and opossum are rarely seen, but they live here. The imported European wild boar is well-adapted to the Smokies and can be dangerous and destructive to many plants. Woodchucks are common along roads.

The most frequently seen bird in the area is the turkey vulture. Groups of these large (six-foot wingspan) black birds soar gracefully and rarely flap their wings. The vee-angle formed by their wings identifies them at great distances. Owls are heard more often than seen. The melodious call of the nocturnal Chuck-will's-widow, or whip-poorwills, can be heard for hours on summer nights near shelters.

Social History

Humans probably came to the southern Appalachians more than 10,000 years ago. They were hunters descended from a race which had crossed a land bridge between Siberia and Alaska during the ice ages. These people hunted mastodon and giant bison and lived as hunter-gatherers for thousands of years. When the great animals became extinct, they hunted deer and elk. Later, they began to hunt smaller game and use vegetation to support a larger and less nomadic population.

About 3,000 years ago, they began growing crops, including corn, squash, beans, and pumpkin. The bow and arrow replaced the spear for warfare and hunting. The natives made pottery and built simple burial mounds. About 1,000 years ago, they began living in villages, which they sometimes ringed with palisades. Ceremonial mounds and temples were constructed. The people in this area formed a loose confederacy of many towns called the Cherokee Nation.

Explorers from Europe first met the Cherokee in 1566 or 1567. At this time, the valley just west of the mountains held the greatest of all Indian trails, "The Great Indian Warpath," which extended from the Creek territory in Alabama to Pennsylvania. Along the Holston and New rivers, pioneers from Pennsylvania made their way to settle Kentucky and Tennessee. The region otherwise presented barriers to immigration from the east.

As early as 1671, two explorers named Batts and Fallam, on one of Colonel Arthur Woods' expeditions, reached the New River from Appomattox. A century later, Daniel Boone went from his home on the Yadkin River across the ranges to the westward valleys by at least six different routes. His and others' explorations resulted in a flood of immigration to Kentucky along the Wilderness Road across upper eastern Tennessee. The pioneers from the Carolinas to the western settlements along the Watauga, Holston, and Nolichucky rivers came mainly by two routes: one, Bright's Trace, climbing Yellow Mountain and crossing the divide just east of the Roan; the other, passing through Iron Mountain Gap between Roan and BigUnaka mountains.

Gradually, the frontier receded under the unceasing pressure of the immigrants, but this region was to be the scene of desperate and destructive Indian warfare. The southwestern trend of settlement was in violation of the Indian treaties with the colonial government and was resisted by the authorities, but, by 1770, a considerable settlement had developed on the Watauga River, near the present site of Elizabethton, Tenn.

The settlers were too busily engaged in securing the eastern Tennessee wilderness against the Indians to participate actively in the Revolutionary War. Yet, two campaigns by these frontiersmen had far-reaching effects. In September 1780, when British Major Patrick Ferguson's threat to bring fire and sword to their doors alarmed the transmountain settlements, the frontiersmen gathered at Sycamore Shoals and marched east. They followed Bright's Trace, crossing from Tennessee into North Carolina by Yellow Mountain Gap. Then followed the battle of Kings Mountain, in which the British and Tory force was defeated.

In March 1781, the frontiersmen assembled in Greasy Cove, near the town of Unicoi, Tenn. Colonel John Sevier, later governor of Tennessee, and Major Jonathan Tipton led them across the ranges, destroyed the villages of the Middle Cherokees, and completely broke the power of that nation. This campaign ended the threat of Indian invasion of the southern states at British instigation. Their route crossed the future A.T. at Coxes Cove Gap, now Spivey Gap, and followed the Cane, Ivy, and Tuckasegee rivers into western North Carolina.

The last flare-up of this frontier spirit was the formation of the little-known independent state of Franklin, which, under Sevier, maintained its sovereignty from 1784 to 1788 before yielding to the claims of North Carolina.

Thus, the Watauga settlements became a part of eastern Tennessee. The burnings, massacres, and more severe hardships of the frontier settlements and Indian villages ended.

Tennessee became a state of the United States in 1796. In 1799, a party led by John Strother surveyed the Tennessee-North Carolina border. Due to the rough terrain, the surveyors only made it to Hot

Springs. The remainder of the state line, including the Smokies, was not surveyed until 1821.

By the early 1800s, the Cherokees had ceded all their land to the settlers in various treaties. These treaties were usually misunderstood and broken. A Cherokee named Sequoyah realized that the settlers held a great advantage with their written word. He developed a phonetic alphabet for the Cherokee language, which soon enabled most Cherokees to read and write their native language. The newspaper *Cherokee Phoenix* was printed in both Cherokee and English.

By 1838, the white men decided the Cherokee must leave. The Cherokee were assembled and ordered to march to the Oklahoma Territory during winter. The families had lived in houses on farms and were ill-prepared for the march. They suffered greatly and a quarter of them died on the march now called "The Trail of Tears." Some of the Cherokee escaped the roundup and fled to the mountains. An agreement was made with a Cherokee prince, Tsali; two of his sons surrendered and were hung for murder. In return, the search was stopped for the other escapees. Much later, the Qualla Indian Reservation was established for their descendants. (Many tourists now visit the reservation, including the town of Cherokee at the southern edge of the Great Smoky Mountains National Park.)

The mountains remained a barrier in many ways, and life changed very slowly for the people living among them. The politics were Whig; the book was the Bible; the farms were small and rough; and the tools, clothes, and buildings were what the settlers could make for themselves. These people were strongly independent.

As the nation divided over slavery and secession, the mountain people lined up strongly antislavery and for the Union. When the vote finally came that made Tennessee the last state to join the Confederacy, eastern Tennessee voted overwhelmingly to stay in the Union. In Sevier County, only one person voted for secession. (That person was John Gatlin, for whom Gatlinburg was named. He left to join the Army and did not return.)

The people of the mountains suffered greatly during the Civil War. On a per-capita basis, they furnished more men to the Union Army than did the counties in the North. Although Knoxville and Chattanooga were held by the Union Army, eastern Tennessee and western North Carolina were generally held by the South. The beleaguered Confederacy could scarcely maintain order in this hostile land and spent considerable effort trying to stop the flow of volunteers to the

Union Army. Outlaws hid in the coves. The only roads across the Smokies were improved by the Cherokees so that saltpeter for gunpowder for the Confederacy could be brought from Alum Cave on Mt. LeConte, by sled over Indian Gap.

After the war, the people remained isolated and self-reliant. Until quite recently, transportation was difficult. About 1880, railroads began to penetrate the mountains to bring out logs and iron ore. Just south of U.S. 19E, the Trail passes Wilder Mine, which produced iron ore from this time period until 1918. The railroad carried ore from the Wilder Mine and a much larger one in Cranberry, to a smelter in Johnson City, Tenn.

Early tourists traveled into the mountains by train. Resorts opened in the Smokies, at Hot Springs, as well as other places. Retired General John Wilder, who had opened the iron mine, built the Cloudland Hotel on Roan Mountain. (In Laurel Fork Gorge, the Trail follows an old logging railroad grade, abandoned in 1920 when most of the area had been logged. Some large clear areas are the result of great brush fires after the logging.)

The Great Smoky Mountains National Park was established after World War I to preserve these largely uncharted and unsettled mountains for the public to enjoy. The U.S. Forest Service, set up in 1911 to constructively manage public timber lands, established many early training centers in this region. Its role has been expanded by Congress to include many other activities, including protection of the Appalachian Trail in national forests.

The coming of electricity with the Tennessee Valley Authority (TVA) during the New Deal era, the interstate highways, industrial plants, and universities helped bring the mountain areas fully into modern America. The times when people had to make do with their own handiwork are now remembered by many groups who strive to preserve their heritage by crafts, such as quilting, weaving, making flintlock rifles, and preserving log cabins.

The Appalachian Trail, meanwhile, is deeply rooted in the history and leaders of the post-logging decades here. The foresters, park superintendents, and surveyors were also leaders and Trail designers of the new ATC and its southern clubs. And, A.T. conceptualizer Benton MacKaye was one of the first planners on the TVA staff.

Trail Route

A study of Arnold Guyot's 1863 manuscript, "*Notes on the Geography of the Mountain District of Western North Carolina*," reveals, as noted earlier, that the southern Appalachians east of the Tennessee Valley and Cumberland Mountains form an enormous oval, extending from southern Virginia to northern Georgia connected by high, parallel transverse ridges. The A.T. utilizes portions of both forks and a connecting transverse ridge, the Nantahala Mountains.

Beginning at Damascus, the Trail route south follows Holston and Iron mountains, short ridges in northern Tennessee parallel to, but west of, the main ridges of the oval. It reaches the crest of the western fork on the summit of Hump Mountain on the Tennessee-North Carolina state line. Beyond, the route follows the state line, generally at high elevations, traversing Big Yellow, Roan, and Unaka mountains. It crosses the Nolichucky River at the end of its deep and wild gorge and then climbs to the crest of the Bald Mountains. The Trail then crosses Big Bald (5,516 feet), one of the outstanding southern Appalachian balds. The ridgecrest, which forms the state line, is extremely circuitous, trending south, west, and north. At Big Butt, the route resumes its southwesterly course.

Between Big Bald and Big Butt is Devil Fork Gap, where a well-maintained USFS trail through the Pisgah National Forest begins. The area from here to the French Broad River is almost entirely publicly owned. Its outstanding features are Camp Creek Bald and Rich Mountain.

Beyond Hot Springs, where the French Broad River breaks through the range, the Forest Service has constructed a superb 30-mile section of Trail culminating on Bluff, Walnut, and Snowbird mountains. As if approaching its climax, the ridge increases in elevation and ruggedness as it nears Davenport Gap, the end of the section.

Between Davenport Gap and the Little Tennessee River to the south lies the highest, wildest, and most primitive terrain of the entire Appalachian range, called by Guyot "the master chain" of the southern Appalachians: the Great Smoky Mountains. The A.T. in this section is entirely within Great Smoky Mountains National Park.

The Great Smokies section terminates at the gorge of the Little Tennessee River, and the route turns back toward the eastern fork of the Blue Ridge. It accomplishes this by leaving the crest of the Great Smokies at Doe Knob, crossing the Little Tennessee River at Fontana Dam, and climbing to the summit of Yellow Creek Mountain. Beyond, the route leads east.

National Forests

Since 1968, the U.S. Forest Service has been purchasing land to protect the A.T. corridor within national forest designation boundaries. All but a few miles of Trail now traverse public lands in Tennessee and North Carolina. From the Virginia line to the Tennessee-North Carolina line near Elk Park, N.C., the A.T. lies within the Cherokee National Forest. South of Elk Park, the Trail meanders back and forth across the ridgetops along the Tennessee-North Carolina line as well as the boundaries between the two national forests: the Cherokee in Tennessee and the Pisgah in North Carolina.

Great Smoky Mountains National Park

The park is in both Tennessee and North Carolina, and the Trail follows the high ridgetops along the state line. Administrative boundaries for the northern and southern sections of the park coincide with the state boundaries. District park ranger offices are in Bryson City, N.C., and Gatlinburg. The main park headquarters is in Gatlinburg.

Dogs are prohibited in the park. For a copy of other regulations and permit procedures, contact ATC or the Smoky Mountains National Park, Gatlinburg, Tenn. 37738.

Game Preserves

Game preserves and cooperative wildlife-management areas occur in many sections covered by this guide. In the game preserves, hunting is prohibited; in cooperative wildlife-management areas, hunting is subject to special restrictions, and special licenses are required. Travel on the A.T. in these areas is not restricted, although it is dangerous to move along the Trail during deer-hunting season unless conspicuously dressed in red or orange cap and shirt. Red- and yellow-paint blazes on trees in these areas indicate hunting boundary lines and should not be confused with Trail markers.

All posted restrictions must be carefully observed. Under no circumstances can firearms be carried legally (except on the cooperative wildlife-management areas, in accordance with the regulations). In most of these areas, unleashed dogs are forbidden also.

Maps

This guide mentions relevant ATC, Tennessee Valley Authority (TVA), U.S. Geological Survey (USGS), and U.S. Forest Service (USFS) maps for each section. You may want to have the TVA, USGS, and USFS maps, in addition to ATC maps, because of their expanded detail of the areas that the A.T. passes through. However, you should not use them for route navigation without consulting ATC maps, because current A.T. locations rarely appear on them.

Shelters

This section of the Trail has a continuous chain of shelters. Their names and locations are given in the summary of distances (page 249). Details of each one's facilities are provided in the Trail data for the appropriate section.

All of the structures on the A.T. were built after 1937. With some exceptions, they were constructed by the NPS or USFS. They are well-built and usually give complete protection from rain, an essential in the southern Appalachians.

Shelters are the only type of overnight accommodation along the part of the A.T. covered in this guide. Public accommodations such as inns and farmhouses, available near the Trail in other sections, are not found frequently in the southern Appalachians, because of the greater wilderness, elevation, and extent of the forested terrain.

Listed under each A.T. section are public accommodations or localities where such may be found. Check in advance, since these facilities often change without notice.

Suggestions for Extended Trips

The major divisions of the Trail data in this guide form a basis for planning trips of more than one or two days' duration.

South from Damascus, the four sections of Trail along Holston and Iron mountains allow a long two-day or a moderate three-day journey on graded trails, with the only changes in elevation near the two ends. In contrast, Sections Five to Eight, from the crossing of U.S. 321 to Iron Mountain Gap, are characterized by many steep ascents and descents on a mostly ungraded Trail. This part of the Trail is extremely scenic and varied. Sections Five, Six, and Seven, containing the rugged Laurel Fork Gorge, the extensive balds of the Yellow Mountains, and the rhododendron-covered Roan Mountain, provide an outstanding three-to four-day trip. The Trail from U.S. 19W to Sams Gap is not graded and is subject to prolific summer growth.

Although shelters are generally located no more than a day's hike apart, they may be crowded. A tent or other emergency shelter should be carried.

Another 75-mile unit (Sections 12 to 16) lies between Sams Gap and Davenport Gap. Davenport Gap and the entire 75-mile unit is fully equipped with shelters. It is divided near midway by the French Broad River at Hot Springs, where provisions may be obtained and a post office is located. From Hot Springs south to the Smokies, a three-day trip may be made; north to Sams Gap, a four-day trip. Travelers desiring a longer trip of the same character may combine this unit with the Great Smokies section to the south.

The Great Smokies afford a superb 70-mile trip on the Trail, or the section may be broken into two shorter trips: the eastern half (Pigeon River to Newfound Gap) of 32 miles and the western half (Newfound Gap to Fontana Dam) of 38 miles. Because of the great popularity of hiking in the Great Smokies, hikers are required to obtain permits to stay overnight at the shelters or elsewhere along the Trail. Hikers planning trips of more than one day in the Great Smoky Mountains National Park, should write to the Superintendent, GSMNP, Gatlinburg, Tenn. 37738, for the current shelter-use and camping regulations.

In planning trips, other divisions of the Trail covered by this guide can readily be made by referring to the summary of distances along the Trail (page 249). In it, road crossings, shelters, and notable physical features along the Trail are tabulated for quick reference.

Services for Hikers

For a list of individuals and organizations providing services for hikers (shuttling, dog-sitting, package holding, and drop-off, *etc.*), send a self-addressed, stamped envelope to the Appalachian Trail Conference, P.O. Box 807, Harpers Ferry, W.Va. 25425.

Damascus, Virginia, to Sams Gap, Tennessee-North Carolina
137.5 miles

Southward from Damascus, the A.T. climbs Holston Mountain and, after three-and-a-half miles, enters Tennessee. It follows the level crest of Holston Mountain southwestward for some 18 miles, then continues for a similar distance along the parallel crest of Iron Mountain. At this point, the Trail descends 1,300 feet to cross Watauga Dam. From here, it leads along Watauga Lake, over Pond Mountain, through the spectacular gorge of the Laurel Fork, along White Rocks Mountain, several valleys and low mountains, then climbs to Doll Flats at the Tennessee-North Carolina line.

From this point, the Trail generally follows the main crest of the Unaka Mountains southwestward along the state line, passing over a succession of high balds that culminate in Roan Mountain (6,285 feet), famed for its massive rhododendron displays and spruce-fir covering. The summits of Little Rock Knob, Little Bald Knob, and Unaka Mountain follow. After descending and crossing the Nolichucky River (1,700 feet), the Trail climbs sharply, skirts No Business Knob, and ascends to the high, grassy summit of Big Bald (5,516 feet). It follows this crest to Sams Gap (U.S. 23).

The TVA maps (seven-and-a-half-minute quadrangles) covering the Trail described in this chapter are Damascus, Laurel Bloomery, Shady Valley, Doe, Carter, Watauga Dam, Elizabethton, White Rocks Mountain, Elk Park, Carvers Gap, Bakersville, Iron Mountain Gap, Unicoi, Huntdale, Chestoa, Bald Creek, and Sams Gap. These maps show the region in great detail. They may be purchased from: Map Sales, Tennessee Valley Authority; the U.S. Geological Survey; and some retail stores.

The Trail north from Damascus is described in the *Appalachian Trail Guide to Central and Southwest Virginia*; south of the Smokies, in the *Appalachian Trail Guide to North Carolina-Georgia*. Both are published by and available from ATC.

Side trails along portions of the Holston and Iron mountains offer interesting and scenic hiking opportunities in the Watauga District of the Cherokee National Forest. A 7.7-mile maintained side trail on

Holston Mountain leads from the A.T. to Holston High Knob. (Trail data are given in Section Two.) On Iron Mountain, a blazed trail maintained by the USFS leads 16 miles to near Damascus. (The route and connection with the A.T. are indicated in Section Three.)

A well-spaced series of shelters lies along the Trail to provide sleeping accommodations for hikers. Water is usually available from nearby springs, but they may be unreliable in dry weather.

This section of Trail starts in Damascus on city streets, crosses land bought for the A.T. by the National Park Service (NPS), enters the Mt. Rogers National Recreation Area of Jefferson National Forest, and reaches the Virginia-Tennessee state line.

For much of the distance between the Virginia state line and the Great Smoky Mountains National Park, the Trail passes through Cherokee National Forest in Tennessee and the Pisgah National Forest in North Carolina.

Damascus to U.S. 421
(Low Gap, Tennessee)
Section One
14.8 Miles

Brief Description of Section

The northern end of this section begins at Damascus Town Hall on Laurel Avenue (U.S. 58) at Reynolds Street, one block south of the post office. It continues along Laurel Avenue through the center of Damascus. After an initial climb of about 1,400 feet from Damascus to the Tennessee line (3.5 miles from the post office), the Trail follows the crest of Holston Mountain over the remainder of the section with no major change in elevation. This section was constructed by the U.S. Forest Service. It has an excellent footway on easy grade and leads through a pleasing forest growth.

From south to north, there is a moderate amount of climbing, a total of 2,100 feet. Because of the difference in elevation of the two ends of the section, the climbing from north to south is appreciably greater, a total of 3,600 feet.

Points of Interest

The main ridges of Holston Mountain and Iron Mountain in Tennessee are of almost equal height and parallel each other in a southwesterly direction for approximately 35 miles. At their centers, they are connected by Cross Mountain to form a gigantic letter H. The Trail follows Holston Mountain from the Virginia-Tennessee line, then traverses Cross Mountain to Iron Mountain, which it follows to the southwestern terminus (see Sections Two and Three).

Four miles southwest from Damascus, by Va. 716 and Tenn. 133, is a USFS recreation area and campground at Backbone Rock, with picnic tables, drinking water, toilet facilities, and trails to scenic features. Backbone Rock itself is a high, narrow ridge with sheer vertical walls perpendicular to the general course of Beaverdam Creek. The stream circles around the end of the rock at its base; Tenn. 133 was tunneled

43

through its thin wall. This area is well worth a visit, by vehicle from Damascus or by a 1.5-mile side trail from the A.T.

Damascus (population 1,500) is situated at the junction of two mountain streams and three major mountain ridges.

Northeast of Damascus is the Feathercamp Ridge of Iron Mountain, which the A.T. traverses. To the south, divided from Feathercamp Ridge by Laurel Creek, is the continuation of Iron Mountain in Tennessee. To the southwest, separated from Iron Mountain by Beaverdam Creek, is Holston Mountain, which the A.T. traverses for some 18 miles.

A Trail registration and information station is maintained at the post office in Damascus, one block north of Laurel Avenue on Reynolds Street and 0.4 mile from the intersection of U.S. 58 and Va. 91, the former division between this Trail section and the one to the north.

In 1987, Damascus celebrated the fiftieth anniversary of the completion of the A.T. with a week of special events. The festival was so successful that it is now an annual event in May, attracting many hikers, politicians, and A.T. and USFS officials.

Road Approaches

The northern end of this section in Damascus on U.S. 58 is 14 miles east of Abingdon, Va., and 51 miles west of Independence, Va. It is also on Tenn./Va. 91, 13 miles south of Glade Springs, Va., and 12 miles north of Mountain City, Tenn. Abingdon and Glade Springs are on I-81.

The southern end of this section is on U.S. 421 at Low Gap, 18 miles east of Bristol, Tenn.-Va., 3.0 miles west of Shady Valley, Tenn., and 14 miles west of Mountain City. Shady Valley is also 23 miles northeast of Elizabethton, via Tenn. 91, and 14 miles southwest of Damascus, via Tenn. 133.

An intermediate point of this section may be reached by gravel USFS 69. It crosses the Trail on Holston Mountain at McQueens Gap, 3.7 miles from the southern end of this section. To reach McQueens Gap from Shady Valley, travel 3.0 miles northeast on Tenn. 133 to the community of Crandull, Tenn., turn left on USFS 69, and proceed 3.0 miles to McQueens Gap. (Automobile vandalism occasionally occurs, even during the daytime, at McQueens Gap.)

Maps

Refer to Map One with this guide for route navigation. For additional area detail, refer to USGS Abingdon, Virginia, quadrangle, or TVA Damascus, Virginia; Laurel Bloomery, Tennessee; and Shady Valley, Tennessee-Virginia, quadrangles.

Shelters, Campsites, and Water

This section has one shelter:

Abingdon Gap Shelter: Concrete-block shelter built in 1959 by USFS; 10.0 miles from northern end of the section; bunk space for 5; spring 275 yards to south.

Next shelter: north 19.4 miles (Saunders Shelter); south 8.2 (Double Springs Shelter).

Springs near the shelter and at two other places are the only dependable sources of water close to the Trail.

An old shelter on McQueens Knob is suitable for emergency use. It is not maintained and does not have water.

Jacobs Creek Recreation Area, maintained by USFS, is located at the foot of the mountain, on the South Holston Lake side near the end of the section. From Bristol, turn left from U.S. 421 (15.2 miles from Bristol city limits) onto USFS 32 (this point is 2.6 miles from the end of the section in Low Gap via U.S. 421). Follow USFS 32 for 1.4 miles and then turn left on Jacobs Creek Road. The recreation area, with camping, picnicking, and swimming facilities, is 0.5 mile farther.

Public Accommodations and Supplies

Stores, restaurants, and a laundromat are readily available in Damascus. A hostel on Laurel Avenue is maintained by the Damascus United Methodist Church, which is next door. Hot water, showers, and lodging are provided. The hostel is patrolled by the local police. Payment for services is by donation. Directions to other suitable lodgings and information about the Trail may be obtained at the post office.

History

Damascus was once known as Mock's Mill, after a man named Mock who came there from North Carolina in 1821. He acquired land and built a mill and a home where he lived the rest of his life. The country was unspoiled, the virgin stands of timber uncut. In that beautiful mountain setting, Mr. Mock reared three families (he married three times and had 33 children).

Confederate General John D. Imboden, who had been one of Robert E. Lee's chief lieutenants, was instrumental in developing the coal, iron, and lumber industries in southwestern Virginia. In 1886, he promoted the building of a railroad from Abingdon into this timber region and acquired the Mock lands. Imboden is said to have named the town at Mock's Mill for Damascus, the ancient capital of Syria, because of the surrounding mountains with their wealth of iron ore, manganese, timber, water, and coal. This was the last of the many enterprises the old gentleman promoted. He had a home in Damascus and died there in 1895.

Precautions

In this section, the Trail passes through, or borders on, three game management areas: Kettlefoot on Holston Mountain, Laurel Fork on White Rocks Mountain, and Flattop on Unaka and Flattop mountains. These areas are on national forest land but are managed in cooperation with the Tennessee Wildlife Resources Agency (Kettlefoot and Laurel Fork) or the North Carolina Wildlife Resources Commission (Flattop). Regulations in these areas forbid firearms and unleashed dogs. A special permit for fishing is required for many of the streams in these areas. Fishing tackle may be carried in the pack. No special pass or permit is needed for hiking.

Trail Description, North to South

Miles   **Data**

0.0   Section begins at Damascus Town Hall on Laurel Avenue (U.S. 58) at Reynolds Street, one block south of the post office. Proceed west-northwest.

0.1 Cross Beaverdam Creek and, in 100 feet, turn left onto smooth gravel path beside split-rail fence. Proceed south through town park.

0.4 Pass under arch, and turn right on Water Street. Immediately cross Mercedes Street, and proceed straight ahead, west, on Rural Street.

0.5 In one block, leave street, and enter woods (straight ahead) on National Park Service land. In 20 feet, make sharp right turn onto old railroad grade. In 250 feet, leave grade and climb back to left.

0.6 Reach old field, and make sharp left uphill. In 250 feet, enter woods.

0.9 Reach woods road, and go left on it, uphill.

1.0 Make sharp right on dug Trail, which ascends small sag by switchbacks.

1.2 Return to woods road at top of sag on crest.

1.7 At corner of barbed-wire fence at edge of saddle, Trail leaves National Park Service land and enters Jefferson National Forest. Ascend toward crest.

1.9 Blue-blazed trail leads downhill to left 0.1 mile to spring at abandoned homestead. Continue along well-worn road with little change in elevation.

3.5 Cross Virginia-Tennessee state line (3,200 feet), and enter Cherokee National Forest. Beyond, Trail gradually narrows and is graded.

4.4 Side trail enters from left and leads about 1.5 miles to Tenn. 133 near Backbone Rock. Beyond, Trail continues through pleasant, mature forest.

5.3 Side trail (3,600 feet) entering from right (may be obscure) leads 1.5 miles to Denton Valley Road. Continue along Trail with varying ascents and descents.

8.9 Pass A.T. register on left of Trail in sag. Please sign register.

9.9 Reach Abingdon Gap, where old Abingdon Road once entered from left; ascend.

10.0 Reach **Abingdon Gap Shelter**; spring located in hollow 275 yards due south from shelter on blue-blazed side trail. (Across from shelter, Maple Springs Trail, which may be obscure, descends 3.5 miles to Denton Valley Road.) From shelter, ascend.

11.1   Reach McQueens Gap (3,653 feet) and USFS 69 (road to left leads to community of Crandull on Tenn. 133; to right, to Denton Valley Road). Continue along main crest. Pass locked steel gate, and ascend McQueens Knob on gravel road.

11.4   Pass small log shelter on left. (Built in 1934, this shelter was the first on Holston Mountain on A.T. It is no longer maintained and has no water or bunks but could provide emergency shelter for three or four persons.)

11.5   Reach McQueens Knob (3,885 feet). Descend gradually along wooded crest following wide trail.

12.3   Bear left from crest, and descend gradually across broad ridgetop of weeds and sparse trees.

12.4   Enter denser woods, and descend.

12.5   Reach gap and old farmstead with overgrown fields. Twenty yards before reaching center of gap, note old rock wall in woods to left; spring (undependable) is on other side of wall. (Avoid old road tracks leading left from gap down hollow.) Ascend cleared knoll (south); descend through old apple orchard now grown into woods. Continue on wide trail.

12.9   Reach Double Spring Gap. Unreliable water source here.

13.2   Start descent along comparatively narrow ridgecrest to southwest. Trail is narrower here.

13.4   Pass through sag. At low point, stone wall parallels Trail for a short distance. Continue on narrow crest, ascending steadily for 0.4 mile.

13.9   Reach slight gap with overgrown field on left. (From gate on left is winter view up valley. Whitetop Mountain with bald crest is visible.) From gap, Trail is wide and well-worn. Generally follow crest, skirting below summits of knolls.

14.2   Enter pine grove.

14.3   Pass between posts of old fence. Pine grove ends here.

14.6   Barbed-wire fence enters from left, and gate is barricaded. Make sharp right, and go straight down side of ridge; swing left, and skirt right side of ridge, descending gradually.

14.8   Reach U.S. 421 about 150 feet downhill (northwest) from Low Gap (3,384 feet). This is the end of Section One. (Tennessee Department of Highways roadside park, with picnic tables and concrete-boxed spring, is just across highway. The crest southwest of Low Gap, about 0.1 mile on the Trail into the next section, has an excellent **campsite**.)

Trail Description, South to North

Miles	Data

0.0   Trail drops down steep bank into hollow at side of U.S. 421, about 150 feet downhill (northwest) from Low Gap (3,384 feet), and then ascends gradually, skirting left of ridgecrest.

0.2   Make sharp right turn straight up side of ridge, and soon come to old road on crest. Barbed-wire fence is on right, with gate barricaded by poles. Make sharp left, and continue on old road, generally ascending on crest but skirting summits of knolls.

0.5   Pass between posts of old fence, and enter pine grove.

0.8   Veer to left in fork; skirt to left of summit (avoid right fork, wide trail leading almost straight ahead); descend slightly.

0.9   Enter slight gap with overgrown field on right. (Winter view up valley; Whitetop Mountain with bald crest is visible.) Trail becomes narrower. Ascend.

1.0   Reach summit of knob. Descend steadily for next 0.4 mile; following narrow ridgecrest to northeast.

1.5   Stone wall parallels path on right for short distance. Ascend.

1.9   Reach Double Spring Gap, with unreliable water source. Ascend northwest out of gap. Reach crest shortly, and continue on wide footway.

2.2   Bear right, and climb through old apple orchard grown into woods, emerging onto cleared knoll.

2.3   Reach brush-filled gap. (Old road track leads back to right down hollow.) Bear right, and ascend slope. Twenty yards beyond center of gap, note old rock wall in woods to right; spring (dependability uncertain) is on other side of wall. Continue up slope.

2.4   Emerge onto broad crest with weeds and sparse trees. Ascend gradually along wooded crest.

3.3   Reach McQueens Knob (3,885 feet). Descend along crest on gravel road.

3.4   Pass small log shelter on right. (Built in 1934, this shelter was the first on Holston Mountain on A.T. It is no longer maintained and has no water or bunks but could provide emergency shelter for three or four persons.)

3.7   Reach McQueens Gap (3,653 feet) and USFS 69 (to right, road leads to community of Crandull on Tenn. 133; to left, Denton Valley Road). Ascend gradually from McQueens Gap for 0.9 mile following old road track, sometimes skirting right of crest. From high point attained, swing right, and descend to southeast.

4.8   Reach **Abingdon Gap Shelter**; spring located in hollow 275 yards due south from shelter on blue-blazed side trail. (Across from shelter, Maple Springs Trail, which may be obscure, descends 3.5 miles to Denton Valley Road.)

4.9   Reach Abingdon Gap, where old Abingdon Road once entered from right.

5.9   Pass A.T. register on right of Trail in sag; please sign register. Descend gradually for about one mile, slowly swinging north, and follow ridgecrest with little change in elevation for next several miles.

9.5   Side trail (3,600 feet) enters from left (may be obscure; leads 1.5 miles to Denton Valley Road). Descend steadily for 0.8 mile, and then ascend somewhat.

10.4   Side trail enters from right (descends 1.5 miles to Tenn. 133 near Backbone Rock). From here, descent is more or less steady to end of section. Trail gradually widens to old road.

11.3   Cross Tennessee-Virginia state line, and enter Jefferson National Forest. Descend steadily.

11.8   From this point, well-worn road becomes almost level for about one mile.

12.9   Blue-blazed trail to right leads 0.1 mile downhill to spring at abandoned homestead. Descend gradually on old road along crest. At bottom of descent, next to corner of barbed wire fence, leave Jefferson National Forest, and enter National Park Service land.

13.6   Where road turns right to circle knob, go straight ahead on footpath, which descends small sag by switchbacks.

13.8   Return to woods road, and continue downhill.

13.9   Leave old road, which angles down to right on footpath into woods.

14.1   Reach field. In 250 feet, make sharp right turn down bank into woods on old railroad grade.

14.2　In 250 feet, make sharp left turn from railroad grade. Then, in 20 feet, leave National Park Service land, and enter Rural Street in Damascus.

14.4　In one block, turn left, passing under arch. Follow gravel path through level, grassy park.

14.7　Reach Laurel Avenue (U.S. 58), and turn right. In 100 feet, cross Beaverdam Creek.

14.8　At Reynolds Street, reach Damascus Town Hall and end of section. (To continue on Trail, see *Appalachian Trail Guide to Central and Southwest Virginia*.)

U.S. 421 (Low Gap) to Tenn. 91
Section Two
6.9 Miles

Brief Description of Section

Proceeding north to south from U.S. 421 at Low Gap, the Trail ascends gradually along the main crest of Holston Mountain on a graded treadway through forest growth. After skirting Rich Knob, it bears left and descends steadily along Cross Mountain, first on Double Springs Road and then through woods to Tenn. 91.

In both directions, the Trail has a moderate amount of climbing, about 1,800 feet. The grade also is moderate.

Points of Interest

Southwest of Rich Knob, the Holston Mountain Trail (maintained by the statewide Franklin Group of the Sierra Club) provides an interesting side trip; see description after this section.

Road Approaches

The northern end of this section is on U.S. 421 at Low Gap, 18.0 miles east of Bristol, 3.0 miles west of Shady Valley, and 14.0 miles west of Mountain City. Shady Valley is also 23.0 miles northeast of Elizabethton, via Tenn. 91, and 14.0 miles southwest of Damascus, via Tenn. 133.

The southern end of this section is on Tenn. 91, 4.0 miles southwest of Shady Valley, and 19.0 miles northeast of Elizabethton.

Maps

For route and area detail, see Map One with this guide and TVA Shady Valley, Tennessee-Virginia, and Doe, Tennessee, quadrangles.

Shelters, Campsites, and Water

This section has one shelter:

Double Springs Shelter: Concrete block shelter built by USFS in 1960; 3.4 miles from northern end of section; accommodates 6; water available from spring.

Next shelter or campsite: north 8.2 miles (Abingdon Gap Shelter); south 8.0 miles (Iron Mountain Shelter).

This section also has a campsite with a good spring 4.4 miles from the northern end of the section.

Public Accommodations and Supplies

Public accommodations are not available at or near either end of the section.

Precautions

From the northern end of this section to Rich Knob, 3.3 miles, the Trail approximates the boundary of the Kettlefoot Game Management Area, which is to the northwest. Accordingly, no firearms or unleashed dogs should be taken through this portion. The exact boundary is posted with orange- and black-lettered signs.

Trail Description, North to South

Miles　　　　　　　　　**Data**

0.0　　From roadside park (picnic tables and concrete-boxed spring) on U.S. 421 about 150 feet northwest of Low Gap (3,384 feet), climb several feet up steep slope; make sharp right, and skirt end of ridge on graded trail. Trail here is in Kettlefoot Game Management Area. (The southeastern boundary of the management area generally follows the crest of Holston Mountain.) Ascend gradually while swinging to left in a long curve.

0.1　　Reach ridgecrest and excellent **campsite**, and make a sharp right turn. Proceed generally southwest, on or near crest.

1.3   Veer left, and follow edge of open field for 50 yards. Good views to the north and the east.

1.4   Cross old Shady Valley Road (obscure). Continue along crest on somewhat narrower trail.

2.3   Very old rail fence is on left of the Trail for about 0.1 mile.

2.6   Barbed-wire fence starts on left. Pass over Locust Knob (4,020 feet).

3.1   Reach gap. Soon, bear right at corner of barbed-wire fence, and ascend, skirting to north of Rich Knob.

3.4   Reach trail junction at gap (4,080 feet). A.T. leaves Holston Mountain. Blue-blazed Holston Mountain Trail, formerly the A.T., continues straight ahead, leading to Flint Rock at 6.0 miles from A.T. and Holston High Knob firetower, 4,140 feet, at 7.7 miles. From junction, bear left on A.T. down draw. **Double Springs Shelter** is located on right about 200 feet beyond (spring 100 yards farther down draw, beyond shelter). From shelter, ascend out of draw, skirting west of Rich Knob on old road. Direction is nearly south.

3.7   Reach crest of Cross Mountain, and descend along it.

4.2   At fork in Trail, make sharp left turn. (Old Trail continues straight ahead on Old Road Ridge, reaching Tenn. 91 in about 2.5 miles.) Descend, skirting crest of hill.

4.3   Spring is located in swampy area.

4.4   Good spring and **campsite** are located on left. Fifty feet beyond, take right fork, and follow crest of Cross Mountain southeast, descending gradually on Double Springs Road.

4.8   Veer to right off road, and continue for the remainder of the section through woods, keeping slightly to right of ridgeline most of the way.

5.3   Pass large rocks to left of Trail. Trail crosses numerous streams, which may be dry in summer months. Water is of questionable quality, since drainage is from pasture area to north.

6.9   Reach Tenn. 91 (3,450 feet) about 0.1 mile south of ridgecrest. A.T. continues diagonally to right across road and then ascends through woods.

Trail Description, South to North

Miles   Data

0.0   From Tenn. 91 (3,450 feet) about 0.1 mile southwest of ridgecrest, descend into woods on graded trail along road bank. Continue generally northwest, crossing numerous small streams, which may be dry in summer months. Water is of questionable quality since drainage is from pasture area. Keep just to the left of ridgecrest.

1.6   Pass large rocks on right.

2.1   Join Double Springs Road.

2.5   Reach fork (3,900 feet) in road, and turn left. (Good spring and **campsite** are on right of Trail 20 yards beyond fork.) From fork, ascend on dirt road to west, skirting crest of hill.

2.6   Pass second spring in swampy area.

2.7   Reach ridgecrest in slight gap. (Avoid old Trail to left, which follows Old Road Ridge, descends, and reaches Tenn. 91 at about 2.5 miles.) Turn right, and ascend ridge to north.

3.2   In slight gap, leave ridgecrest, and skirt left side of Rich Knob.

3.4   Reach **Double Springs Shelter** on left of Trail in draw (spring 100 yards to left, down draw).

3.5   Reach gap (4,080 feet). Here, A.T. joins Holston Mountain Trail. (Blue-blazed Holston Mountain Trail, formerly the A.T., approaches on left. On this trail, it is 7.7 miles to Holston High Knob firetower, 4,140 feet, and 6.0 miles to Flint Rock.) To continue on A.T. from glade, descend to east, skirting north of Rich Knob. (From here to end of section, the crest of Holston Mountain is the southeastern boundary of Kettlefoot Game Management Area.)

3.8   Pass through gap. Here, bear left along ridgecrest and barbed-wire fence. Pass over Locust Knob (4,020 feet).

4.3   Reach end of wire fence.

4.6   Very old rail fence is on right for 0.1 mile.

5.5   Cross old Shady Valley Road (obscure).

5.6   Views to north and east across farm clearing.

6.8   Reach level area and excellent **campsite** on ridgecrest; Trail makes sharp left turn. Descend gradually, while swinging to right in long curve, then climb down steep slope at side of

U.S. 421 to a point about 150 feet downhill (northwest) from Low Gap (3,384 feet).

6.9   Section ends here at Tennessee Department of Highways roadside park (picnic tables and concrete-boxed spring). Trail continues directly across highway. See Section One.

Holston Mountain Side Trail

At a point 3.4 miles south of Low Gap, A.T. leaves Holston Mountain and heads southeast over Cross Mountain to Iron Mountain. From this point, a blue-blazed trail continues southwest along the crest of Holston Mountain to Holston High Knob. Before 1954, this was the A.T. Its abandonment as the A.T. route, while necessary to avoid the wide valley crossings to the south, was nevertheless undertaken with some reluctance because of the considerable beauty and ease of traverse. For 13.1 miles, this trail follows the mountain crest through pleasant forest growth with no major change of elevation. Outstanding features are Flint Rock, a high rock outcropping near Flint Mill Gap overlooking the Holston River Valley and South Holston Lake, Holston High Knob with a USFS firetower, which has splendid views, and Holston High Point, the site of a U.S. government radar station. To preserve access to this region for hikers, this former A.T. route is blue-blazed as far as Holston High Knob and maintained by the Franklin Group of the Sierra Club.

Road Approaches to Side Trail

From Tenn. 91, 12 miles northeast of the city limits of Elizabethton, turn left (northwest) on USFS 56, passable by car (hard-surfaced for one mile, gravel beyond). Follow USFS 56 for 5.6 miles to Holston High Knob. Near crest of Holston Mountain, USFS 56A leads left to Low Gap and Holston High Point. (At Low Gap, 2.8 miles from road junction, is USFS Low Gap Campground with tables, fireplaces, four tent platforms, four pit toilets, and a piped water supply, which must be boiled or purified.) Keep right, and follow road east for 0.8 mile. At last switchback, with USFS firetower on summit of Holston High Knob (4,140 feet) within sight 250 feet farther up road, blue-blazed Holston Mountain Trail commences on right. (Tower allows splendid view. Prominent are Holston Valley and Clinch Mountain to the north, Iron Mountain and Roan Mountain to the south, and Unaka Mountain to the southwest.)

Side Trail Data, North to South

Miles   Data

0.0   Leaving A.T. in glade, proceed west, generally following crest of Holston Mountain.

1.1   In sag, take left fork, and descend steeply to southeast.

1.4   Reach Spanish Oak Gap. Generally follow ridgecrest.

3.2   Pass through Little Deep Gap.

3.9   Start steep descent.

4.0   Where ridgecrest again becomes almost level, Josiah Trail approaches from left. Via the Josiah Trail, it is 3.5 miles to Tenn. 91. At trail junction, side trail to right leads 50 yards to spring. Continue along level crest.

4.3   Josiah Trail leads to right and reaches Flatwoods Road in about 2.5 miles. Continue on crest, and descend.

5.5   Reach Flint Mill Gap (3,380 feet). (Several trails lead from gap. Sharp and due-west to the right, blue-blazed foot trail leads downhill, passing after 100 yards, spring and **campsite**, where it reaches Flint Rock, with outstanding views of South Holston Lake, at about 0.5 mile. Old Flint Mill Trail continues on, descending very steeply. Bearing right, southwest, out of Flint Mill Gap is old woods road.) To follow Holston Mountain Trail, bear left in gap. Old Flint Mill Trail descends and leads to the left to reach Tenn. 91 in 2.5 miles. Bear right, and ascend crest by switchbacks. Trail then becomes level.

7.6   Enter gravel USFS 56, passable by car. Straight ahead, within sight, is USFS firetower on summit of Holston High Knob (4,140 feet); tower affords splendid view.

Side Trail Data, South to North

Miles   Data

0.0   From road, follow foot trail along mountain crest.

1.9   At end of ridgecrest, bear left, and descend by switchbacks.

2.2   Reach Flint Mill Gap (3,380 feet). (Several trails lead from gap. At southern end of gap is Old Flint Mill Trail, descending back to right, 2.5 miles to Tenn. 91. Beyond, old road leads southwest back to left. Foot trail, also blue-blazed, leads left, west, downhill, passing after 100 yards, spring and **campsite** where it reaches Flint Rock, with outstanding views over South Holston Lake, at about 0.5 mile. Old Flint Mill Trail continues, descending very steeply.) From gap, ascend ridge to northeast.

3.4   Holston Mountain Trail is joined by Josiah Trail, which descends left to reach Flatwoods Road in about 2.5 miles.

3.6   Just before ascent, Josiah Trail leads to right 3.5 miles to Tenn. 91; at trail junction, side trail leads 50 yards to spring on left.

4.4   Reach Little Deep Gap.

6.3   Pass through Spanish Oak Gap.

7.6   Join A.T. in glade (to right, A.T. leads 3.5 miles to Tenn. 91; straight ahead, it is 3.4 miles to U.S. 421).

Tenn. 91 to Watauga Dam Road
Section Three
15.6 Miles

Brief Description of Section

Beginning at the northern end of this section, the Trail completes in the first mile, the crossover from Holston to Iron Mountain via Cross Mountain. Then, for nearly 15 miles, it follows the comparatively narrow crest of Iron Mountain in almost a straight line southwest. The traverse from north to south involves a climb of 2,600 feet, none of it strenuous. An elevation gain of 732 feet from the beginning of the section to its highest point is accomplished over 5.6 miles. The Trail continues for another 7.0 miles with only minor changes in elevation before beginning a 1,300-foot descent in 3.0 miles on the southwestern end of the mountain. Because of this descent, traverse from south to north is correspondingly more difficult, with a total climb of 3,900 feet. The route along Iron Mountain is through forest growth on a well-graded trail constructed by USFS. Nettles and briars grow thickly on the southern half of this section in mid-summer. Long pants are recommended for hikers. The southern six miles of this section are in the Big Laurel Branch Wilderness Area.

Points of Interest

From numerous vantage points, this section allows fine views over the Watauga River Valley and the TVA Watauga Lake.

In the southern half of the section, the double parallel crests of Iron Mountain are apparent. The southeastern crest, which is the A.T. route, varies only slightly in elevation and divides the watershed of Stony Creek from that of the Watauga River. Its southeastern slope is uniformly very steep, descending directly to Watauga Lake at its lower end. In contrast, the northwestern crest is cut into a series of short ridges and knolls by the streams that drain its slopes; from these knolls, side ridges extend northwestward for a mile or more into Stony Creek Valley.

From 0.2 mile southwest of the intersection of Cross and Iron mountains (1.2 miles on A.T. from Tenn. 91), the crest of Iron Mountain may be followed on a side trail back to the northeast to near Damascus, Va., providing (with Sections One and Two of the A.T.) an interesting circuit of the Beaverdam Creek watershed. To traverse this section from the A.T., turn left (north) on the former A.T. for 0.6 mile to join Doe Valley Road. Turn right (east) on Doe Valley Road, and continue for 3.0 miles to Shady Gap; then follow the graded Iron Mountain Trail 16 miles to Methodist Camp on Tenn. 91, 3.0 miles southeast of Damascus.

Three miles from the northern end of the section, a grave and stone monument are in the woods 15 yards to the north of the Trail. The monument bears the inscription, "Uncle Nick Grindstaff—born Dec. 26, 1851—died July 22, 1923—lived alone, suffered alone, and died alone." Orphaned at three, Nick Grindstaff was robbed and beaten at 26 years of age on a trip to the West. Disillusioned, he became a hermit and lived the remaining 45 years of his life on Iron Mountain with only his dog as a companion.

Road Approaches

The northern end of this section is on Tenn. 91, 4.0 miles southwest of Shady Valley, Tenn., and 19 miles northeast of Elizabethton, Tenn. Shady Valley is also on U.S. 421, 21 miles west of Bristol, Tenn., and 11 miles east of Mountain City, Tenn.

The southern end of this section is on Watauga Dam Road, 9.0 miles east of Elizabethton via Siam Valley. To reach this end of the section from Elizabethton, follow the blue-and-white TVA signs to Watauga Dam. The Trail is 0.9 mile before the Watauga Dam visitors building.

Maps

Refer to Map One with this guide for route navigation. For additional area detail, refer to TVA quadrangles for Doe, Tennessee; Carter, Tennessee; and Watauga Dam, Tennessee.

Shelters, Campsites, and Water

This section has two shelters:
Iron Mountain Shelter: Concrete-block shelter built by USFS in 1960; 4.5 miles from the northern end of the section; accommodates 6; water available 0.2 mile south on A.T.

Next shelter: north 8.0 miles (Double Springs Shelter); south 6.7 miles (Vandeventer Shelter).

Vandeventer Shelter: Concrete-block shelter built by USFS in 1961; 11.2 miles from the northern end of the section; accommodates 6; water available 0.5 mile on side trail.

Next shelter: north 6.7 miles (Iron Mountain Shelter); south 6.3 miles (Watauga Lake Shelter).

Reliable sources of water are available at four other places, noted in the Trail descriptions.

A good tentsite, but no water, is 6.5 miles south of the northern end of the section. The area near a spring (unreliable in summer) 7.3 miles south of the northern end also provides a good tentsite.

Public Accommodations and Supplies

No accommodations are available at the northern end of the section near the Trail crossing of Tenn. 91 or in Shady Valley.

At the southern end of the section, the nearest accommodations are in Elizabethton, 9.0 miles west.

Trail Description, North to South

Miles   **Data**

0.0   From eastern side of Tenn. 91 (3,470 feet), enter woods, and ascend gradually.

0.2   Pass spring (unreliable).

0.4   Cross USFS logging road. (Doe Valley Road is 200 yards to the left beyond gate.)

0.5   Cross first of a series of log-and-plank bridges through swampy area.

0.7   Here, and again in another 100 yards, cross a bog bridge over a sluggish stream. *Water must be purified; residences are located upstream.*

1.2   Bear right, southwest, onto crest and old woods road. (To left, it is 0.6 mile northeast to Doe Valley Road. From that junction, it is 1.0 mile northwest to Tenn. 91 and 3.0 miles east to Iron Mountain Trail.)

1.5   Reach top of rise.

1.9   Veer left from crest, ascending, and follow switchbacks back to crest and old road. Ascend steadily.

2.7   Pass over a summit (4,120 feet).

2.9   Blue-blazed side trail to right leads 100 yards to spring.

3.2   At top of ascent, Nick Grindstaff grave and stone monument are 15 yards to left. Continue along ridgecrest with only minor changes in elevation.

4.5   Reach **Iron Mountain Shelter** (water located 0.2 mile farther south on A.T.).

4.7   Pass spring on right. A more reliable spring is 100 yards to left on blue-blazed trail.

5.0   Reach top of broad summit.

5.2   Cross under powerlines in cleared strip. From top of ridge to left are views of fields around Doeville, Tenn.

5.6   Reach summit (4,190 feet). Ridgecrest becomes very level.

5.8   Avoid blue-blazed trail to right. (Wide trail, used for maintenance access, descends 3.5 miles, via Hurley Hollow, to Tenn. 91 in Stony Creek Valley.) A.T. swings left and descends steeply.

6.2   Reach Turkeypen Gap (3,970 feet), now grown into mature woods. Ascend through white pines.

6.4   Avoid wide trail to right, which leads 4.0 miles via Elliott Hollow to Tenn. 91 in Stony Creek Valley. (In next 0.2 mile, avoid several trails to right.) Trail ascends along crest to southwest.

6.5   Reach grassy, level area with good **tentsites** but no water. (Wide trail to right, northwest, leads 4.0 miles via Elliott Hollow to Tenn. 91.) Continue southwest along crest through woods.

7.2   Avoid wide trail to right. Continue easy descent through white-pine forest.

7.3   In boggy sag grown to a thicket, piped spring (may fail in summer) is 100 yards to left beyond small bog. (Good **tentsites** are 175 yards ahead.) Trail ascends rutted road to left of knoll.

7.4   At top of rise, in grassy junction, A.T. bends to the left and continues southwest on or near crest. (Avoid wide trail to right leading 3.5 miles via Elliott Hollow to Tenn. 91.) Good **tentsites**.

7.6   Old road tracks diverge to right, skirting side of ridge. Keep left, and ascend through woods and blackberry thickets.

7.7   Enter more mature woods. From here, Trail generally follows ridgecrest through woods to end of section. After short distance, Trail narrows to footpath.

8.2   Horselog Ridge Trail descends to right.

9.8   Sharp summit dividing Peters Branch from Lower Nidifer Branch may be seen on right. Begin series of switchbacks. Enter Big Laurel Branch Wilderness.

10.9 Pass lookout point to left.

11.2 Reach **Vandeventer Shelter**. Behind shelter, cliff allows view across Watauga Lake. To reach water, continue south on A.T. for 300 feet, and then turn right on blue-blazed trail and descend steeply to right on old roadtrack 0.2 mile to saddle; bear right off roadtrack 0.3 mile into hollow, and reach spring. From shelter, continue ascent. Soon, pass blue-blazed trail to spring. (This is beginning of little-used Vandeventer Trail, which descended to Stony Creek Valley.)

12.0 Pass massive rock formation on left.

12.6 Pass to right of summit (3,560 feet) at head of Face Camp Branch. Descent is more or less continuous from here to end of section.

12.8 On side of hill, Iron Mountain Trail leads to right. (Iron Mountain Trail continues down mountain, reaching hard-surfaced road at Blue Spring School in about 3.5 miles.) From Iron Mountain Trail junction, circle to left downhill, then swing right into draw.

12.9 Pass spring. One hundred feet below spring, turn left, cross stream, and ascend, skirting crest.

14.9 Skirt left (south) of summit (3,000 feet).

15.6 Reach Watauga Dam Road (2,240 feet), end of section and end of Big Laurel Branch Wilderness. To continue on A.T., cross road, bear right about 100 feet, climb bank, and ascend along ridgecrest.

Trail Description, South to North

Miles   **Data**

0.0   From Watauga Dam Road (2,240 feet), climb bank at highest point in gap, and follow wide trail. Enter Big Laurel Branch Wilderness. Turn left after about 50 feet, avoiding old grade, which continues straight. (A.T. follows wide trail along well-defined ridgetop for first 14.4 miles of section. First 8.0 miles are in woods. Trail often skirts summits and is graded in many places.) Ascend steadily on graded trail, generally on southern slope of mountain.

0.7   Pass to the right of summit (3,000 feet), and soon gain crest.

2.7   Reach draw. Turn right, and ascend through draw, soon passing spring.

2.8   Reach Iron Mountain Trail leading to left. (Iron Mountain Trail continues down mountain, reaching paved road at Blue Spring School in about 3.5 miles.)

2.9   Come back onto crest.

3.0   Pass to left of summit (3,560 feet) at head of Face Camp Branch.

3.6   Pass massive rock formation on right.

4.0   Reach rock overlook on right with excellent views of Watauga Valley to southeast.

4.4   Pass blue-blazed trail on left to spring. (This is beginning of little-used Vandeventer Trail, which descended to Stony Creek Valley. To reach water, descend steeply on old track 0.2 mile to saddle; there, turn right off roadtrack into hollow, and reach spring in 0.3 mile.) In 300 feet, reach **Vandeventer Shelter**. Behind shelter, cliff allows view across Watauga Lake. Continue to follow crest on well-defined trail.

4.7   Pass lookout point. Begin series of switchbacks.

5.8   Sharp summit dividing Peters Branch from Lower Nidifer Branch may be seen on left. Leave Big Laurel Branch Wilderness.

7.4   Horselog Ridge Trail (may be obscure) descends sharply left.

8.2   In open, grassy junction, Trail bends right and soon descends. (Avoid wide trail to left, which descends along a side ridge 3.5 miles via Elliott Hollow to Tenn. 91 in Stony Creek

Valley.) Good **tentsites**; water available 175 yards ahead to the right of boggy sag.

8.3   In boggy sag grown into a thicket, piped spring (may fail in summer) is 100 yards to right, beyond small bog. Beyond sag, Trail ascends gently through woods of mostly white pine.

8.4   Avoid wide trail coming in from left and back.

9.0   Enter grassy, level area with good **tentsites** but no water. (Wide trail to left, northwest, leads 4.0 miles via Elliott Hollow to Tenn. 91. In next 0.2 mile, avoid several trails to left.) Continue northeast on or near crest.

9.1   Pass benchmark at high point (4,105 feet) of knoll.

9.2   Side trail back to left leads 4.0 miles via Elliott Hollow to Tenn. 91.

9.5   Descend through white pines to Turkeypen Gap (3,970 feet), now grown into mature woods. Trail rises out of gap, gently at first, then steeply through a long curve to the right.

9.8   After 90 degrees of curve, turn to right, near top of climb. (Wide blue-blazed trail to left, used for maintenance access, leads 3.5 miles via Hurley Hollow to Tenn. 91 in Stony Creek Valley.) A.T. continues generally northeast along crest through woods.

9.9   Follow nearly level crest to northeast.

10.0 At high point (4,190 feet) of broad summit, Trail turns east and continues east for next quarter-mile.

10.4 Cross under powerline in cleared strip. (From top of ridge to right are limited views of fields around Doeville, Tenn.)

10.9 In small hollow, pass spring on left. (A more reliable spring is 100 yards to right on blue-blazed trail. This is the water supply for **Iron Mountain Shelter**, 0.2 mile ahead.) Trail ascends along rutted road.

11.1 Reach **Iron Mountain Shelter**. Continue along broad crest with little change in elevation.

12.4 Nick Grindstaff's grave and stone monument are located in woods 15 yards to right of Trail.

12.7 Blue-blazed trail to left leads 100 yards to spring. Pass over summit (4,120 feet), then descend more or less steadily.

13.8 Take switchback to right. (**Caution:** Roadtrack continues straight here.) Then, take switchback to left, and continue descent on southeastern slope.

13.9   Pass through gap where woods road rejoins Trail. Reach next summit. Descend sharply, with view of Cross Mountain straight ahead and to left.

14.4   Turn left. (Former A.T. goes straight ahead on road 0.6 mile northeast to Doe Valley Road. From that junction, it is 1.0 mile northwest to Tenn. 91 and 3.0 miles east on Tenn. 91 to Iron Mountain Trail.) A.T. continues generally north.

14.9   Here, and again in another 100 yards, cross bridge over sluggish stream. *Water must be purified, because residences are located upstream.* (This is the first of a series of plank-and-log bridges through swampy area for next 0.2 mile.)

15.3   Cross obscure, old woods road. In 50 yards, cross USFS logging road (Doe Valley Road is 200 yards to right, beyond locked gate).

15.4   Pass intermittent spring.

15.6   Reach paved Tenn. 91 (3,450 feet) and end of section (ridge-line of Cross Mountain, 4,510 feet, is about 0.2 mile to right.) To continue on A.T., go directly across road, and then descend to right into woods on graded trail.

Watauga Dam Road to Dennis Cove Road
Section Four
14.5 Miles

Brief Description of Section

The northern end of this section starts at the gap in Iron Mountain through which the access road to the Watauga Dam visitors building passes. From there, the Trail goes 0.4 mile along a ridgeline and then 0.5 mile on the service road to Watauga Dam. Next, the Trail crosses the top of Watauga Dam. It contours for 2.3 miles, paralleling the western shore of Watauga Lake but, for the most part, not in sight of it. Nearing U.S. 321, the Trail turns east and follows close to the highway and the lake for 1.3 miles, passing through a picnic area and passing a boat-launch area on U.S. 321, 3.6 miles east of Hampton, Tenn. Most of the land the A.T. passes through here is part of TVA's Watauga Dam Reservation.

From U.S. 321, the Trail climbs 1,700 feet in 1.3 miles to the crest of Pond Mountain. It follows the crest westward for 5.1 miles and then drops steeply into Laurel Fork Gorge. Most of the land here is in the Pond Mountain Wilderness, where logging, roads, and development are prohibited. The A.T. proceeds upstream in the gorge for 2.8 miles to the end of the section at Dennis Cove Road.

This section has considerable climbing in both directions, primarily over Pond Mountain. From north to south, the ascents total 4,000 feet; from south to north, they total 3,600 feet.

Note: A major relocation is planned in this section. See Trail data on pages 72 and 76.

Points of Interest

The views from Watauga Dam are spectacular, and the glimpses of the lake along the Trail are rewarding. Watauga Dam, 320 feet high and 840 feet long, was completed in 1949. It is made of an impervious core of rolled earth with heavy layers of rock that provide weight and stability. Watauga Lake is 16.3 miles long and 0.8 mile wide at its widest point and covers 6,430 acres. The powerhouse was built one-half mile downstream from the dam to take advantage of an additional 35-foot fall in the river.

From the top of the dam, U.S. 321 can be seen across the lake to the south with the summit of Pond Mountain (4,329 feet) on the horizon (south-southeast). On the eastern bank of the lake, just above the dam, is the 128-foot-diameter spillway. Looking downstream, Holston Mountain (4,140 feet) can be seen to the north. Angling up to the right behind the emergency spillway is an edge-on view of the great Iron Mountain Fault. This fault is about 44 miles long. The rocks of Holston Mountain and Iron Mountain slid to the northeast on this fault. The rock above the fault is older than the rock below the fault.

The outstanding feature of this richly varied section is the wild and rugged gorge of Laurel Fork, through which the Trail passes for 2.7 miles. With its sheer cliffs and wooded slopes, its rhododendron and mountain laurel, waterfalls and rapids, and its ever-changing direction and appearance, the gorge possesses a natural beauty that is one of the highlights of the A.T. It lies within the Pond Mountain Wilderness. A new footbridge across the river—built of native materials without hardware or power tools by ATC volunteers—won a national primitive-skills award in the early 1990s from the U.S. Forest Service. (Mile point 13.7 southbound.)

Laurel Fork twists its way down the narrow defile between Pond and Black mountains, carrying an average 26 million gallons of water per day from an annual rainfall of 54 inches in the valley above. In its course, it passes over rapids and waterfalls, the largest being Laurel Falls, about 40 feet high. From the streambed, the wooded slopes rise steeply and uninterrupted to the mountaintops 1,200-1,600 feet above, while, in places, cliffs rise vertically from the water's edge as much as 150 feet. Toward the middle or end of May, flowering shrubs can be found blooming in profusion, including Catawba rhododendron (otherwise found in this region only on the tops of the higher mountains, such as Roan), Carolina rhododendron, and mountain laurel. Many other flowers are found in season. A stand of virgin timber remains in the gorge in a very steep hollow above Laurel Falls, so inaccessible that it did not warrant cutting when the rest of the gorge was timbered. (See page 71.) This hollow is not, however, easy to reach from the Trail.

The gorge is accessible only on foot, and the A.T. is the only maintained trail through it.

A side trip to Potato Top is worthwhile. This is a large, rocky projection in the shape of a potato hill, almost surrounded by nearly vertical cliffs that drop to Laurel Fork (see TVA Elizabethton, Tenn., quadrangle map). The views of the gorge from this point are outstanding.

Road Approaches

The northern end of this section is on Watauga Dam Road, 9.0 miles east of Elizabethton, Tenn., by road, via Siam Valley. From Elizabethton, go south on U.S. 19E and 321 to Valley Forge, and turn left (east) following the blue-and-white TVA signs toward Watauga Dam. The Trail crosses Watauga Dam Road 0.9 mile before the Watauga Dam visitors building.

By special arrangement with TVA, A.T. hikers may cross the dam, but other visitors may not. Do not use the old TVA construction and maintenance road as a shortcut to the dam.

The southern end of the section is at Dennis Cove, 3.0 miles southeast of Braemar, Tenn., and U.S. 321 via USFS 50. Hampton, Tenn., is 0.5 mile west of Braemar on U.S. 321 and Tenn. 67.

At the southwestern corner of Watauga Lake, the Trail is easily accessible from U.S. 321. Here, the Trail is a few yards north of the highway, between the road and the lake. This point is 2.8 miles east of Hampton, Tenn., on U.S. 321.

The Trail crosses U.S. 321 near USFS Rat Branch Recreation Area, 3.6 miles east of Hampton. Cars may be left here at a motel for a nominal charge.

Note: A planned relocation will move the A.T. crossing of U.S. 321 almost a mile north toward Hampton, at the Shook Branch Recreation Area.

A midpoint of the section is accessible by a one-mile blue-blazed trail up Laurel Fork where U.S. 321 crosses the stream east of Hampton. Vandalism of cars occurs frequently at night at the Trailhead parking lot, however.

Maps

Refer to Map One with this guide for route navigation. For additional area detail, refer to TVA Elizabethton and Watauga Dam, Tennessee, quadrangles.

Shelters, Campsites, and Water

This section has two shelters:

Watauga Lake Shelter: Built in 1980 by USFS; 1.9 miles from the northern end of the section; accommodates 6; water available.

Next shelter: north 6.3 miles (Vandeventer Shelter); south 10.7 miles (Laurel Fork Shelter).

Laurel Fork Shelter: Stone shelter built in 1966 by Tennessee Eastman Hiking Club; 12.6 miles from the northern end of the section; accommodates 6; water available 150 feet from shelter.

Next shelter: north 10.8 miles (Watauga Lake Shelter); south 7.7 miles (Morehead Gap Shelter).

Two good campsites are available—one at the crossing of Griffith Branch near Watauga Lake, and the other at a spring on Pond Mountain, 9.2 miles from the northern end of the section. Water is also available in the picnic area along the southern shore of Watauga Lake.

Public Accommodations and Supplies

From the northern end of the section, the nearest accommodations are in Elizabethton, 9.0 miles west.

At the crossing of U.S. 321 is a combination restaurant, motel, and service station where tent space may be rented and limited supplies obtained. To the west, it is 3.6 miles on U.S. 321 to Hampton, which has restaurants, groceries, and a laundromat.

Rooms may be rented in Braemar and Hampton. Transportation is available from Hampton Cab or local drivers.

History

Laurel Fork, which joins the Doe River in Hampton after leaving its torturous gorge, drains a high valley (14,528 acres) lying between White Rocks Mountain on the south and Pond and Walnut mountains on the north. Laurel Fork Valley was timbered from 1911 to 1925. In 1911, a railroad was built from Braemar up through the gorge into the valley, requiring three high trestles and 32 miles of track. Spur tracks were moved from place to place as the timber was removed. (The railroad bed now serves as the route of the A.T. for some distance through the gorge.)

The logs were transported to the mill at Braemar in 80,000-pound-capacity flat cars, hauled by 70-ton Shay locomotives. The bark and extract wood were hauled out in boxcars. During the 14 years of operation, more than 200 million board-feet of lumber were manufactured. About 60 percent of this was hemlock. The remainder consisted of hardwoods: oak, chestnut, poplar, maple, wahoo, cucumber, birch, and sassafras.

A few mountaineers have lived in Laurel Fork Valley all their lives and, until recent times, walked down to Hampton and back for supplies.

Except for the small mountain community of Dennis Cove, the valley is forested, most of it within the Unaka District of the Cherokee National Forest. The upper portion (8,000 acres) now constitutes the Laurel Fork Game Management Area.

Precautions

Explorations in Laurel Fork Gorge off the A.T. should be undertaken with caution because of the extreme ruggedness of the terrain and the presence of poisonous snakes in some seasons.

Trail Description, North to South

Note: A relocation on Pond Mountain is planned that will shorten the A.T. by 3.0 miles (by going more directly to the ridgecrest) and eliminate the walk through developed areas beside Watauga Lake. The segment listed here as miles 3.1 to 9.2 will be changed radically. Please follow the white blazes.

Miles   Data

0.0   From high point of Watauga Dam Road (2,240 feet), climb western bank on stone steps. Ascend on ungraded Trail through woods.

0.2   Reach ridgetop, and follow rocky crest.

0.3   Reach summit (2,480 feet). Continue straight ahead (south) along crest. Soon, descend steeply along rocky slope, which burned in 1970.

0.5   Turn right onto paved dam-access road. (Road to left, closed to public, leads 0.2 mile to steel gate and junction with

Watauga Dam Road.) Descend on road. In about 0.2 mile, powerhouse can be seen to the right.

0.9   Walk across Watauga Dam to western end, and turn left along nearly level construction road. Near eastern end of dam is concrete emergency spillway. Behind the spillway, the large Iron Mountain Fault is visible.

1.3   At end of road, make sharp right on short, steep ascent. Continue on level, graded trail.

1.5   Cross hollow that drains into small inlet of lake. Climb steeply to crest of small side ridge, then descend.

1.9   Turn right onto old road paralleling stream. Beyond, where Trail crosses stream, blue-blazed trail leads right 50 yards uphill to **Watauga Lake Shelter**. Soon turn left away from water, and ascend to crest of small ridge.

2.2   Join road coming down hollow from right, cross Griffith Branch (possible **campsite**), and continue on road. Soon leave road at junction of roads, and skirt left.

2.4   Enter grove of white pines. Near end of ridge, cross dirt road, leave white pines, and descend.

2.8   Cross through draw where dirt road comes down from right. (Dirt-and-gravel beach is 100 yards to left.) Soon, pass through boaters' picnic area.

3.0   Swing right onto dirt road, and continue with little change in elevation.

3.1   Pass around steel gate, then go straight ahead with unpaved roads to right and left. For next 0.3 mile, Trail passes between lake to left and residential area to right; for next 1.0 mile beyond, U.S. 321 is to the right of Trail.

3.2   Cross unpaved lake-access road.

3.4   Cross small stream and paved lake-access road, then swing left and start paralleling to left of U.S. 321. Cross log footbridge over storm-water ditch. In 130 yards, enter USFS Shook Branch Recreation Area, with picnic tables, sandy beach, water, and toilets; open in warm weather.

4.0   Start ascent to summit of short ridge; cross, and descend.

4.3   Emerge from woods into USFS Rat Branch Recreation Area (lake access). Continue along upper edge of grassy field.

4.4   Turn right onto paved lake-access road, and go directly across U.S. 321. (Located here is combination service station, restaurant, and motel.) Turn left along U.S. 321.

4.5   Turn right away from highway, and ascend into woods. (For next 3.7 miles, the Trail passes over a series of small summits and through shallow gaps as it ascends a side ridge south-southwest to crest of Pond Mountain.)

4.7   Pass under powerline. (Powerline easement is northern boundary of 4,365-acre Pond Mountain Wilderness Area. Trail traverses wilderness area for 9.0 miles and exits at upper end of Laurel Fork Gorge, about 0.3 mile north of Dennis Cove.) Continue ascent through switchbacks.

5.7   Pass over three summits.

8.2   Near head of steep, semicircular drainage, Big Pond Trail enters from left and back. (Big Pond Trail leads east 1.1 miles to Bear Stand, 4,040 feet, 0.3 mile south of Pond Mountain Summit, 4,329 feet; views east, west, and south.). Continue skirting right on less steep ascent.

8.3   Descend gently along narrow crest for 0.6 mile. Reach crest of western ridge of Pond Mountain, and bear right.

9.2   After circling to right of large knob on level path, reach The Pond Flats. Excellent **campsites** located here. (In the blocky, white quartzite boulders around the spring and campsite are what appear like short—three inches long—outlines of straight shoestrings. These are the filled holes of animals, perhaps worms, called "skolithus," who drilled their burrows straight down in tidal sands of the seashore about 550 million years ago. The sands have since changed to hard quartzite.)

9.3   Spring located in rocky bottom (3,700 feet) of drainage. Water may rise farther down the drainage in dry weather.

9.5   Leave The Pond Flats on ascent of small knoll.

9.7   Start down steep nose of side ridge heading northwest.

9.9   Pass through Horseridge Gap (3,300 feet). (Hazelwood Hollow Trail, somewhat obscure, leads to the right 1.2 miles to U.S. 321, east of Hampton, Tenn.) Winter views of Watauga Lake to right.

10.2   Start steady, sometimes steep, 1.5-mile descent.

10.5   Switch back to right. Straight ahead are fine views of Laurel Fork Gorge; winter views of Hampton to the right. In the next 0.2 mile, pass two more ledges that afford good views of White Rocks and Roan mountains to the south and Hampton to the west.

10.7	Old A.T. bears right.
10.9	Turn left off crest, and leave road. (**Caution:** Straight ahead, road leads into posted property.) Start descent through several switchbacks to Laurel Fork.
11.1	From this turn there is a good view of Potato Top, south-southwest.
11.5	Switch back to right, descending.
11.8	Turn left on level trail near Laurel Fork. (Blue-blazed trail to right, former route of A.T., leads 1.0 mile downstream to U.S. 321 at eastern end of Hampton, Tenn. Impressive "Buckled Rock," a high cliff, can be seen across Laurel Fork at 0.4 mile along this trail.) Continue upstream and, in 140 yards, bear left on old road entering from right across stream. A few yards to right, Pine Tree Spring overflows from foot of large pine at water's edge. Continue upstream on wide trail.
12.0	Cross footbridge over stream. Veer left, and continue upstream on wide trail through rhododendron growth.
12.2	Make second crossing on footbridge. Continue upstream.
12.3	Pass Waycaster Spring on left. Leave wide trail, and bear left through dense rhododendron growth. Ascend steeply on narrow, ungraded trail.
12.6	Reach summit of low, narrow ridge. (This ridge, covered with pine, Catawba rhododendron, and mountain laurel, allows fine views of rocky gorge walls. Stream circles end of ridge and is visible to the right.) Continue along ridge. (Continue up ridgecrest from this point about 300 feet to reach **Laurel Fork Shelter**. Water is reached by following path 150 feet to stream in hollow from left, north of shelter. To right of shelter, blue-blazed trail follows old railroad grade south about 0.5 mile to reconnect with A.T. beyond Laurel Falls at about mile 13.4 on A.T.; it is intended to be used when high water floods the Trail below Laurel Falls.)
12.7	A.T. bears right from ridgecrest and descends.
12.8	Reach wide trail near edge of stream and continue upstream.
13.1	Skirt base of cliff on built-up rock walk at edge of stream. *Caution:* If the walk is flooded, return to old railroad grade and use blue-blazed high-water route.
13.3	Reach Laurel Falls. From falls, leave stream temporarily. Turn back sharply left away from falls, up rough-graded trail.

13.4   Reach old railroad grade, and make sharp right. (Blue-blazed
       trail to left, on railroad grade, leads about 0.5 mile to reconnect
       with A.T. at mile 12.6.) In 0.1 mile, pass vista. Proceed up
       grade, alternately passing through cuts and along side of
       gorge.
13.6   Rough trail to right (west-southwest) leads 0.2 mile to sum-
       mit of Potato Top, which offers a fine view of Laurel Falls to
       the north.
13.7   Where railroad originally crossed trestle over stream, turn
       left, and descend to stream; cross log footbridge over stream
       (Koonford Bridge).
13.8   Regain railroad grade; turn left, and follow grade upstream.
13.9   Leave Pond Mountain Wilderness.
14.5   Pass through rustic fence, and cross USFS parking lot (2,533
       feet) to paved USFS 50 in Dennis Cove, end of section. (To
       right, USFS 50 leads 4.1 miles to U.S. 321 at Braemar, near
       Hampton, Tenn. To left, it is 1.0 mile to USFS Dennis Cove
       Recreation Area on Laurel Fork with **campground** and run-
       ning water; road beyond continues to Buck Mountain Road
       via Walnut Mountain.) To continue on A.T., cross road
       diagonally to left, and climb bank into woods.

Trail Description, South to North

*Note: A relocation is planned for Pond Mountain that will shorten the A.T.
by 3.0 miles (by going more directly to the ridgecrest) and eliminate the walk
through developed areas beside Watauga Lake. The segment listed here as miles
5.3 to 11.4 will be changed radically. Please follow the white blazes.*

Miles   **Data**

0.0   At northern edge of USFS parking lot, walk through rustic
       fence, and continue straight ahead through woods on old
       railroad grade. Proceed downstream, northwest, with Lau-
       rel Fork on the right.
0.6   Enter southwestern corner of 4,365-acre Pond Mountain
       Wilderness Area. (Trail traverses wilderness area for 9.0
       miles and exits at powerline easement about 0.2 mile south of
       U.S. 321, near Rat Branch.) Continue on old railroad grade.

0.7 Where railroad originally crossed trestle over stream, turn right, descend to stream, and cross log footbridge over stream (Koonford Bridge).

0.8 Return to railroad grade. Proceed down grade, alternately passing through cuts and along rim of gorge.

0.9 Pass vista with spectacular view into gorge. Rough trail to left (west-southwest) leads 0.2 mile to summit of Potato Top, which offers unsurpassed views of the gorge.

1.1 Turn back sharply left down rough-graded trail. (Blue-blazed trail straight ahead follows railroad grade north about 0.5 mile to **Laurel Fork Shelter** and reconnects with A.T. at mile 1.9. It is intended to be used when high water floods the Trail below Laurel Falls.)

1.3 Reach Laurel Fork near base of Laurel Falls, and turn right. Skirt base of cliff on built-up rock walk at stream's edge. (**Caution:** If the walk is flooded, return to old railroad grade, and follow blue-blazed trail downstream.)

1.5 Trail widens to old roadbed.

1.9 Bear right off wide trail, and ascend on narrow, graded trail to crest. (Trail up ridgecrest to right leads 300 feet to **Laurel Fork Shelter**. Water can be reached by following path 150 feet to stream from left, north of shelter. Blue-blazed trail to right of shelter follows old railroad grade south about 0.5 mile to reconnect with A.T. at mile 1.7.) Proceed to left, west, along crest. (This ridge, covered with pine, Catawba rhododendron, and mountain laurel, allows fine views of rocky gorge walls. Stream circles ridge and is visible upstream.) Descend steeply from point of ridge through pines and rhododendron.

2.0 Rejoin wide trail close to stream, and continue downstream.

2.2 Pass Waycaster Spring. This is last dependable water source before crest of Pond Mountain (mile 5.1), where spring may fail in summer. Next water is located at U.S. 321, at mile 10.0.

2.3 Cross footbridge over stream.

2.5 Recross footbridge over stream. Continue downstream, keeping to right of stream. At bend of Trail to right, where old roadbed continues straight and crosses stream, Pine Tree Spring overflows from foot of large pine at water's edge. Watch for turn in 140 yards.

2.7 Make sharp right. (Blue-blazed trail straight ahead leads 1.0 mile downstream to U.S. 321 at Hampton, Tenn. Impressive "Buckled Rock," a high cliff, can be seen across Laurel Fork at 0.4 mile along this trail.) Ascend steeply.

2.8 Turn left onto old railroad grade, and pass through notch cut in rocks for railroad.

3.0 Switch back to left, ascending.

3.4 From this turn, there is a good view of Potato Top, south-southwest.

3.6 Reach crest of ridge. Make sharp right on old road, and ascend. (**Caution:** Straight ahead is posted property.)

3.8 Trail bears right as old A.T. enters from left rear. Pass rock ledge. In the next 0.2 mile, pass two additional ledges, with good views of White Rocks and Roan mountains to the south and Hampton to the west.

4.0 Switch back to left. To right are fine views of Laurel Fork Gorge; winter views of Hampton to the right. Old A.T. enters from right rear. Steep climb ahead on ridgecrest.

4.2 Trail continues straight ahead, while old A.T. bears off to the right.

4.6 Reach trail junction in Horseridge Gap (3,300 feet). (Hazelwood Hollow Trail leads left 1.2 miles to U.S. 321, east of Hampton, Tenn.) Continue straight, east, along ridge, climbing.

5.0 Descend southeastern end of knoll, and enter The Pond Flats, which has excellent **campsites.**

5.1 Spring located in rocky bottom (3,700 feet) of drainage. Water may rise farther down the drainage in dry weather. (In the blocky, white quartzite boulders around the spring and campsite are what appear to be short—three inches long—outlines of straight shoestrings. These are the filled holes of animals, perhaps worms, called "skolithus," who drilled their burrows straight down in tidal sands of the seashore about 550 million years ago. The sands have since changed to hard quartzite.)

5.3 Leave The Pond Flats, and circle to left of knob on level path.

5.6 Start easy 0.6-mile ascent along narrow crest.

6.2 Veer left off crest at 3,760 feet, and skirt left, descending gently.

6.3   Near top of steep, semicircular drainage, Big Pond Trail ascends to right. (Big Pond Trail leads east 1.1 miles to Bear Stand, 4,040 feet, with good views to east, south, and west). A.T., to left, continues skirting left, and descends steeply.

6.9   Turn left off crest, and descend very steeply by switchbacks. In the next 2.9 miles, pass over several summits and through small gaps in generally steep descent.

9.8   Pass under powerline. Leave Pond Mountain Wilderness.

10.0   Reach U.S. 321. Turn left, and follow shoulder of highway 150 yards to entrance of a combination restaurant, service station, and motel. Turn right, and cross highway into USFS Rat Branch Recreation Area (lake access). Turn left, and proceed along upper edge of grassy field.

10.2   Enter woods, turn right, and climb small ridge.

10.5   Descend side of ridge to side of highway. For next 0.6 mile, U.S. 321 generally parallels Trail on left.

10.7   Make sharp right onto paved access road to USFS Shook Branch Recreation Area (picnic tables, sandy beach, water, and toilets; open in warm weather).

11.0   Leave recreation area, cross log footbridge over storm-water ditch, and continue along wooded shoulder of U.S. 321. In 130 yards, circle to right, cross paved lake-access road and small stream, then turn right again. For next 0.3 mile, the Trail goes between lake to the right, and residential area to the left.

11.3   Cross unpaved lake-access road.

11.4   Approach dirt road, pass around steel gate, and continue on level dirt road.

11.5   Leave dirt road as it circles to left. Ascend, and then proceed on level trail. Pass through boaters' picnicking and camping area. Soon, bear away from lake, and ascend.

11.7   Cross old road through draw. (Dirt and gravel beach is 100 yards to right.) Ascend away from lake. Continue through grove of white pines along low ridge, crossing two dirt roads.

12.1   Where road comes uphill from right, cross road at junction, and continue on side road, descending. Cross Griffith Branch (possible **campsite** here), and turn right, away from road; continue up narrow hollow.

12.4   Join old road trace coming down from left. Bear right, and descend.

12.6   Blue-blazed trail leads left 50 yards uphill to **Watauga Lake Shelter**. Cross small stream tumbling down from left, and continue descent on old road parallel to stream. In 130 yards, turn left from road, and ascend around side ridge.

13.2   Enter end of dam construction road, and proceed along road beside lake for 0.2 mile.

13.4   Descend metal stairs to western end of Watauga Dam. Proceed across dam. Near eastern end of dam is concrete emergency spillway. Behind spillway, large Iron Mountain Fault is visible.

13.6   Turn left at eastern end of dam on access road; ascend steadily on paved road for 0.3 mile. From a turn in this road, the powerhouse can be seen downstream.

13.9   At gap, make sharp left off access road. (Straight ahead, access road leads 0.2 mile to steel gate and junction with Watauga Dam Road.) Once in woods, immediately turn right, and ascend steeply on rocky slope through area burned over in 1970.

14.1   End steep climb at summit (2,480 feet). Continue straight ahead, northeast, along narrow, rocky crest.

14.3   From end of ridge, start steep descent on ungraded trail.

14.5   Descend bank on stone steps to high point of Watauga Dam Road and end of section. To continue on A.T., cross road, bearing right about 100 feet, and ascend bank on concrete steps. Leave TVA land.

Dennis Cove (USFS 50)
to U.S. 19E at Bear Branch Road
Section Five
19.4 Miles

Brief Description of Section

At the northern end of this section, the A.T. starts in Dennis Cove, 3.5 miles southeast of Hampton, Tenn., and climbs 1,000 feet in 2.8 miles to White Rocks Mountain firetower. It follows the crest for 4.1 miles eastward and then passes over numerous small side ridges for another 5.9 miles until it crosses Walnut Mountain Road. Then, it goes over Big Pine Mountain, turns south into Sugar Hollow, and in 5.0 miles comes out on a road at Mill Creek. It follows several roads and trails, ending on U.S. 19E.

This section requires considerable climbing in both directions: 6,600 feet from north to south, and 6,500 feet from south to north. Several parts are steep, especially the northern end of White Rocks Mountain and in Sugar Hollow.

Points of Interest

The Trail from Dennis Cove to the ridgecrest of White Rocks Mountain is of particular and varied interest, passing through open fields, scenic viewpoints, interesting rock formations, and pleasing forest growth. White Rocks firetower has good views of the Holston Mountain and Iron Mountain ranges to the north, Beech and Grandfather mountains to the east, the entire Roan massif to the south, and Unaka Mountain to the southwest. Coon Den Falls, a small, pretty cascade, can be reached by a blue-blazed side trail. South of Moreland Gap, the Trail leaves major ridge lines and passes over many small side ridges to avoid farms and roads.

Road Approaches

The northern end of the section at Dennis Cove is 3.0 miles southeast of Braemar, Tenn., and U.S. 321 via USFS 50 through Cedar Gap.

Hampton, Tenn., is 0.5 mile west of Braemar on Tenn. 57, U.S. 321, and U.S. 19E. Cars can be parked at business establishments near the Trail, after permission is obtained. Vandalism is common on cars parked overnight at Trail crossings.

The southern end of the section is on U.S. 19E, 0.9 mile into Tennessee from the Tennessee-North Carolina state line, 16 miles east of Hampton, Tenn., and 2.5 miles west of Elk Park, N.C.

The Trail crosses Walnut Mountain Road 6.7 miles from the southern end of the section. To reach this crossing from Roan Mountain, Tenn., proceed east 1.5 miles on U.S. 19E to Shell Creek. There, turn left (north) on Buck Mountain Road (marked "Walnut Mountain Road" on TVA quadrangle map) and proceed 4.0 miles to junction with Walnut Mountain Road; turn left on Walnut Mountain Road, and go about 1.0 mile to Trail crossing, just north of Laurel Fork.

Maps

Refer to ATC Tennessee-North Carolina Maps One and Two for route navigation. For additional area detail, refer to TVA Watauga Dam, Tennessee; White Rocks Mountain, Tennessee/North Carolina; and Elk Park, North Carolina-Tennessee, quadrangles.

Shelters, Campsites, and Water

This section has one shelter:

Moreland Gap Shelter: Concrete-block shelter built in 1960 by USFS; 5.8 miles from northern end of section; accommodates 6; spring nearby.

Next shelter: north 7.7 miles (Laurel Fork Shelter); south 14.1 miles (Apple House Shelter).

Good campsites are just south of White Rocks Mountain firetower and in Sugar Hollow south of Big Pine Mountain. The campground at USFS Recreation Area in Dennis Cove, about 1.0 mile from the A.T., may be used. Shelters, campsites, and several other places along the Trail have springs and stream branches.

Public Accommodations and Supplies

At the southern end of the section, on U.S. 19E, the nearest facilities are to the east, with several grocery stores between 1.2 and 4.0 miles, a restaurant at 2.0 miles, a post office (Elk Park) at 2.5 miles, a motel at 3.0 miles, and a campground at 3.5 miles. Similar facilities, notably a motel/hiker hostel with shuttle service (at 4.0 miles from the Trailhead), are located at Roan Mountain, Tenn., west on 19E.

Precautions

Between Moreland Gap and U.S. 19E, many streams flow across the Trail. Many of them come from nearby pastures not visible from the Trail, so water from streams must be purified before use—always the safest course anywhere on the Trail.

Trail Description, North to South

Miles   **Data**

0.0   From USFS parking lot in Dennis Cove, cross USFS 50 diagonally to the left (south), and climb bank into woods. (This is the start of a relocation by the ATC Konnarock Crew and TERC Hiking Club completed in 1988. The blue-blazed trail to the left, former route of A.T., proceeds 0.6 mile through Dennis Cove on the paved road, ascends 0.5 mile to Coon Den Falls and beyond, 0.8 mile to a ridge, 3,320 feet, on the northern end of White Rocks Mountain, where it connects with this relocation. The blue-blazed trail, combined with the relocation, forms a 3.6-mile loop.) Continue through woods to a shed near chalet.

0.1   Leave woods, and proceed up road to the left of pond.

0.3   Swing left, and cross (right) fence into white pine forest. Continue parallel to fence for several yards, then turn right, and cross short ridge into another drainage. Turn left, and ascend beside a small stream. In next 0.6 mile, cross stream several times.

0.9   In head of hollow, swing left. Proceed along sidehill trail, skirting left for 0.1 mile.

1.2   Cliff at end of spur permits view to north and west. Turn right, and ascend ridge.

1.4   Veer to right of cliff, and ascend through rhododendron.

1.5   Cliff to right provides views to west and north.

1.7   Turn right, and ascend. (Blue-blazed trail to left, former A.T., leads to Coon Den Falls, 0.8 mile, and Dennis Cove Road, USFS 50, 1.3 miles.)

2.8   Reach White Rocks Mountain firetower on summit (4,105 feet). Follow USFS road southeast, descending.

3.3   Where road swings to right off crest, leave road, and follow Trail straight ahead, ascending.

3.6   Reach edge of field in gap. (Avoid trail to right, which descends in 3 to 4 miles to U.S. 19E.) Go directly southeast across field, passing former site of old Canute Place, named for its first settlers; possible **campsite**. Only some foundation stones remain, mostly covered by a thicket of briars.

3.7   Just before entering woods and ascending, blue-blazed trail to right leads 200 yards to spring. About 50 feet beyond blue-blazed trail, reach remains of old fence, enter woods, and ascend.

3.8   Continue to left of old fence.

4.4   At fence corner, turn right and pass through gap in fence. Beyond, follow nearly level trail to left, east-southeast, through woods along main crest of White Rocks Mountain. Reach highest point of White Rocks Mountain (4,206 feet).

4.9   Descend steadily on woods road, following main ridge.

5.8   Reach Moreland Gap (3,813 feet) and **Moreland Gap Shelter**; spring short distance down hollow opposite shelter). Woods road bears to right, 50 feet past shelter. Continue east on ridge, ascending steeply.

6.1   Last major summit (4,121 feet). From here, Trail generally follows ridgetop, descending gradually for 0.7 mile.

6.8   In middle of a long, sweeping curve to right, turn left, and ascend. In about 100 yards, pass through small sag; begin lengthy descent.

7.2   Pass to left of large rock outcrop, and enter rhododendron thicket. Descend steeply to left of crest. In about 100 yards, reach excellent **campsite** where several small streams converge. (Purification is recommended for water in this area and for next several miles. Most of the streams are polluted to some extent because of human or animal habitation upstream.)

7.3   Cross small stream. About 30 feet to right are remnants of moonshine still. Cross low, narrow ridge and two more streams. (Water from these sources should be purified before drinking.)

7.4   Cross boggy branch, and turn right. Trail has several small climbs and descents.

7.7   Avoid old road that turns right. Descend along spur.

7.8   Cross small boggy stream (purification recommended). Ascend, skirting left on steep ridge.

8.4   Make sharp right down side of ridge, and soon make sharp left onto old road.

8.5   In small sag, make sharp right away from old road, which turns left.

8.6   Cross small cascade in stream (purification recommended) that comes down from right. Soon, cross boggy stream (purification recommended).

8.7   Cross spring, and enter grove of white pines. Ascend, skirting left of steep slope.

8.8   Cross crest, and leave white pines.

8.9   Cross boggy stream (purification recommended). About 30 feet above are remnants of another moonshine still. Ascend generally along crest. Then descend.

9.1   Pass spring. Continue level, skirting left.

9.3   Among large rhododendrons, cross small stream (purification recommended). Ascend steeply.

9.6   Cross crest. Located here are faint signs of old homestead. (Paths lead off to north-northeast and south-southwest.) Join old road, and descend to south through rhododendron.

10.0   Cross USFS logging road. To right, road leads 0.2 mile to locked gate, which allows pedestrian traffic, and 0.2 mile beyond to paved Buck Mountain Road (marked "Walnut Mountain Road" on TVA White Rocks Mountain quadrangle). Ascend through large white pines. Trail crosses several small or intermittent streams.

10.3   Turn left on old logging road for 25 yards; then make hard right.

10.4   Trail crosses undulating terrain in woods with several springs and possible **campsites**.

10.7   Descend ridge by switchbacks, reach road parallel to Laurel
       Fork (not recommended for drinking), and turn right. (Here,
       Laurel Fork tumbles over a small cascade, and there is a cliff
       across creek.) Ascend beside stream, which flows from south,
       for about 0.1 mile.

10.9   Cross log bridge over Laurel Fork, and ascend steeply through
       rhododendron.

11.0   Reach crest.

11.2   Pass through break in old fence at northwest of broomsedge
       field. Follow level path through field. (Fine view to right,
       south, encompassing Hump, Little Hump, and Yellow moun-
       tains and Grassy Ridge, Jane Bald, Round Bald, and Roan
       High Knob. Straight ahead along Trail to east is view of Buck
       Mountain. To its right in distance is rugged crestline of
       Grandfather Mountain.) At southeastern edge of field, enter
       woods, and start steep descent.

11.4   Reenter woods.

11.5   Cross downed barbed-wire fence, and continue south-south-
       east through heavy rhododendron and woods. Cross stream
       (purification recommended).

11.6   Traverse open area surrounded by rhododendron. (Located
       here is campsite suitable for several tents.) Soon, make short,
       steep descent.

11.7   In next 50 yards, cross three streams. Ascend through moun-
       tain magnolias and large hemlocks. In next 0.4 mile, Trail
       travels on and passes over several small side ridges.

12.1   Cross two streams; cross old road.

12.4   Pass through broad, relatively level area. Cross two narrow
       streams in 0.1 mile.

12.7   Reach gravel Walnut Mountain Road. To right, paved Buck
       Mountain Road (marked "Walnut Mountain Road" on TVA
       White Rocks Mountain quadrangle) is 1.5 miles; Walnut
       Mountain is to left. Ascend to left, north, along road for 10
       yards, then turn off road to right. Descend easily, crossing
       traces of two old roads. Soon, turn straight down side of
       ridge.

12.9   Turn right onto gravel road, ascend road for 15 yards, then
       turn left into woods. Skirt around head of drainage.

13.0   Reach crest of spur and turn left, downhill, onto old road.
       Descend along crest.

13.1   Turn right off crest down side of hill. Descend steeply, and cross boggy seep in bottom of narrow hollow. Continue on easy grade.

13.2   Turn left onto old gravel road in Slide Hollow. Follow road across main stream in hollow, and continue east along road as it starts up left side of slope above stream valley. (*Stream is contaminated; do not use.*)

13.3   At sharp curve to left, leave road, and head up hollow on wide path.

13.4   Reach ruins of moonshine still; turn left, north, away from stream. Climb through short switchbacks, then angle up side of hill, skirting left to level shoulder of ridge. Continue gentle ascent, skirting left.

13.5   Turn up end of ridge, and ascend more steeply.

13.6   Reach northeastern summit of Big Pine Mountain. (To left, east-southeast, is a winter view of the sharp peak of Beech Mountain. To right of Beech, southeast, and at almost twice the distance, is rugged crest of Grandfather Mountain.) Continue through shallow sag and over a higher summit (about 3,700 feet) in long curve to left. Join old road approaching from left and back. Soon make sharp left, and descend east-southeast for almost a mile.

14.4   Make sharp right away from crest. Avoid faint trail continuing straight ahead. Skirt left, and descend into Sugar Hollow.

14.7   Turn right on old logging road in bottom of Sugar Hollow. Ascend gently along road near stream. Soon, come to good campsite.

14.9   Trail turns sharply left down steep stream bank. (Upstream 0.1 mile is former site of Don Nelan shelter, built by TEHC in 1981 and burned by vandals in 1990.) A.T. crosses Sugar Branch on rustic bridge and starts steep ascent of southern side of Sugar Hollow.

15.1   Cross seep on stone beam. Continue climb out of Sugar Hollow by switchbacks and wooden steps.

15.4   Make sharp right on crest of spur. Ascend along spur to large hemlock, then skirt left on old road.

15.5   Cross crest, and head down side of ridge. Go through two sags, and cross two rises; in each sag, bear left at junction of trails.

15.7   Cross old road at right angle. (To left, road leads 1.1 miles to the Elk River; to right, 0.1 mile to steel gate near end of Campbell Hollow Road.) Descend road bank, and soon cross small, boggy stream (*water contaminated—do not use*). Fifty yards farther, cross log footbridge over Jones Branch. (This is the second of five crossings of Jones Branch or its tributaries. *All the water in this area is contaminated and must not be used.*) Continue through boggy area under rhododendron, hemlocks, and hardwoods.

15.9   Cross plank bridge over Jones Branch. (*Contaminated water; do not use.*) Climb through overgrown field, and turn left onto paved Campbell Hollow Road. Continue on road, generally west, for 0.5 mile.

16.3   Turn left from Campbell Hollow Road, and climb bank into overgrown field. Cross field to south, enter woods, and cross small, boggy stream. *Contaminated water—do not use.* Climb through rhododendron to pine-covered crest of low ridge, and descend other side.

16.5   Cross small stream. *Water contaminated—do not use.* Ascend side of hill by switchbacks.

16.6   After steep, short climb, leave woods and USFS lands, and turn left onto paved Buck Mountain Road. In a few yards, turn right into field opposite High Point Memorial Baptist Church. For next 0.3 mile, ascend gently as Trail meanders through meadows and woods of former farm.

16.9   Reach northwestern corner of Isaacs Cemetery. Proceed along western side of cemetery, turn right into woods, and ascend on switchbacks.

17.0   South of cemetery, cross old road, and ascend into woods, steeply at first, then more gently through grassy field with white pines.

17.3   Reach summit (about 3,820 feet). (This is the high point on the Trail between White Rocks Mountain and Doll Flats. White Rocks Mountain can be seen to the west, Beech to the east. To the south and southwest are the peaks of the Roan massif: Hump, Little Hump, Yellow Mountain, Grassy Ridge, Jane Bald, Round Bald, and Roan High Knob.) Continue south, descending steeply through field and then young woods.

17.5   Turn right in narrow, grassy hollow, and descend. At cross fence (at junction with larger hollow), a spring, walled in with rough stones, is 10 yards to right. Turn left (south) into main hollow.

17.6 Spring is located at base of tree near ruins of house on left. Trail follows nearly level old road for next 0.4 mile. Skirt left, around end of several spurs.

18.0 In curve of road to right, turn left down spur, and, in 45 yards, cross fence to right on pole stile. Descend side of hill, turn right, cross another fence on plank stile, and skirt left through woods.

18.1 Leave woods near top of long, grassy hollow, and switch back to left. Descend through Bishop Hollow. USFS permits cattle to graze here at times, to preserve open field.

18.6 Veer right away from center of hollow, and soon skirt right on level trail.

18.7 Cross fence on stile, and continue on nearly level path. Soon, switch back to right, and ascend spur.

18.8 Turn left off crest of spur. Cross to another spur, and turn left. Descend into Bear Branch Hollow by switchbacks and steep trail. Pass under two powerlines.

19.1 Cross Bear Branch. *Water contaminated—do not use.* Climb out of hollow, and soon cross paved Bear Branch Road, diagonally to the left.

19.2 Pass concrete pigpen on the left, and soon cross high point of ridge. Descend to U.S. 19E.

19.4 Cross U.S. 19E to A.T. sign on southern side of highway and end of section. To continue on Trail, descend into hollow 25 yards east of A.T. sign.

Trail Description, South to North

Miles   **Data**

0.0 From A.T. sign on southern side of U.S. 19E, go straight across highway. Trail enters woods and ascends small ridge by sidehill trail.

0.2 Cross high point of ridge. Pass concrete pigpen 35 yards ahead on right. Soon, cross paved Bear Branch Road diagonally to the left.

0.3 Cross Bear Branch (*water contaminated*), and ascend steeply through switchbacks. Pass under two powerlines.

0.5   Turn left onto crest of spur, and ascend. In 0.1 mile, cross over to another spur, and descend.

0.7   Use switchback to left on nearly level trail, cross fence on stile, and continue on level trail, skirting right. Soon, reach grassy field near bottom of Bishop Hollow.

0.8   Swing to left, and ascend through middle of grassy hollow. USFS permits cattle grazing here, to preserve open field.

1.2   Near head of hollow, switch back to right, and enter woods. Skirt right through woods, ascending.

1.4   Cross fence on plank stile, and ascend to left. In 90 yards, cross fence on pole stile, and turn left again. Turn right into curve of old road. Follow road for 0.4 mile as it contours right around several spurs with little change in elevation.

1.8   Pass to left of house ruins. (Spring is located at base of tree near house foundation.) Continue up center of hollow. In about 100 yards, turn right (east) toward side hollow.

1.9   Go through downed cross fence at bottom of side hollow. Spring, walled in with rough stone, is 10 yards to left. Ascend through short hollow. At head of hollow, switchback to left, and skirt left. Ascend through young woods and overgrown field.

2.1   Summit, about 3,820 feet. (This is the high point on the Trail between Doll Flats and White Rocks Mountain and has excellent views. White Rocks Mountain can be seen to the west, Beech Mountain to the east. To the south and southwest are the peaks of the Roan massif: Hump, Little Hump, Yellow Mountain, Grassy Ridge, Jane Bald, Round Bald, and Roan High Knob.) Continue north on a gentle descent through grassy field overgrown with white pines.

2.3   Make sharp right off old roadtrack into thick stand of young white pines. Descend through woods by switchbacks.

2.4   Exit woods, cross rough road, and make a switchback to the southwest, near corner of Isaacs Cemetery. Head north along western edge of the cemetery and, in 0.3 mile, after a slight rise, descend gently as the Trail meanders through the meadows and woods of a former farm.

2.7   Opposite High Point Memorial Baptist Church, turn left onto paved Buck Mountain Road. In 25 yards, turn right off Buck Mountain Road, and descend steeply into USFS woods.

2.9   Cross small stream. (*Water contaminated—do not use.*) This is the first of five crossings of Jones Branch or its tributaries. (*All the water in this area is contaminated and must not be used.*) Continue straight ahead to top of low, pine-covered ridge; turn right, then left, and descend other side through rhododendron.

3.0   Cross plank bridge over small stream. *Contaminated water— do not use.* Veer left, and cross overgrown field to Campbell Hollow Road.

3.1   Descend steep road bank, and turn right onto paved Campbell Hollow Road. Proceed on road, generally east, for 0.5 mile.

3.5   Turn right off Campbell Hollow Road, descend through overgrown field, and cross plank bridge over Jones Branch. (*Water contaminated—do not use.*) Continue through bog under rhododendron, hemlocks, and hardwoods.

3.7   Cross log footbridge over Jones Branch. (*Contaminated water—do not use.*) In 50 yards, cross another boggy stream (*water contaminated—do not use*), then climb a road bank, and cross old road. (By this road, the Elk River is 1.1 miles to right; to left, steel gate near end of Campbell Hollow Road is 0.1 mile.) Ascend straight up side of hill, north, on old roadtrack. Cross two rises, and go through two sags; in each sag, keep right at junction of trails.

3.8   Intersection of old trails; cross crest, the southern rim of Sugar Hollow, and turn left. Skirt right on gullied road.

3.9   Descend along crest for 90 yards, and turn left off spur. Descend steeply by wooden steps and switchbacks into Sugar Hollow.

4.2   Cross seep on stone beam. Continue descent on more gentle grade.

4.5   Cross rustic bridge over Sugar Branch, and climb steep bank to old logging road. (Upstream 0.1 mile is former site of Don Nelan Shelter, built by TEHC in 1981 and burned by vandals in 1990.) Turn right, and descend along road near stream. Soon, pass good **campsite**.

4.6   Turn left, away from road, and ascend on graded trail, generally skirting right.

4.9   Make sharp left onto crest of Big Pine Mountain, and begin long climb to summit.

5.5   At long curve to right, turn left off road, and soon cross
       summit (about 3,700 feet) of Big Pine Mountain. Continue
       nearly level, and pass through sag to minor summit.

5.8   Northeastern summit of Big Pine Mountain. (To right, east-
       southeast, is winter view of the sharp peak of Beech Moun-
       tain. To the right of Beech, southeast, and at almost twice the
       distance, is the rugged crest of Grandfather Mountain.)
       Descend end of ridge, then turn left, and skirt right, south-
       west, on gentle grade.

5.9   Reach flat shoulder of spur ridge. Go diagonally across crest,
       and start gentle descent; trail soon becomes steep and de-
       scends through switchbacks.

6.0   At stream, to left of moonshine still, turn hard right, and
       continue straight down hollow.

6.1   Turn left into sharp curve of dirt road. Proceed along road,
       skirting right on slight downgrade.

6.2   Cross main stream in Slide Hollow. (*Water contaminated—do
       not use.*) In 25 yards, turn right off road, and enter woods on
       narrow trail. In 50 additional yards, cross boggy seep in
       bottom of narrow hollow, then ascend steeply.

6.3   Reach crest, and turn left on old roadtrack. Ascend along
       crest. In 100 yards, turn right off crest, and circle to right; turn
       right on gravel logging road. Follow it 100 feet, and turn left
       onto Trail.

6.4   Ascend side of ridge, crossing traces of two roads.

6.6   Reach Walnut Mountain Road. (To left, it is 1.5 miles to Buck
       Mountain Road, marked "Walnut Mountain Road" on TVA
       White Rocks Mountain quadrangle; Walnut Mountain is to
       right.) Descend diagonally to left across road, and ascend
       bank on opposite side.

6.7   Cross rounded knoll; continue through woods, and cross
       several small or intermittent streams. Cross several old roads.
       Possible **campsite**.

8.0   Ascend through woods, and enter broomsedge field over-
       grown with briars and yellow poplar. Cross field on level
       path. (To left, south, is magnificent view of Hump Mountain
       on left and Roan High Knob on right, with summits of Hump,
       Little Hump, Yellow Mountain, Jane Bald, and Round Bald
       between. To back, east-southeast, is view of sharp peak of
       Beech Mountain. To the right of Beech, southeast, and almost

twice the distance, is the rugged crest of Grandfather Mountain.)

8.2   On western side of field, enter woods, and continue on level Trail. Soon, bear right onto crest, and cross downed fence.

8.3   Make sharp right, and proceed straight down side of ridge.

8.5   Cross log bridge over Laurel Fork (not recommended for drinking). Turn right on parallel trail, and descend gently beside stream.

8.6   Beside small cascade, turn left away from stream, and ascend steeply.

8.7   Reach end of ridge in grove of white pines.

8.8   Leave white pines where Trail levels and joins old road.

8.9   Where road turns left up ridge, go straight ahead across head of hollow, which drains to right. (To right, just after Trail leaves road, is faint trail down hollow to bog and possible spring. To right of hollow is good **campsite** among boulders.) Ascend gently, skirting right; avoid faint descending trail.

8.0   Cross crest of spur, and descend to old road. Turn left on road, ascending; in 25 yards make sharp right, away from road.

9.2   Make sharp left across small stream; descend through large white pines.

9.3   Cross stream (not recommended for drinking), and soon cross USFS logging road (via this road, it is 0.2 mile south to locked gate, which permits pedestrian traffic, and 0.2 mile beyond to paved Buck Mountain Road). Ascend west through beech and oak woods and large rhododendron.

9.4   Turn north on old, obscure road.

9.6   In short descent, avoid old trail to left. Continue on old road through draw, where path goes to left down drainage.

10.0   Make sharp left on intersecting trail and, in 70 yards, cross small stream (purification recommended). Soon cross crest, descend other side of ridge, and cross small branch (purification recommended).

10.2   Spring is in sloping rock to left of Trail.

10.4   Cross boggy branch (purification recommended). About 30 feet to left are remnants of moonshine still. Soon, descend through white pines.

10.6   Cross small boggy branch (purification recommended).

10.7   Cross small stream, climb over low ridge, and then cross larger stream tumbling over boulders (water from these sources must be purified before drinking).

10.8   Follow road 100 yards left, then turn right up side of ridge.

11.5   Cross small stream in rhododendron thicket.

11.9   Cross small stream and two sluggish branches (all water should be purified).

12.1   Cross small stream (purification recommended), and start steep ascent.

12.5   Turn right. (To left, former route of A.T. follows crest of White Rocks Mountain, east-southeast.) Trail follows crest of White Rocks Mountain for next 4.0 miles.

13.3   Reach first major summit (4,121 feet).

13.6   Reach Moreland Gap (3,813 feet). Woods road enters from left. Located here is **Moreland Gap Shelter** (spring short distance down hollow opposite shelter). Continue west along crest.

14.5   Reach highest point (4,206 feet) of White Rocks Mountain.

15.0   Pass corner of old field bordering ridgecrest.

16.1   USFS road enters from left. Join road, and follow it straight ahead.

16.6   Reach White Rocks Mountain firetower (4,105 feet). From tower, descend steadily to northwest.

17.7   Turn left, and proceed west across broad ridge. (Blue-blazed trail straight ahead, former A.T., leads 0.8 mile north to Coon Den Falls and 0.5 mile more to USFS 50 and proceeds west 0.6 mile on paved road through Dennis Cove to end of section. The blue-blazed trail, combined with the relocation, provides a loop of 3.6 miles.)

17.9   Cliff to left provides views to west and north. Skirt left on ridge, descending.

18.1   Veer right, to center of ridge, and continue descent through woods.

18.2   Cliff at end of ridge permits a view to the west. Turn left, and skirt right on graded trail for next 0.1 mile.

18.4   Turn right (north) down head of hollow. In next 0.6 mile, reach stream, and cross it several times.

19.0   Turn right off old road, away from stream, ascend bank into white-pine woods, and cross short ridge. Turn left, and parallel fence before crossing it; turn right down hollow.

Continue descent through old farmstead, and pass to right of pond.

19.3   Below pond, turn left above gate, pass to left of shed, then turn right into woods.

19.4   Descend steep bank to paved USFS 50 in Dennis Cove. Cross road diagonally to left (north) to USFS parking lot and end of section. To continue on A.T., pass through opening in rustic fence at northwestern edge of parking lot, and proceed downstream on broad, level path beside Laurel Fork.

U.S. 19E to Carvers Gap
(Tenn. 143-N.C. 261)
Section Six
13.0 Miles

Brief Description of Section

This section traverses the high balds of Hump Mountain, Yellow Mountain, and the eastern portion of Roan Mountain. The Trail passes over five summits more than 5,400 feet above sea level and skirts the shoulders of Big Yellow Mountain and Grassy Ridge. Several of the finest remaining southern Appalachian balds, with their open, grassy summits, are found in this section.

The northern end of this section is in Tennessee at U.S. 19E. The Trail enters North Carolina at Doll Flats and returns to the state line at Bradley Gap. The Trail is on or near the Tennessee-North Carolina state line for the remainder of this section. This section is on USFS land, although the corridor from U.S. 19E to Doll Flats is very narrow.

Beginning at the northern end of the section at U.S. 19E, the Trail climbs through Wilder Mine Hollow to Doll Flats and ascends gradually on a graded trail (dug by the Konnarock Crew and the TERC in 1983 and 1984) to the open, grassy eastern ridge of Hump Mountain. The Trail crosses Hump Mountain on open balds, descends to open Bradley Gap, circles left to climb to the southern peak of Little Hump Mountain, crosses the end of Yellow Mountain, and descends to Yellow Mountain Gap. The Trail climbs from the gap over a small knob and through two sags to another knob, which provides outstanding views. After a short descent, a long climb through woods skirts the northern end of Grassy Ridge.

The Trail then follows the crest westward through open fields, passing over the summits of Jane Bald and Round Bald.

Because of the ascent of the Hump from U.S. 19E, travel from north to south involves much more climbing than from south to north. Total climbing going south is 5,680 feet; north, it is 2,400 feet.

Points of Interest

The mountaintops of this section are treeless meadows, providing superb views. In late June, this section is enhanced by rhododendron and flame azalea in bloom, as well as Gray's lily, or orange bell lily, a rare plant found in few places besides these balds. From this section's eastern end, Grandfather, Beech, and White Rocks mountains are especially prominent. The western peaks provide views of the North Toe River Valley and the Black Mountains, including Mt. Mitchell to the south and southwest, and the upper Doe River Valley, Little Rock Knob, and Ripshin to the north.

Grassy Ridge is the only peak close to the A.T. that is both above 6,000 feet and has a natural 360-degree view. All others have trees or man-made structures at the top.

At Yellow Mountain Gap, the Overmountain Victory Trail crosses the A.T. This is the historic Bright's Trace, used by frontiersmen on their way from Sycamore Shoals (Elizabethton, Tenn.) to defeat the British army at Kings Mountain, S.C., during the Revolutionary War. That defeat saved the South and was a turning point in the war.

The USFS land for the A.T. and strips below it on both sides have been designated as the "Highlands of the Roan" because of the unique natural features of the area. The Southern Appalachian Highlands Conservancy is active in obtaining private land in the designated strips in order to preserve the area from development.

The Trail in Wilder Mine Hollow passes through the ruins of Wilder Mine. Magnetic iron ore was mined here from 1880 until 1918. Numerous open pits and underground tunnels were dug. The mine was served by a spur line of a railway to a much larger mine in Cranberry, N.C. A stone quarry was operated here between 1952 and 1960. The rock is pretty, with pink feldspar, white quartz, and green epidote.

Road Approaches

The northern end of the section is on U.S. 19E, 0.9 mile into Tennessee from the Tennessee-North Carolina state line, 16 miles east of Hampton, Tenn., and 2.5 miles west of Elk Park, N.C. Cars can be parked at business establishments near the Trail, after permission is obtained. Vandalism is common on cars parked overnight at the Trail crossing.

The southern end of this section is at Carvers Gap on the Tennessee-North Carolina state line, 14 miles south of Roan Mountain, Tenn., on Tenn. 143 and 14 miles north of Bakersville, N.C., on N.C. 261. Vandalism occurs with cars parked overnight at the Trail crossing.

Maps

Refer to ATC Tennessee-North Carolina Map Two for route navigation. For additional area detail, refer to TVA Elk Park, North Carolina-Tennessee; White Rocks Mountain, Tennessee-North Carolina; and Carvers Gap, North Carolina-Tennessee, quadrangles.

Shelters, Campsites, and Water

This section has three shelters:

Apple House Shelter: Rebuilt in 1984 by the TERC Hiking Club and Cherokee National Forest staff; 0.5 mile from northern end of section; water available at spring 0.3 mile south of shelter.

Next shelter: north 14.1 miles (Moreland Gap Shelter); south 7.8 miles (Overmountain Shelter).

Overmountain Shelter: Also known on some trail maps as Yellow Mountain Barn; located at Yellow Mountain Gap, 8.3 miles from the northern end of section; accommodates 20; fires and cooking permitted on ground floor only; water available.

Next shelter: north 7.8 miles (Apple House Shelter); south 1.7 miles (Roan Highlands Shelter).

Roan Highlands Shelter: Wooden shelter located at Low Gap built in 1977 by USFS; 10.0 miles from northern end of section; accommodates 6; water available at nearby spring 100 yards to the left.

Next shelter: north 1.7 miles (Overmountain Shelter); south 4.3 miles (Roan High Knob Shelter).

Fine campsites are available near the springs at Doll Flats, Bradley Gap, the sag between Hump and Little Hump mountains, Yellow Mountain Gap, and Grassy Ridge.

Public Accommodations and Supplies

The northern end of the section has a grocery store 1.2 miles east on U.S. 19E. Other grocery stores are within the next few miles. The post office in Elk Park, N.C., is 2.5 miles east of the Trail. A motel is 3.0 miles and a campground is 3.5 miles east of the Trail; restaurants are 2.0 and 3.0 miles from the A.T. Similar facilities, notably a motel/hiker hostel with shuttle service (at 4.0 miles from the Trailhead), are located at Roan Mountain, Tenn., somewhat farther to the west on U.S. 19E.

No public accommodations are available at the southern end of this section. Roan Mountain State Park (campgrounds, cabins, restaurant) is approximately 9.0 miles north of Carvers Gap on Tenn. 143.

Precautions

Trail marking across the balds is difficult. Blazes on posts mark the Trail on the bald of Hump Mountain. For the most part, the Trail route is obvious in clear weather. However, extreme caution should be taken, especially in fog and particularly in the vicinity of the Hump Mountain summit, which has ridges not followed by the A.T., and Big Yellow Mountain and Grassy Ridge, which have side ridges extending south, higher than the main crest. Frequent reference to the detailed Trail data is advised, even in good weather. Nettles are abundant on some parts of this section in summer. Long pants are recommended.

When traveling this section from north to south, ample allowance should be made for the considerable climbing involved.

Do not enter the underground mines in Wilder Mine Hollow. The air may be foul, and roof falls can occur.

Trail Description, North to South

Miles   **Data**

0.0   From U.S. 19E (2,880 feet) 0.9 mile northwest of the North Carolina state line, descend to southeast on former driveway, cross pole bridge over stream, and turn west.

0.2   Turn south on old mine road, and head up Wilder Mine Hollow. Soon, pass abutment of former railroad bridge, and ascend on road.

0.5   **Apple House Shelter** is on right. (First constructed in 1952, it was used to store explosives for the quarry in the hollow, and tools for the nearby orchard. Seasonal spring is 0.3 mile south, up the hollow.) Level ground near shelter is a good space for tents. Cross stream, and continue on road.

0.6   Cross small stream (seasonal). Soon, pass pit of former stone quarry on right. Spoil banks of iron mine are on left. (**Caution:** Do not enter underground mines. They may contain foul air or poisonous gas, and roof falls occur frequently.)

0.7   Where two hollows join in grove of white pines, take trail to left.

0.8   Small spring to left. Continue ascent through two parallel drainages. Farther on, skirt to right around spur on graded trail.

1.0   Cross head of hollow under powerline, then cross road on crest, and continue on level road to south; in 100 yards, road starts steep rise.

1.1   Switch back to left, and descend into head of hollow, skirting right on road.

1.2   At end of road, ascend steeply on path, skirting right at first. Ascend by switchbacks to cliff, and turn to left onto end of road.

1.3   Turn right away from road, and climb bank to steep, graded trail. Ascend steeply through switchbacks, then skirt right of crest.

1.4   Cross old road that runs across ridge, pass by rock outcrop, soon turn left uphill, and reach old road on crest. Proceed on grassy road, then veer right into wide path.

1.5   Cross fence, pass through grassy sag, and reenter woods. Soon, fence enters from right and back; continue to left of fence.

1.7   In sag where fence goes off to right, go past fence corner, then cross fence, and ascend, skirting right.

1.9   Follow contour around to right on steep hillside; soon pass through rock field below cliffs.

2.0   Start steep ascent in rich woods; climb through switchbacks toward cliffs.

2.1   Climb through gap in low cliff, and reach crest. Switch back and forth beside rocky hollow, then cross rock field on level path.

2.2   Where Trail swings right through broad drainage, pastoral valley is in view to northwest. Swing back to left at base of cliff, then right.

2.3   Cross crest of rocky spur. (Overlook is 50 feet to right.) Turn
      up middle of steep hollow, and climb over narrow stone
      escarpment to broad crest.

2.4   Ascend gradually to southeast on long curve to left.

2.6   Enter Doll Flats (4,560 feet). Grassy, overgrown field with
      boulders and scattered old trees offers many excellent **camp-
      sites**. Pass boulder, and reach old roadtrack and fence. To
      right, south, follow old road for 60 feet, then turn right, west,
      and descend 240 yards to spring. Pass through break in fence,
      and enter grove. In trees, turn right, south, leave trees, and
      follow level path across open grassy field.

2.8   Reenter woods. For next 1.3 miles, Trail goes south, then east
      as it climbs gently while skirting left (northern) slope of ridge.

4.1   At boulder, turn right (south), and ascend narrow spur.

4.2   Reach grassy, open field, and continue south.

4.3   Turn right (west) onto old roadtrack in center of ridgecrest
      and continue west, then northwest for 0.75 mile, ascending
      along bald eastern ridge of Hump Mountain.

5.0   Cross summit of Hump Mountain (5,587 feet). (From here
      there is magnificent panoramic view of Doe River Valley to
      northwest, Whitetop and Mt. Rogers in Virginia to northeast,
      Beech Mountain to east-northeast, and Grandfather Moun-
      tain with multiple peaks to east. Nearby and to west-south-
      west are Grassy Ridge and Roan High Knob.) In 100 yards,
      turn left.

5.1   Descend to southwest along broad ridge. Trail follows old
      roadtrack, generally to right of crest. Small, intermittent
      spring on western side of Hump may be reached by turning
      back to right at top of first rock outcropping and following
      contour through field (no trail). Spring is below large, marked
      rock near edge of woods.

5.9   Reach wide, grassy Bradley Gap (4,960 feet), which has good
      campsites and numerous springs that may be trampled by
      cattle. (Well-defined trail to right descends 1.5 miles to upper
      end of gravel road to Shell Creek, Tenn. A seep spring is
      about 0.2 mile along this trail. Another spring, source of
      Horse Creek, is about 100 yards left, southeast. *All water in this
      area must be treated*.) Go west through gap, following worn
      cattle trail. Begin gradual ascent. At fork, take left (lower)

trail, which leaves main crest and proceeds across field directly toward wire fence at point just above edge of woods.

6.3   Pass through opening in fence. Spring is just a short distance ahead and below Trail. Continue on path through field close to woods on left, skirting left of northern peak of Little Hump Mountain.

6.5   Reach small gap. (Avoid wide trail leading to left and slightly down.) Pass straight through woods, then ascend through field on main ridgecrest. (Here, Trail joins state line.) Bear right, and ascend steeply through brush to flat, grassy summit of Little Hump Mountain (5,459 feet), with outstanding views and **campsites**. Descend broad, grassy slope to southwest. Trail is marked with occasional cairns.

6.9   Pass large rock formation on left. Continue descent, following center of ridge.

7.1   Reach saddle. A spring (source of Little Horse Creek) is about 100 yards left (southeast). *Water must be boiled or purified.*

7.3   Cross fence on stile, picking up old roadtrack entering from left. Keep right, and follow rutted road through beechwoods with fence on right.

7.9   Leave old road, which bears left, and continue along fence.

8.0   Old road reenters next to Trail. Descend through field, and then swing right into woods.

8.3   Reach Yellow Mountain Gap (4,682 feet), which has good **campsites**. (Historic Bright's Trace crosses through gap. Road is not passable by car. To left, it descends via Roaring Creek to U.S. 19E at Toe River, N.C.; to right, it descends via Hampton Creek to U.S. 19E at Roan Mountain, Tenn. A spring of uncertain dependability is about 300 yards down trail to right. To left and back, southeast, along old Bright's Trace, is another spring at about 300 yards.) Blue-blazed trail through fence to the left, leads 0.3 mile downhill past spring to **Overmountain Shelter**. (The loft of the barn is intended for sleeping only.) To continue on A.T., cross through gap into woods, and ascend steeply northwest, keeping to right of fence.

8.5   Make sharp left turn, and reach a summit (4,907 feet). (Excellent views of Hump Mountain, Big Yellow, Grassy Ridge, Roan High Knob, and Little Rock Knob.) Descend gradually on, or near crest of narrow ridge, keeping to right of fence.

9.0 Old woods road goes off to right via Heaton Creek to Roan Mountain, Tenn.

9.2 In saddle (Buckeye Gap, 4,730 feet), overgrown road enters on right from Heaton Creek and proceeds straight ahead. Beyond saddle, skirt to right of ridge to spur, then switch back to left to return along spur to ridge. Follow ridge a short distance, then bear left through gap in fence, and ascend, skirting left of ridge.

9.7 Switch back to right.

9.8 Reach summit of Elk Hollow Ridge (5,180 feet) at top edge of field. Pass through opening in fence, and descend along edge of field, keeping to right of fence.

10.0 At bottom of field, near fence corner, reach Low Gap (5,050 feet) and **Roan Highlands Shelter** (spring is about 100 yards to left down side of ridge). From shelter, ascend through woods.

10.1 Pick up old road, which Trail follows or parallels for next 0.1 mile.

11.0 At top of steep rise, turn right in scrub growth. Skirt northern slope of Grassy Ridge at nearly constant elevation through alder growth and occasional fir.

11.3 Pass spring on left, and then several small springs along Trail.

11.4 Reach open main ridge and old roadtrack. Located here is good **campsite**. Flat summit of Grassy Ridge (6,189 feet) may be reached by following wide trail track back to left, then turning to right across grassy bald. Gap, 6,050 feet, surrounded by Catawba rhododendron about 0.2 mile south of summit, provides excellent **campsite**. Spring is a short distance down on eastern side of gap.

11.9 Reach Jane Bald summit (5,807 feet).

12.0 Pass rock formation; good views.

12.2 Pass through Engine Gap (named for an abandoned sawmill engine), and swing left onto graded trail.

12.4 Turn left onto old roadtrack on ridgecrest.

12.6 Pass slightly to right of Round Bald summit (5,826 feet).

12.7 Pass clump of spruce, planted many years ago as a test to see if spruce would grow in a bald area. Soon, reach wooden steps built in 1976 by crew from Appalachian Mountain Club, contracted by USFS and Southern Appalachian Highlands Conservancy.

13.0   Cross rail fence, and descend stone steps to Tenn. 143/N.C. 261 through Carvers Gap (5,512 feet). USFS picnic area, with spring and toilets, is beyond parking area straight across highway. To continue on A.T., cross highway, and walk to right of pole fence along left edge of drive to parking lot.

Trail Description, South to North

Miles   **Data**

0.0   From Tenn. 143/N.C. 261 through Carvers Gap (5,512 feet), ascend stone steps, cross rail fence, and ascend east directly up open slope of Round Bald. Ascend on gravel trail with log steps. Near summit, pass clump of spruce, planted many years ago to see if spruce would grow in a bald area.

0.4   Pass slightly to left of Round Bald summit (5,826 feet), and descend on old roadtrack.

0.6   Turn right onto graded trail on North Carolina side of the ridge.

0.8   Pass through Engine Gap (named for an abandoned sawmill engine), then ascend.

1.0   Pass rock formation that affords good views.

1.1   Reach Jane Bald summit (5,807 feet), and start easy descent.

1.6   Trail narrows. Leave main ridgecrest, and bear left onto footpath through alder brush. (Flat summit of Grassy Ridge can be reached by following wide trail straight ahead, then turning right near summit through open field scattered with alder. Gap, 6,050 feet, surrounded by Catawba rhododendron about 0.2 mile south of summit, provides excellent **campsite.** Spring is short distance down on eastern side of gap. About 0.2 mile south of gap is rock outcropping with excellent views.)

1.7   Pass spring on right. Continue skirting northern slope of Grassy Ridge.

2.1   Reach eastern shoulder of Grassy Ridge, and make sharp left turn. Descend steeply.

2.9   Old woods road enters on left. Trail follows or parallels road for next 0.1 mile. Continue on crest, descending.

3.0   Reach **Roan Highlands Shelter** in Low Gap (5,050 feet).
        Spring is about 100 yards to right, down side of ridge.) From
        shelter, ascend along crest to left of fence.
3.2   At top of field, reach summit of Elk Hollow Ridge (5,180 feet),
        pass through opening in fence, and descend to left of crest.
3.3   Switch back to left, and continue descent.
3.4   Pass through gap in fence, and turn right onto old roadtrack.
        Descend on old road for short distance, then turn left, and
        follow crest of spur (north-northwest).
3.7   Near end of spur, swing back to right, and continue descent
        to east.
3.8   Rejoin old road, and turn left.
3.9   In saddle (4,730-foot Buckeye Gap), overgrown road appears
        on left from Heaton Creek. A.T. continues straight ahead.
4.0   Bear away from fence. Avoid old road, which goes left to
        Heaton Creek. Trail continues north, skirting left of crest.
4.5   Reach a summit, 4,907 feet, that provides excellent views of
        Hump Mountain, Big Yellow Mountain, Grassy Ridge, Roan
        High Knob, and Little Rock Knob. Descend from summit,
        and make sharp right turn. (Avoid trail on crest of spur ridge
        straight ahead.) Descend steeply, keeping to left of fence.
4.7   Reach Yellow Mountain Gap (4,682 feet), which has good
        campsites. (Historic Bright's Trace crosses through gap.
        Road is not passable by car. To right, it descends via Roaring
        Creek to U.S. 19E at Toe River, N.C. To the left, it descends via
        Hampton Creek to U.S. 19E at Roan Mountain, Tenn. A
        spring of uncertain dependability is about 300 yards down
        trail to left. Level trail straight ahead, skirting right of ridge,
        leads 300 yards southeast to spring.) Blue-blazed trail to right
        through fence, leads 0.3 mile downhill past spring to
        Overmountain Shelter. (The loft of the barn is intended for
        sleeping only.) Cross through gap into woods, and ascend
        through field at edge of woods.
5.7   Where road approaches from right, and old field opens up on
        left, cross fence on stile. (**Caution:** Watch for turn. Old
        roadtrack continues ahead and then bears right along south-
        ern extension of Big Yellow Mountain.) Ascend on footpath
        near edge of woods on left, gradually diverging from fence.
        Ascend through field.

5.9   Reach saddle. A spring, source of Little Horse Creek, is about 100 yards right (southeast). *Water must be boiled or purified.* Turn left, and follow footpath up broad slope of Little Hump Mountain, proceeding northeast.

6.2   Pass large rock formation. Continue ascent following center of ridge to flat, grassy summit of Little Hump Mountain (5,459 feet), with outstanding views and **campsites**. Bear left, northeast, and descend steeply on rough trail through scrub growth and then woods.

6.5   Soon, reach small gap. (Avoid wide trail leading to right and slightly descending.) Ascend gradually from gap through scrub woods.

6.6   Emerge from woods, and proceed on footpath through field, keeping along edge of woods. Spring is below Trail in woods to right. Trail skirts right of northern peak of Little Hump Mountain.

6.7   Pass through opening in fence, and continue gentle descent through grassy field.

7.1   Pass through Bradley Gap (4,960 feet), which has good **campsites** and numerous springs that may be trampled by cattle. (Well-defined trail to left descends 1.5 miles to upper end of gravel road to community of Shell Creek, Tenn. A seep spring is about 0.2 mile along this trail. Another spring, source of Horse Creek, is about 100 yards right, southeast. *All water in this area must be treated.*) From Bradley Gap, ascend broad, rocky crest of Hump Mountain, proceeding northeast. There are several parallel footpaths or animal paths—avoid old paths leading to right around side of Hump Mountain. From top of last rock outcropping, on trail to summit, a small intermittent spring on western slope may be reached by bearing left from Trail and following contour through field (no trail); spring is below large, marked rock near edge of woods. Continue ascent to northeast along broad ridge. Trail follows old road, generally to left of crest.

8.0   Make sharp right (east), and, in 100 yards, cross summit of Hump Mountain (5,587 feet). (From here is magnificent, panoramic view of Doe River Valley to northwest, Whitetop and Mt. Rogers in Virginia to northeast, Beech Mountain to east-northeast, and Grandfather Mountain, with multiple peaks, to east. Nearby and to west-southwest are Grassy

Ridge and Roan High Knob.) Descend 0.7 mile, first south-east, then east on old roadtrack along broad bald on eastern ridge of Hump Mountain.

8.6   Turn left (north), leave roadtrack, and proceed through grass to sparse woods at edge of bald.

8.8   Enter scrub growth, and descend narrow spur.

8.9   At boulder, turn left (west). In about 50 feet, side trail leads 100 yards to right to cliff overlooking Elk Park, N.C. Follow graded trail, first west, then north, as it descends gradually along northern slope of ridge.

10.2 Leave woods, and enter Doll Flats (4,560 feet). Continue to left of fence, then follow level path across grassy field.

10.3 Enter woods, turn left, and, in 40 yards, pass through break in fence.

10.4 Cross old roadtrack. Grassy, overgrown field with boulders and scattered old trees offers many excellent **campsites**. Follow old roadtrack to left 60 feet, then turn right, south, and descend 240 yards to spring. Proceed straight ahead (west), passing to right of boulder. Soon, head down side of broad ridge descending to northwest, in long curve to right.

10.7 Leave broad ridgetop, and descend steeply over narrow stone escarpment. Descend through middle of steep hollow, turn right, and cross crest of rocky spur. (Overlook is 50 feet to left. Pastoral valley is within view to northwest.) Descend to base of cliff, then cross broad drainage.

10.8 Cross rock field, descending steeply.

10.9 Descend through gap in low cliff, and head straight down side of hill. Turn left, then turn right at base of small cliff.

11.0 Cross narrow spur, and continue descent through switch-backs to rich woods.

11.1 Trail crosses rock field in hollow. Short cliff is 250 feet to right. Soon, descent becomes less steep.

11.3 At bottom of sag (fence goes off to left from corner), cross fence from left to right. Continue to right of fence (northeast).

11.4 Veer right away from fence, and skirt left.

11.5 Leave woods, pass through grassy sag, and cross fence into woods. Soon, turn left off crest, turn right, and skirt left, paralleling crest. Pass rock outcrop, and cross old road, which runs across ridge.

11.7   Descend steeply by switchbacks to old road. Turn left on road, and follow it to cliff. Drop off right side of road, and make sharp right turn on graded path. Descend through switchbacks to another road.

11.8   Road swings around head of narrow hollow, then makes sharp right turn, and descends steeply.

12.0   Cross road, which comes straight down crest, then cross clearing under powerline.

12.1   Cross crest of little spur, then switch back to left (northeast). Enter Wilder Mine Hollow.

12.2   Descend along division between two small drainages, and pass spring on right. (This spring is the water supply for Apple House Shelter, 0.3 mile ahead.)

12.3   Where hollow comes together in grove of white pines, join old road. Descend along road across stream, and pass pit of former stone quarry on left. Spoil banks of iron mine are to right. (**Caution:** Do not enter the mines. Abandoned mines are treacherous. They may contain foul air or poisonous gas, and roof falls occur frequently.)

12.4   Continue on road, and cross stream again.

12.5   **Apple House Shelter** on left. (First constructed in 1952, this building was used to store explosives for the quarry in the hollow and tools for the orchards nearby. Spring (seasonal) is 0.3 mile south along the Trail. Level ground near the shelter provides a good space for tents.

12.6   Avoid road that goes straight ahead on level; veer left, and descend.

12.8   Pass abutment of former railroad bridge, and turn right on gravel driveway. Cross pole bridge over stream, and turn left.

13.0   Reach A.T. sign on southern side of U.S. 19E (2,880 feet), end of section. To continue on A.T., cross highway, and ascend bank.

Carvers Gap (Tenn. 143-N.C. 261) to Hughes Gap
Section Seven
4.6 Miles

Brief Description of Section

The Trail route follows close to the Tennessee-North Carolina state line throughout this section. The northernmost 1.8 miles follow the old Carvers Gap-Cloudland Road through dense balsam and rhododendron growth, skirting Roan High Knob summit. A short distance in the middle of the section is an open, grassy area at the Cloudland Hotel site. This is the point of departure for side trips to the rhododendron gardens and Roan High Bluff to the west and southwest. The southernmost 2.6 miles follow the main ridgecrest in woods. Northbound, the hiker gains 2,380 feet in elevation, 2,110 feet of it in the first 2.6 miles. Traveling southward, the amount of climbing is 820 feet.

Most of the section passes through USFS lands, with the Cherokee National Forest (Unaka District) bordering the Trail's northern side, and the Pisgah National Forest (Toecane District) along the south.

Points of Interest

The high point of this section, both in elevation and in scenic splendor, is the Cloudland rhododendron gardens on Roan Mountain, close to the Trail 2.0 miles from the northern end. This area may be reached either on foot from the Trail or by car from Carvers Gap. Here, Catawba rhododendron grow in profusion. These flowering shrubs are not planted or cultivated as the term "gardens" might imply. Rather, this description has come into use because of their massive concentrations and the unusual beauty of their natural spacing and grouping. The purplish-pink blossoms reach their fullest point about the second or third week in June. On certain weekends during this season, the states of North Carolina and Tennessee hold rhododendron festivals in the area. The summit of this part of Roan Mountain is forested with evergreens, predominantly Fraser or balsam fir and, to a much lesser extent, red spruce. For the south-to-north Trail traveler, this is the last fir or spruce encountered in any abundance before reaching New England, except for that on Mt. Rogers in southwest Virginia and an isolated "colony" in the Shenandoah National Park.

Between the fir and the rhododendron are fairly extensive grassy areas. Here, Scotch heather is occasionally found. Snow buntings winter here, as do many other birds normally found much farther north.

The rhododendron gardens and the southwestern end of the mountain, which terminates with Roan High Bluff (6,267 feet), are well worth several hours of exploration.

Road Approaches

The northern end of this section is at Carvers Gap on the Tennessee-North Carolina state line, 14 miles south of Roan Mountain, via Tenn. 143, and 14 miles north of Bakersville, N.C., via N.C. 261.

The southern end of the section is at Hughes Gap, on the Tennessee-North Carolina state line. From Roan Mountain, Tenn., it can be reached by going south 5.3 miles on Tenn. 143 to the Burbank community and then west 3.0 miles on a rural road. Hughes Gap is 4.0 miles northeast of Buladean, N.C., on a rural road. Buladean is 12 miles north of Bakersville, N.C., on N.C. 226, and 14 miles west of Unicoi, Tenn., on Tenn. 107/N.C. 226.

The middle of the section near Roan High Knob is accessible by ascending the paved USFS road from Carvers Gap to Cloudland rhododendron gardens (2.0 miles). From the first parking lot that is reached, the Trail is northwest, at the end of the woods in a small picnic area.

Maps

Refer to ATC Tennessee-North Carolina Map Two for route navigation. For additional area detail, refer to TVA Carvers Gap, North Carolina-Tennessee; Bakersville, North Carolina; and Iron Mountain Gap, Tennessee-North Carolina, quadrangles.

Shelters, Campsites, and Water

This section has one shelter:

Roan High Knob Shelter: Originally a fire warden's cabin; rebuilt by the Cherokee National Forest staff; 1.3 miles from the northern end of section; accommodates 15; water available at spring 50 yards from shelter.

Next shelter: north 4.3 miles (Roan Highlands Shelter); south 5.4 miles (Clyde Smith Shelter).

Water is also available at Cloudland, Carvers Gap, and at Ash Gap (also good tentsites here).

Public Accommodations and Supplies

No public accommodations or supplies are available near the Trail in this section. The closest source of supplies is at a store in Burbank, Tenn., 8.0 miles north from Carvers Gap, and 3.0 miles east from Hughes Gap. Roan Mountain village, west on 19E, has a restaurant, stores, a motel/hiker hostel with shuttle service (at 4.0 miles from the Trailhead). Trailridge Mountain Camp, which provides hot showers, tent space, mail service, and sometimes shelter for hikers, is 2.0 miles from Hughes Gap on Hughes Gap Road in North Carolina. It is open in the summer months. Roan Mountain State Park (campground, cabins, restaurant) is 1.0 mile north of Burbank.

Precautions

Hikers are advised not to leave cars overnight at Hughes Gap because of past incidents of vandalism.

Trail Description, North to South

Miles   **Data**

0.0   From Carvers Gap (5,512 feet), proceed to right of log fence along paved Cloudland rhododendron gardens road. Water is available here at spring below picnic area to right.

0.1   Leave road, and ascend on footpath through weeds and open balsam.

0.2   Reach old road, and turn right. Trail follows old road through balsam and rhododendron from here nearly to Cloudland. Ascend steadily with switchbacks.

1.3   Blue-blazed trail at left leads 0.1 mile to summit of Roan High Knob (6,285 feet) and **shelter**, the highest on the A.T. (Originally the fire warden's cabin, it was abandoned for 20 years and then renovated; spring 50 feet past cabin on blue-blazed trail.) A.T. continues on road.

1.8   Reach open picnic area within sight of road. Keep straight ahead past picnic table and, in 50 feet, enter Trail through rhododendron. At fork 50 feet farther, turn left, and gradually ascend, crossing old trail.

1.9   Cross old cabin site, turn left, and reenter woods in 100 feet, ascending. Keep right, and leave woods again in another 100 feet. Ascend through grassy area to large spruce tree. This is at left front corner of old hotel site (6,150 feet). (Straight ahead and slightly to right on crest is small USFS parking lot. Slightly to left, beyond small lot, is large parking lot built in 1952. Beyond parking lot, road leads to Cloudland rhododendron gardens. Water from drinking fountains is available here. Beyond is Roan High Bluff, 6,267 feet.) Turn right at large spruce tree, and follow old road tracks. Climb rocky bank, and continue north into grassy alcove. (To rear is excellent view of Black Mountains.)

2.0   Enter woods at end of alcove. Immediately make sharp left, and descend steeply through rhododendron. Reach old graded trail in 150 feet, and make sharp right onto it.

2.2   Leave dense fir and rhododendron growth. Trail generally descends ridge in northerly direction from here to Hughes Gap.

2.8   Reach Ash Gap (5,340 feet) with good **tentsites**. To left, faint trail leads 0.1 mile to small spring. Continue straight ahead in gap through beech woods.

3.3   Reach summit of Beartown Mountain (5,481 feet). In 200 feet, side trail 150 feet to left provides excellent views to north and west. From side-trail junction, continue down ridge. Near Hughes Gap, Trail turns right off crest and follows old road down right side of ridge.

4.6   Reach end of section at road through Hughes Gap (4,040 feet). Small spring, trickle from rocks in roadbank, is 700 feet to right at second bend in road. To continue on A.T., veer left across road, and ascend into woods.

Trail Description, South to North

Miles	Data

0.0　From Hughes Gap (4,040 feet), ascend steeply on old road along left side of ridge. In about 0.5 mile, the Trail returns to ridgecrest and then ascends ridge in southerly direction to Cloudland.

1.3　Side trail to right leads 150 feet to overlook with excellent views.

1.4　Reach summit of Beartown Mountain (5,481 feet). Descend gently through beech woods.

1.8　Reach Ash Gap (5,340 feet) with good **tentsites**. To right, faint trail leads 0.1 mile to small spring. Ascend steadily.

2.4　Enter dense spruce and rhododendron.

2.5　Make sharp left off old trail, and ascend steeply.

2.6　At summit (6,150 feet), make sharp right, emerging into grassy alcove. From alcove, go toward open area. (Straight ahead on crest is old hotel site, with excellent views of Black Mountains and small USFS parking lot. To right is larger USFS parking lot, built in 1952. To west beyond parking lots are Cloudland rhododendron gardens and water from drinking fountains. Farther west is Roan High Bluff, 6,267 feet.) Descend rocky bank slightly to left of path to parking lot, and follow old road tracks south to large spruce tree at left front corner of hotel site.

2.7　After sharp left turn down trail, enter woods. In about 100 feet, reach old cabin site. Bearing right, cross toward opposite corner. Beyond site, bear left, and descend through woods.

2.8　Pass picnic table at edge of road. Keep to left, and enter old road. (Do not cross paved road.) Trail follows old road through balsam and rhododendron from here nearly to Carvers Gap.

3.3　Blue-blazed trail at right leads 0.1 mile to summit of Roan High Knob (6,285 feet) and **shelter**, the highest on the A.T. (Originally the fire warden's cabin, it was abandoned for 20 years and then renovated in 1980. Spring is reached by continuing past cabin on blue-blazed trail about 50 feet.) Keep straight on old road, skirting left side of knob. Beyond, descend steadily with several switchbacks.

4.4   Turn left off old road onto footpath, and descend straight downhill to east. Bear slightly right through weeds and open balsam.

4.5   Reach paved USFS Cloudland rhododendron gardens road by large rock. Turn left, downhill, to road junction, keeping to left of pole fence.

4.6   Reach Carvers Gap (5,512 feet) and end of section. USFS parking lot and picnic area, with spring and toilets to left, on Tennessee side. To continue on A.T., cross Tenn. 143/N.C. 261 through gap, climb bank on stone steps, and cross pole fence.

Hughes Gap to Iron Mountain Gap
(Tenn. 107-N.C. 226)
Section Eight
8.1 Miles

Brief Description of Section

The Trail over this section follows the state line along the main crest of the Iron Mountains. From the northern end of the section at Hughes Gap, the Trail ascends through woods to the north and west over two minor knolls, and then climbs steeply up Little Rock Knob, emerging on the cliffs near the summit. From here, it descends westward through laurel and rhododendron and then hardwood growth. The Trail then climbs to the summit of a knoll, which provides good views in winter, and descends to the northwest through beech woods. It enters an old woods road, on which it descends westward to Greasy Creek Gap.

From the gap, it follows a narrow trail along the main crest through forest growth. From a weedy gap, it continues on a dirt road southwest along the main crest to the end of the section.

The grade of this section is difficult in both directions. Hiking southward means a total of 2,200 feet of climbing; hiking northward, 2,600 feet.

Points of Interest

The outstanding feature of this section is Little Rock Knob (4,919 feet). The northern side of this mountain is faced with a high cliff, bordered at the top with a dense growth of mountain laurel. The Trail passes along its top edge, near the summit of the mountain, providing outstanding views of Roan Mountain to the south, Ripshin Ridge to the north, and Unaka Mountain to the west. Several other high, open places also allow fine views.

At a gap 1.7 miles south of Hughes Gap, wildflowers bloom in abundance during mid-May.

Road Approaches

The northern end of this section is at Hughes Gap, on the Tennessee-North Carolina state line. From Roan Mountain, Tenn., it can be reached by going south 5.3 miles on Tenn. 143 to the Burbank community and then west 3.0 miles on Hughes Gap Road. Hughes Gap is 4.0 miles northeast of Buladean, N.C., on Hughes Gap Road. Buladean is 12 miles north of Bakersville, N.C., on N.C. 226, and 14 miles west of Unicoi, Tenn., on Tenn. 107/N.C. 226.

The southern end of the section is at Iron Mountain Gap, on the Tennessee-North Carolina state line, 10 miles east of Unicoi on Tenn. 107 and 4.0 miles north of Buladean on N.C. 226.

Maps

Refer to ATC Tennessee-North Carolina Map Two for route navigation. For additional area detail, refer to TVA Iron Mountain Gap, Tennessee-North Carolina, quadrangle.

Shelters, Campsites, and Water

This section has one shelter:

Clyde Smith Shelter: Wooden shelter built in 1977 by USFS; 2.1 miles from northern end of section; accommodates 6; water available from spring 300 yards from shelter.

Next shelter: north 5.4 miles (Roan High Knob Shelter); south 8.7 miles (Cherry Gap Shelter).

Campsites are available at 3.2, 4.0 and 4.2 miles from the northern end of the section. Water is available at various places throughout the section.

Public Accommodations and Supplies

From Hughes Gap, limited supplies may be obtained at Burbank, 3.0 miles east of the Trail. Lodging and meals are available at Roan Mountain Village, 5.3 miles north of Burbank. Roan Mountain State Park (campground, cabins, restaurant) is 1.0 mile north of Burbank. Trailridge Mountain Camp, which offers hot showers, tent space, mail service, and sometimes shelter for hikers, is open in the summer months. It is located on the road to Buladean, 2.0 miles west of Hughes Gap.

From Iron Mountain Gap, there is a small grocery store about 0.5 mile on the road to Buladean. No accommodations are available near Iron Mountain Gap.

Precautions

Parking cars at Hughes Gap is not advised because of past incidences of vandalism.

Trail Description, North to South

Miles   **Data**

0.0   From Hughes Gap (4,040 feet), follow old woods road uphill, north.

0.2   Reach first summit. Continue through woods on old road, which narrows to trail width.

0.4   Cross second summit, and descend with new fence on right. (Beyond fence is wooded area with heavy chestnut blowdown.) Reach gap, and pass through field now grown into trees. Enter heavy woods, and ascend steeply up southern slope of Little Rock Knob (4,918 feet) on winding trail through laurel growth. Turn left (west), and skirt south of summit.

1.3   Reach top of cliff on Little Rock Knob with excellent views to west and north. From cliff, descend westward through laurel and rhododendron thickets, soon coming onto ridgetop. Follow trail generally along ridge, descending steeply, first through rhododendron, then hardwoods.

1.7   Enter gap. (Trail to right leads 0.1 mile to spring.) Continue west, ascending gradually.

1.9   Skirt right (northern) side of knoll through beech woods, just below summit. (Partly open summit, 4,640 feet, with views in winter, is about 100 yards to left.) From knoll, Trail bears northwest and descends through open woods.

2.0   Make sharp left. (**Caution:** Main ridge with old trail appears to continue north.) Descend gently to west through trees and grassy area.

2.1   Blue-blazed trail to right leads 200 yards to **Clyde Smith Shelter** and to spring at 300 yards.

2.2   Enter old woods road. (To right, road leads 200 yards to spring.) Keep left. Trail follows woods road along main crest from here to Greasy Creek Gap, generally descending.

2.4   Reach shallow gap. Avoid old road to the left.

3.2   Reach foundation of old homestead with row of six large maple trees in front. (Spring is 100 yards down in hollow to right; possible **campsite**.) Continue straight between homestead and row of trees, and ascend part-way up next hill. Then, bear right (north), and continue to follow road, generally descending.

4.0   Reach Greasy Creek Gap (4,034 feet). (To left, dirt road, not passable by car, descends along Greasy Creek to Buladean, N.C., becoming passable by car at 0.9 mile. To right, road, not passable by car, descends about 2.5 miles to Tiger Creek.) Spring and good **campsite** are 300 yards to right on blue-blazed trail. (Beyond, blue-blazed trail returns to A.T. in another 200 yards at 4.2 miles.) Cross road, climb bank, and ascend gradually on broad ridgecrest. Proceed through woods to corner of old field and fence on left. Continue ascent with fence and old field on left and fine views of Roan High Bluff to south and Grassy Ridge to southeast.

4.2   Blue-blazed trail to right descends steeply for 200 yards to spring and good **campsite**; 300 yards beyond, blue-blazed trail returns to A.T. in Greasy Creek Gap.

4.7   Reach summit of knob (4,332 feet), and bear right. Avoid spur ridge extending left (south). Proceed through woods along broad, main crest to northwest, generally descending.

5.3   Pass through gap, and begin steady ascent.

5.8   Pass overhanging rock, which may provide shelter for one or two persons. Shortly, come to high point (4,426 feet). Descend on crest through woods.

6.0   Pick up fence and field on right.

6.4   Trail bears left through woods, leaving ridgecrest. Descend steeply, skirting left slope of ridge and keeping brushy crest above to right.

6.6   Blue-blazed side trail leads steeply downhill and slightly to left about 0.1 mile to small stream; good source of water. At junction with side trail, make sharp right turn.

6.7   Reach weedy gap. From gap, ascend westward up ridge on dirt road, then bear left. Reach orchard and road. Follow road to left, skirting left side of hill. (Trail follows this road to end of section.)

6.9   Woods start on left.

7.1   At end of woods, bear right, avoiding old track downhill on left. Ascend to right, across field.

7.2   Reach crest (4,168 feet), with magnificent views of Unaka Mountain to west, Roan Mountain to southeast, and Little Rock Knob to east. Descend steadily along crest, with woods on left and tree farm on right.

8.1   Pass through gate, and reach paved road through Iron Mountain Gap (3,723 feet) at end of section. To continue on A.T., cross road diagonally to left (south), and continue diagonally across dirt parking lot to southern corner.

Trail Description, South to North

Miles   **Data**

0.0   From paved road in Iron Mountain Gap (3,723 feet), pass through gate, and ascend along gravel road to northeast, skirting left side of ridgecrest. (Trail follows this road generally along ridgecrest for 1.5 miles.)

0.4   Fence and tree farm border road on left, providing fine views back toward Unaka Mountain. Woods on right.

0.9   Woods on right end at this point just below summit, with magnificent views of Unaka Mountain to west, Roan Mountain to southeast, and Little Rock Knob to east. Leave crest, and slant to right downhill on road through field.

1.0   Old track approaches from right. Keep left, and descend gradually along road with woods on right.

1.2   Enter old orchard, and continue on road; pass through slight saddle, and bear right, skirting right side of knoll. (**Caution:** Take care to locate turn. Road continues ahead, descending Tennessee side of mountain.) Descend east through woods, then bear to right, and descend into weedy gap.

1.4   After gap, enter woods, ascending gradually. About 50 feet into woods, Trail turns left uphill, and blue-blazed side trail descends steeply to right about 0.1 mile to small stream; good water source.

1.7   Reach crest. Trail generally follows ridgecrest for next 2.0 miles. Ascend gradually with fence and occasional views to left.

2.1   Reach first major summit.

2.3   Reach second summit (4,426 feet), and continue along almost-level ridgetop. Soon, pass overhanging rock, which could provide emergency shelter for one or two persons.

3.5   Reach summit of knob (4,332 feet). Bear left, avoiding side ridge extending to south. Descend inside edge of woods with wire fence and field on right. (From field are fine views of Roan High Bluff to south and Grassy Ridge to southeast.)

3.8   Reach corner of old field. Descend gradually along broad ridgecrest. (In 50 yards, blue-blazed trail to left descends steeply for 200 yards to spring and good **campsite**; blue-blazed trail continues beyond and, in 300 additional yards, reenters A.T. at Greasy Creek Gap.)

4.0   Reach Greasy Creek Gap (4,034 feet). (To right, dirt road, not passable by car, descends along Greasy Creek to Buladean, N.C., becoming passable by car at 0.9 mile. To left, road, not passable by car, descends about 2.5 miles to Tiger Creek.) Blue-blazed trail to left descends 300 yards to spring and good **campsite**; 200 yards beyond, blue-blazed trail returns to A.T. at 3.8-mile point above.) From gap, continue straight ahead onto old woods road, ascending along ridgecrest for next 1.8 miles.

4.9   Reach foundation of old homestead with row of six large maple trees in front. (From here, spring is 100 yards down hollow to left.) Continue between homestead and row of trees.

5.7   Reach shallow gap. Avoid old road to right.

5.9   Road to left leads 20 yards to spring. A.T. leaves road and becomes footpath.

6.0   Blue-blazed trail to left leads 200 yards to **Clyde Smith Shelter** (trail leads to spring 100 yards beyond shelter). Ascend gradually to east through trees and grassy area.

6.2   Skirt left (northern) side of knoll near edge of woods, just below summit. (Partly open summit, 4,640 feet, is about 100 yards to right.) Descend gradually to east along ridgecrest.

6.4   Reach gap. (Trail to left leads 0.1 mile to spring.) Ascend steeply through hardwood forest.

6.7   Enter rhododendron and laurel growth, and continue steep ascent along ridgecrest, which soon becomes quite narrow.

6.8   Reach top of cliffs on Little Rock Knob, with excellent views to west and north. Proceed east, through rhododendron and laurel thickets, keeping below summit (4,918 feet). Then, bear right, and descend steep, southern slope through laurel and hardwood growth.

7.5   Pass into field in gap partly grown into small trees. Ascend steeply, with new fence on left. (To left of fence is wooded area with heavy chestnut blowdown.)

7.7   Pass over summit. Beyond slight gap, Trail widens gradually to old woods road.

8.0   Pass over second summit.

8.1   Reach end of section at road through Hughes Gap (4,040 feet). (A small spring, a trickle from rocks in roadbank, is 700 feet to left at second bend in road.) To continue on A.T., cross road, veer slightly left, and ascend steeply.

Iron Mountain Gap (Tenn. 107-N.C. 226) to Nolichucky River
Section Nine
19.1 Miles

Brief Description of Section

From Iron Mountain Gap, the Trail ascends steadily through woods along the main crest of the Iron Mountains. After crossing Little Bald Knob, it passes through a beautiful hardwood forest, descends sharply to a gap, skirts the southern slope of Piney Bald, and descends to reach Cherry Gap.

The Trail continues through woods along the main ridgecrest to Low Gap, ascending to the broad summit of Unaka Mountain. Beyond the summit, the Trail continues on the scrub-covered ridge before descending by switchbacks to Deep Gap. It then generally follows the crest through woods, over knolls and balds, and through gaps to Indian Grave Gap.

From Indian Grave Gap, the Trail continues along the ridge with little change in elevation until it reaches Curley Maple Gap. From Curley Maple Gap, it descends steadily along Jones Branch. Upon nearing the Nolichucky River, it bears right and follows a sidehill trail above the right bank of the river, crossing the Clinchfield Railroad and reaching former U.S. 19W and 23. The Trail crosses the river on a walkway on a new bridge and reaches the end of the section.

This section has considerable climbing in both directions: 6,300 feet going northward and 4,300 feet going southward. Both directions have several long, steep grades. The section should therefore be considered difficult, especially when traveled northward.

Points of Interest

Unaka Mountain (5,180 feet) is outstanding among the southern Appalachian Mountains. Although much of the northwestern slope was marred by a severe fire in 1925 and extensive barren rock fields remain, the forest growth is slowly returning. Some of the original forest, untouched by the fire, can be found along the creeks, such as at the head of Dick Creek.

In 1972, 7.4 miles of the Trail was moved off USFS 230 and relocated across the summits. The biggest part of the mountain is covered with scrub growth, but the lower southwestern peak, known as Beauty Spot, is open, grass-covered, and easily accessible; the views from it are superb. Little Bald Knob also has fine views. The Unaka Mountain Wilderness Area lies in the valley, but the Trail does not enter it.

The southern end of the section parallels and then crosses the scenic Nolichucky River. At this point, the river has just emerged from its course through a high-walled, rocky gorge from Poplar, N.C.

Road Approaches

The northern end of the section is at Iron Mountain Gap, on the Tennessee-North Carolina state line, 10 miles east of Unicoi, Tenn., on Tenn. 107 and 4.0 miles north of Buladean, N.C., on N.C. 226. Buladean is 12 miles north of Bakersville, N.C., on N.C. 226.

The southern end of the section is at the Nolichucky River in Chestoa, Tenn., 2.3 miles southwest of Erwin, Tenn., on Tenn. 36, which joins U.S. 23 0.5 mile farther west.

Indian Grave Gap (10.8 miles from northern end) is 6.6 miles southeast of Erwin, Tenn., via Tenn. 395 (designated 10th Street inside Erwin city limits and "Rock Creek Road" outside of city). Along this road at 3.3 miles is USFS Rock Creek Recreation Area. From Indian Grave Gap, the road continues as N.C. 230 to the communities of Poplar, 4.0 miles distant, and Huntdale, N.C., 6.0 miles farther. The buses and trucks of rafts passing through the gap are carrying people to raft the gorge of the Nolichucky River. Indian Grave Gap can also be reached from Unicoi by gravel USFS 230. This road starts from Tenn. 107, 7.4 miles east of Unicoi, ascends the eastern slope of Unaka Mountain, and continues along the crest to Indian Grave Gap. Along the crest, the road closely parallels the Trail and crosses it between Indian Grave Gap and Beauty Spot.

Maps

Refer to ATC Tennessee-North Carolina Map Two for route navigation. For additional area detail, refer to TVA Iron Mountain Gap, Tennessee-North Carolina; Unicoi, Tennessee-North Carolina;

Huntdale, North Carolina-Tennessee; and Chestoa, Tennessee-North Carolina, quadrangles.

Shelters, Campsites, and Water

This section has two shelters:

Cherry Gap Shelter: Concrete-block shelter built in 1962 by USFS; 2.7 miles from northern end of section; accommodates 6; water available at spring 250 feet southwest of shelter.

Next shelter: north 8.7 miles (Clyde Smith Shelter); south 12.2 miles (Curley Maple Gap Shelter).

Curley Maple Gap Shelter: Concrete-block shelter built in 1961 by USFS; located 14.9 miles from northern end of section; accommodates 6; water available at spring 100 feet beyond on A.T.

Next shelter: north 12.2 miles (Cherry Gap Shelter); south 9.9 miles (No Business Knob Shelter).

Good campsites with water are available at Deep Gap and at two places in Beauty Spot Gap.

USFS Rock Creek Recreation Area has picnic and camping facilities. At Indian Grave Gap crossroads, it is 3.3 miles west on Tenn. 395.

Public Accommodations and Supplies

From Iron Mountain Gap, there is a small grocery store about 0.5 mile south on N.C. 226 (towards Buladean). No accommodations are available near Iron Mountain Gap.

Erwin has a large grocery store 2.3 miles from the southern end of the section; a hospital is 3.0 miles, and the post office 4.1 miles from the Trail. Motels are available, as well as stores and restaurants. The YMCA at 3.5 miles (corner of Ohio and Love streets) offers showers for a small fee but no lodging.

Nolichucky Expeditions, a whitewater rafting business near the Trail, offers shuttle service to and from town, river trips and lodging.

Precautions

From Beauty Spot Gap to Indian Grave Gap, the Flattop Game Management Area borders the southern (North Carolina) edge of the Trail. No firearms or unleashed dogs are allowed in this game area.

Beauty Spot is bald, and the Trail on it by necessity is sparsely marked. Use care in fog to avoid getting lost.

Trail Description, North to South

Miles	Data

0.0   From highway at Iron Mountain Gap (3,723 feet), cross small flat area at left of gravel road, and enter woods. Proceed along left side of ridgeline, with gravel road above on crest.

0.5   Reach gravel road. In a few yards, take old woods road straight ahead and uphill.

0.7   Turn right off road, and follow foot trail uphill.

0.9   Reach sag, and soon cross graded trail.

1.0   Pass to right of large outcrop of rock. Cross old logging road; continue ascent.

1.1   Reach level portion of ridgecrest from which Roan Mountain may be seen to south. Continue ascent.

1.2   Reach summit of Little Bald Knob (4,459 feet). Make hard right, and descend. For next 0.4 mile, Trail generally follows top of wide ridgecrest to west.

1.6   While crossing right shoulder of small knob, make hard right. Descend steeply.

1.9   Reach narrow gap. Beyond gap, swing left, and skirt southern slope of Piney Bald at nearly constant elevation. (Summit of Piney Bald is open and offers fine views. It may be reached by proceeding straight up ridgecrest through woods from gap at 1.9 miles.) Regain main ridge, and descend along it.

2.3   Reach Cherry Gap (3,900 feet). (Woods road crosses through gap. To right, road passes seasonal spring in depression on left at about 100 feet and then descends about 0.6 mile to USFS 230. To left, road descends along Bearwallow Creek, later Pigeonroost Creek, passing good spring on right at about 0.3 mile, opposite first abandoned house on left, and reaching Pigeonroost, N.C., 4.0 miles north of Huntdale, at about 6.5 miles.) Ascend wide trail from Cherry Gap.

2.7   Reach **Cherry Gap Shelter** (spring in hollow 250 feet southwest can be reached by blue-blazed trail). From shelter, ascend along main crest, and generally follow it for next mile.

3.7   Reach Low Gap (3,900 feet). (Faint side trail descends to left, passes spring at 200 yards—12 yards to right of trail at base of hemlock tree—and reaches Upper Poplar , at 3.0 miles.) From Low Gap, ascend steadily on graded trail.

4.0   At very sharp switchback, turn uphill to left. Use caution here! (The unmarked, graded trail ahead leads about 0.5 mile to USFS 230 and is former A.T. route.) Ascend from switchback and reach ridgecrest in small gap. Turn sharply right up ridge. After short distance, begin skirting left of ridge while continuing to ascend.

4.7   Reach spring, and continue to ascend through woods on left side of ridge. Enter evergreen woods.

5.4   Pass benchmark on summit of Unaka Mountain (5,180 feet). Continue across broad summit area in relatively open brush. Cross quartzite ledge, and begin gradual descent on broad crest through hardwood forest.

6.2   Turn left from crest, and begin descent to east. Make sharp right at first of several switchbacks with continuing descent.

6.4   At this switchback on the crest, a switchback in USFS 230 is only a few feet to right. (About 0.7 mile uphill on road is junction. From junction, road to left, west, leads 0.4 mile to USFS Pleasant Garden Recreation Area.) Continue descent to edge of field. Follow Trail at edge of field, with USFS 230 on right.

7.0   Reach Deep Gap (4,100 feet). (Marked "Beauty Spot Gap" on TVA Unicoi and Huntdale quadrangles. Meadow to right provides excellent **campsite**. Concrete-boxed spring is on right at eastern end of gap, on old graded trail leading back, to right, into hollow. Trail to left from western end at gap leads about 1.2 miles to Upper Poplar , on Poplar Creek.) From Deep Gap, follow ridgecrest to left of road. Veer away from road, and cross small summit, then descend to gap with field and fence on left and USFS 230 on right. Ascend through woods on ridge, and again veer away from road.

7.7   Reach end of fence.

7.8   Cross summit, then descend.

7.9   Veer left. Soon, cross old woods road (to right is small clearing and about 200 feet beyond is USFS 230). Reenter woods, and soon turn straight down southern side of ridge.

8.0   Reach nearly level Trail. Soon, cross bog. On western side of bog, blue-blazed trail to north leads 150 yards to spring and spacious **campsite** across crest and to USFS 230 at northeastern end of level Beauty Spot Gap (4,300 feet). The camping area is accessible to vehicles.

8.2   Turn right, and soon start gradual ascent, then turn straight uphill.

8.3   Reach end of pole fence, and turn left, keeping to right of fence. In a few feet, reach gate in fence. This is southwestern end of level Beauty Spot Gap. (Blue-blazed trail leads north 50 yards through gate and across USFS 230 to spring. A good **campsite** on small knoll to east is also accessible to vehicles.) Continue along ridge while veering away from fence. Soon, reach open field, and join old roadtrack.

8.5   Reach Beauty Spot (4,437 feet) summit. Beauty Spot is a natural grassy bald, with splendid views in all directions, particularly of Roan Mountain (east), the Blacks (south), Big Bald and Flattop Mountains (southwest), and upper Toe River Valley. The Nolichucky River is also visible in several places. Continue straight along ridge on intermittent roadtrack. Use caution in fog.

8.9   Turn left toward woods, and descend gently. Enter woods, and continue descent.

9.5   Make sharp right, and descend, skirting left of ridge.

9.7   Cross USFS 230, and continue on abandoned road on or near ridgeline.

10.1   Pass under powerline, and continue on or near crest.

10.8   Reach Indian Grave Gap (3,360 feet) and crossroads. [To right, paved road (Tenn. 395, designated 10th Street inside Erwin city limits) descends along right prong of Rock Creek, passes USFS Rock Creek Recreation Area with picnic and **camping** facilities at 3.3 miles and, at 6.6 miles, reaches Tenn. 36, main street of Erwin, 1.2 miles northeast of center of town. To left, road descends about 4.5 miles to Poplar USFS 132 skirts left of ridge straight ahead and terminates in 2.1 miles at Ephraim Place, overlooking Nolichucky River gorge. Back to left and up the hill, USFS 230 crosses Unaka Mountain and intersects Tenn. 107 west of Iron Mountain Gap.] Ascend steps across road in Indian Grave Gap, and reenter woods. Trail follows ridgecrest for a short distance.

10.9   Faint old road enters from left; swing to right, and skirt right
        of ridge. Trail is fairly level and partly on old graded trail.

11.5   Turn sharply to left around side ridge. Leave old graded trail,
        and turn downhill, skirting right of side ridge. Trail becomes
        very rocky.

12.3   Reach trail intersection in gap. Continue straight ahead
        through gap, and descend, skirting left of ridge. Look for
        turn.

12.4   Turn back left in very sharp switchback, and begin skirting
        right of ridge. Trail skirts ridge at nearly constant elevation
        for more than 2.0 miles. Through the trees are overlooks to
        Erwin, Tenn., and Buffalo Mountain.

13.6   Pass spring on left.

13.8   Cross small stream, entering from left.

14.4   Pass spring on left.

14.8   Reach Curley Maple Gap (3,080 feet), with remnant of old
        shelter built by CCC for Cherokee National Forest. (Aban-
        doned USFS road crosses through gap, descending to right
        4.0 miles to Erwin, Tenn., and to left into Jones Branch below
        Ephraim Place.) Pass through Curley Maple Gap, cross road,
        and descend on graded trail through woods.

14.9   Reach **Curley Maple Gap Shelter** on left (spring is 100 feet
        farther down A.T. on left). From shelter, continue gradual
        descent on graded trail, soon following a prong of Jones
        Branch. As stream becomes steeper, Trail skirts high on rocky
        slope and then descends by switchback.

16.1   Reach logging road (built 1960-61), and turn back sharply
        right on it. Descend steadily through rhododendron and
        hemlock forest. Follow road, avoiding side trails. Trail crosses
        Jones Branch occasionally (three times on footbridge) and
        passes several small clearings.

17.8   Bear right with road, away from Jones Branch. Pass Noli-
        chucky Gorge Campground (hiker hostel) and Nolichucky
        Expeditions buildings on left. (Here are views of Temple Hill
        Knob through trees.)

18.1   Begin sidehill traverse of slopes above Nolichucky River.
        Slope is steep and rocky at times and affords views of the
        river below. Parts of the path were carved from the rock using
        a jackhammer.

18.6   Trail turns right away from the river, then left at drainage.

18.7   Pass grove of young Carolina hemlocks, then cross woods road.

19.0   Cross railroad tracks (**Caution: cross with care!** Trains descending from North Carolina, left, are particularly quiet and may not signal approach. If the train is stopped, *do not cross under or between cars.*) Trail parallels tracks, then emerges from woods road onto paved road (former U.S. 19W and 23, as shown on 1939 edition of TVA Chestoa quadrangle). Cross highway bridge on TEHC-designated Ray Hunt Walkway over the Nolichucky River.

19.1   Reach end of section at western end of the Nolichucky River bridge (1,700 feet) in Chestoa, 2.3 miles southwest of Erwin. A.T. turns left on road along river.

Trail Description, South to North

Miles   **Data**

0.0   From western end of new highway bridge across Nolichucky River (1,700 feet), cross TEHC-designated Ray Hunt Walkway over river.

0.1   Cross road at eastern end of bridge. Enter woods. Soon, Trail bears right, paralleling railroad tracks. Then, Trail turns left and crosses tracks. (**Caution: cross with care!** Trains descending from North Carolina, right, are particularly quiet and may not signal approach. If the train is stopped, *do not cross under or between cars.*)

0.4   Cross woods road. Soon, pass grove of young Carolina hemlocks.

0.5   Trail turns right at drainage. Soon, bear left, and begin traverse of steep cliff above the Nolichucky River (views of river and railroad bridge) on sidehill trail, portions of which were carved from the rock by jackhammer.

1.0   Trail bears away from the river, traversing a more gentle slope.

1.3   Pass Nolichucky Gorge Campground (hiker hostel) and Nolichucky Expeditions buildings on right. Bear left away from riverbank. Follow road up Jones Branch to northeast. Trail crosses Jones Branch occasionally (three times on footbridges) and passes several small clearings. Avoid side trails.

2.4   Hemlock and rhododendron forest begins here.

3.1   Turn back sharply left, up graded trail above road cut. (**Caution:** Turn may be obscured by summer growth.) Ascend, then, high above stream, switch back to right, and ascend steadily on graded trail, soon returning to prong of Jones Branch.

4.2   Pass spring on right of Trail, and 100 feet beyond, reach **Curley Maple Gap Shelter.**

4.3   Reach Curley Maple Gap, 3,080 feet. (Abandoned USFS road crosses through gap descending to left 4.0 miles to Erwin, Tenn., and to right, leading into Jones Branch below Ephraim Place.) Cross road through gap, and skirt left of ridge.

4.8   Pass spring on right.

5.3   Cross small stream entering from right.

5.5   Pass spring on right.

6.8   Cross trail intersection in gap, and ascend gradually on rocky trail.

7.6   Turn sharply right around side ridge.

8.2   Reach crest, and cross old road.

8.3   Reach Indian Grave Gap (3,360 feet) and crossroads. (To left, paved road, Tenn. 395, designated 10th Street inside Erwin city limits, descends along right prong of Rock Creek, passing USFS Rock Creek Recreation Area, with picnic and **camping** facilities, at 3.3 miles, and, at 6.6 miles, reaching Tenn. 36, main street of Erwin, 1.2 miles northeast of center of town. To right, road descends about 4.5 miles to Poplar USFS 230 ascends ridge just across gap, crosses Unaka Mountain and intersects Tenn. 107 west of Iron Mountain Gap. Back to right, USFS 132 skirts left of ridge and terminates 2.1 miles at Ephraim Place, overlooking Nolichucky River gorge.) To continue on A.T., cross road, and enter woods.

9.0   Cross under powerline, and join abandoned road, with other abandoned roads crossing Trail.

9.4   Cross gravel USFS 230, and ascend, skirting right side of ridge.

9.5   Reach crest, make sharp left, and continue ascent.

10.2   Reach open field, follow roadtrack, and turn right (southeast). Roadtrack is intermittent and obscure. Use caution in fog. In about 100 yards, bear left (northeast) around small knoll, and continue through sag.

10.6   Reach Beauty Spot (4,437 feet) summit. (Beauty Spot is a natural grassy bald, with splendid views in all directions, particularly of Roan Mountain, east, Black Mountains, south, Big Bald and Flattop Mountains, southwest, and upper Toe River Valley. The Nolichucky River is also visible in several places.) Continue straight ahead on crest on old roadtrack, descending. Soon, leave field and road, and enter woods.

10.8   Reach gate in pole fence where USFS 230 enters on left. (This is southwestern end of level Beauty Spot Gap, 4,300 feet. Blue-blazed trail leads 50 yards north through gate and across road to spring. Small knoll to east has a good **campsite**, accessible to vehicles.) Veer right, keeping to left of fence, and, a few feet from end of fence, turn straight, downhill, for a short distance. Swing left, and descend.

10.9   Trail levels and soon turns left. Continue on level Trail through open woods.

11.1   Cross narrow bog. (Just before bog, on western side, blue-blazed trail leads 150 yards to spring and spacious **campsite**, north across crest, and to USFS 230 at northeastern end of Beauty Spot Gap. This area is accessible to vehicles.) Ascend along side of ridge.

11.2   Cross old woods road (to left is small clearing and about 200 feet beyond is USFS 230). Reenter woods, and turn right on crest.

11.6   Reach field on right with road on left. Bear away from road, then cross small summit.

12.1   Reach Deep Gap, 4,100 feet (marked "Beauty Spot Gap" on TVA Unicoi and Huntdale quadrangles). Meadow to left provides excellent **campsite**. Concrete-boxed spring is on old graded trail (just across road) at eastern end of gap. From western end of gap, trail to right leads about 1.2 miles to Upper Poplar , on Poplar Creek. Where road bears away to left, leave road, and begin ascent on ridge toward summit of Unaka Mountain. (Road ascends to skirt left of summit.)

12.6   At switchback on crest, switchback in USFS 230 is only a few feet to left; about 0.7 mile uphill on road is junction. Road to left, west, from junction leads 0.4 mile to USFS Pleasant Garden Recreation Area. To continue on Trail, ascend right (southern) slope with switchbacks.

12.9   Reach crest. Ascend gradually through woods across broad crest. Cross quartzite ledge onto broad summit area with relatively open brush.

13.7   In evergreen woods, reach benchmark at summit of Unaka Mountain (5,180 feet). Descend gradually; evergreens change to hardwoods. Soon, descend steeply to southeast. Reach spring. Continue steep descent.

15.1   Reach trail junction. (Unmarked, graded trail to left leads about 0.5 mile to USFS 230 and is former A.T. route.) Turn back sharply right, and follow graded trail, skirting left of ridge.

15.4   Reach Low Gap (3,900 feet). (Here, faint side trail descends to right, passing spring in 200 yards—12 yards to right of trail at base of hemlock tree—and reaching Upper Poplar , at about 3.0 miles.) From Low Gap, A.T. generally follows Tennessee/North Carolina state line to end of section. Ascend to east from Low Gap.

16.4   Reach **Cherry Gap Shelter** (spring located in hollow 250 feet southwest, reached by blue-blazed trail.) From shelter, continue east along almost-level ridgecrest.

16.8   Reach Cherry Gap (3,900 feet). (Woods road crosses through gap. To left, in 100 feet, road passes seasonal spring and descends about 0.8 mile to USFS 230. To right, road descends along Bearwallow Creek, later Pigeonroost Creek, passes good spring on right at about 0.3 mile opposite first abandoned house on left, and reaches Pigeonroost, N.C., 4.0 miles north of Huntdale, in about 6.5 miles.) From Cherry Gap, ascend on ungraded trail.

17.0   Skirt right (southern) slope of Piney Bald. Summit of Piney Bald is open and offers fine views. It can be reached by proceeding straight up ridgecrest through woods (no trail) instead of skirting summit on southern slope.

17.2   Bear right into narrow gap. Beyond, ascend steeply up ridge to southeast.

17.5   While crossing left shoulder of small knob, make hard left. Descend east through mature forest. Trail mostly follows top of broad ridgecrest to east with gentle ascents and descents.

17.9   Reach Little Bald Knob (4,459 feet). From summit, descend along ridge to northeast, keeping alongside and to left of fence. Roan Mountain may be seen from edge of woods.

18.1   Cross old logging road; then pass to left of large rock outcrop. Descend steeply; then cross graded trail.

18.2   Reach sag, which is subject to extremely heavy summer growth. Ascend slightly, coming close to fence on right. Beyond, bear right from ridgecrest, and descend on foot trail.

18.4   Reach old woods road, and bear left.

18.6   Enter gravel road, passable by car. In a few yards, veer right onto foot trail into woods. Proceed along right side of ridgeline, with gravel road above on crest.

19.1   Reach paved highway (Tenn. 107/N.C. 226) through Iron Mountain Gap (3,723 feet). A.T. continues on dirt road to left of ridgecrest across highway.

Nolichucky River, Tennessee, to Spivey Gap, North Carolina
Section Ten
10.2 Miles

Brief Description of Section

The northern end of this section begins at the western end of the highway bridge across the Nolichucky River. The Trail climbs almost immediately from the Nolichucky River and ascends the narrow crest of Cliff Ridge. The climb is continuous for almost 2.0 miles, during which the Trail gains 1,500 feet. Beyond, there is relatively little change in elevation to the end of the section. From the top of Cliff Ridge, the Trail follows Temple Ridge south and descends into Temple Hill Gap.

From Temple Hill Gap, the Trail skirts first the northern and then the eastern side of No Business Knob on graded trail. The eastern slope is characterized by many sharp ridges, around which the Trail winds back and forth. The Trail reaches Devils Creek Gap, ascends sharply, and skirts the side of Flattop Mountain. It then descends along Oglesby Branch to reach U.S. 19W 0.3 mile east of Spivey Gap.

Because of the initial climb, travel from north to south is considerably more difficult than travel in the opposite direction. Traveling southward requires 3,300 feet of climbing in this section. Traveling northward, the climbing totals 1,500 feet.

Points of Interest

The Nolichucky River Gorge has walls so sheer that no highway has been built through it. The all-freight Clinchfield Railroad, running from Elkhorn City, Ky., to Spartanburg, S.C., follows the southern riverbank in its climb to the crest of the Blue Ridge at Alta Pass, N.C.

The small, completely isolated mountain community of Lost Cove, N.C., is located about 4.0 miles southeast of Unaka Springs. The community once had a small number of permanent residents, for whom, after the discontinuance of railroad passenger service, the only mode of travel in and out of the area was by foot or horseback. (The Lost Cove area is now posted private property.)

This section includes the unusual scenery from Cliff Ridge, close by the Nolichucky River, and the interesting circuit of No Business Knob, leading through the upper elevations of the isolated Devils Creek watershed. No Business Knob was named by a man who tried without success to climb it when it was overgrown with thick underbrush, which developed after a severe fire burned the knob to bedrock. He concluded that he had "no business" on that knob. There are fine views from the Trail at Cliff Ridge and along No Business Knob.

The Trail is within the Unaka District of the Cherokee National Forest from the point where it leaves the road near the Nolichucky River to the state line east of Devils Creek Gap. From that point to the end of the section, it lies within the Toecane District of the Pisgah National Forest (National Forests in North Carolina).

Road Approaches

The northern end of the section is on the western side of the Nolichucky River at Chestoa, Tenn., 2.3 miles southwest of Erwin, Tenn., via Tenn. 36, which joins U.S. 23 0.5 mile farther west.

The southern end of the section crosses U.S. 19W near Spivey Gap on the Tennessee-North Carolina state line, 16 miles south of Erwin via U.S. 19W and 27 miles northwest of Burnsville, N.C., by U.S. 19E and U.S. 19W.

Maps

Refer to ATC Tennessee-North Carolina Map Two for route navigation. For additional area detail, refer to TVA Chestoa, Tennessee-North Carolina, quadrangle.

Shelters, Campsites, and Water

This section has one shelter:

No Business Knob Shelter: Concrete-block shelter built in 1963 by USFS; 5.7 miles from northern end of section; accommodates 6; water available from spring 400 yards south on A.T.

Next shelter: north 9.9 miles (Curley Maple Gap Shelter); south 10.1 miles (Bald Mountain Shelter)

Water is available at four other places along the section, all south of the shelter.

At the southern end of the section, going north up the highway, it is 0.3 mile to Spivey Gap and Bald Mountain Campground (USFS facility with spring, picnic tables, fireplaces, and toilets, but no shelters). North Carolina wildlife checking station is at campground entrance.

Public Accommodations and Supplies

Erwin has a large grocery store 2.3 miles from the northern end of the section, a hospital (3.0 miles), and a post office (4.1 miles). Motels, stores, and restaurants are available. The YMCA is 3.5 miles from the northern end of the section (corner of Ohio and Love Streets) and offers showers for a small fee, but no lodging.

From the southern end of the section at Spivey Gap, the closest accommodations are still in Erwin. Ample accommodations are also available in Asheville, N.C., more than 30 miles to the south.

Precautions

The North Carolina portion of the section is also within the Flattop Wildlife Management Area. No firearms or unleashed dogs should be taken into this area.

Trail Description, North to South

Miles	Data
0.0	From western end of highway bridge across Nolichucky River (1,700 feet), turn left on road along riverbank. (Paved road to right, northwest, leads through several turns over 0.9 mile to U.S. 23 and beyond, left, southwest, an additional 0.7 mile to a restaurant and service station/grocery with limited selection of supplies.) Follow river road upstream for 250 feet (road continues 0.8 mile along river to Unaka Springs), then turn right, and climb steep bank on steps. Enter graded trail, which skirts steep hillside through dense rhododendron.
0.1	Field and house are below on right.
0.2	Start ascent by switchbacks.

0.5   Reach crest in saddle (avoid side trail downhill to left). Trail ascends lightly wooded (predominantly pine and laurel) crest of Cliff Ridge for next 1.0 mile. There are numerous switchbacks and many fine views of Nolichucky River and surrounding area.

0.7   Pass rock on overlook and, in 0.1 mile, pass another.

1.2   Unaka Springs can be seen almost directly below. Continue ascent; forest growth changes to more mature hardwood.

1.6   In saddle, old graded trail (obscure) enters from right (leads down side ridge).

1.9   Reenter crest at elevation of 3,240 feet. For next 0.6 mile, continue south along crest of Temple Ridge, with alternating short ascents and descents.

2.6   Reach access road (3,250 feet) to site of former Temple Hill firetower. A.T. follows road to left, descending. (Straight ahead, access road ascends 0.5 mile to summit of Temple Hill, 3,710 feet. No view.)

3.3   Enter Temple Hill Gap (2,850 feet). (To left, road impassable by car descends via Mine Flat, reaching Unaka Springs at 2.1 miles and Nolichucky River bridge at beginning of this section at 3.0 miles. To right, road descends 1.0 mile to Granny Lewis Creek.) From Temple Hill Gap, follow logging road to left for 50 yards. Then, bear right off road on graded trail, which skirts left side of crest. Ascend steadily for 0.3 mile.

3.6   Bear right around shoulder of ridge; behind is impressive view of Temple Hill. Continue on graded trail, which skirts well below summit of No Business Knob (4,160 feet). Next 1.5 miles have practically no change in elevation.

5.6   Enter trail junction. (Unblazed trail to left, north, descends 0.5 mile to end of gravel USFS road, passable by car; leads back 5.0 miles to Unaka Springs.) Turn back sharply right (south).

5.7   Reach **No Business Knob Shelter** (nearest water is spring about 200 yards ahead on A.T.). From shelter (3,180 feet), descend gradually down draw to south.

5.9   Spring is to right of Trail in hemlock grove. (For next 2.5 miles, Trail skirts eastern slope of No Business Knob, making numerous sharp switchbacks with little change in elevation. Direction is generally southern. Along route are several vistas that provide views of Flattop Mountain to east over Devils Creek drainage.)

6.5   Cross small creek.

6.8   Cross stream at switchback to left.

8.3   Reach old logging road through Devils Creek Gap (3,400 feet). (To right, road descends to Kan Lot and U.S. 19W; to left, it descends into Devils Creek watershed and ends.) Follow Trail along crest (east) directly across road.

8.4   Cross state line into North Carolina, and enter Flattop Wildlife Management Area. (Side trail leads downhill to right.) Soon, ascend sharply up ridgecrest through dense rhododendron.

8.6   Reach small gap on crest. Here, bear left, and skirt side of hill on graded trail into hollow.

8.8   After steep 400-foot ascent through head of hollow, reach wildlife management-area dirt road (3,770 feet). (To right, road leads to Spivey Gap. To left, road forks; right fork circles around wildlife opening and continues east along side of Flattop; left fork descends northwest.) Cross road, and follow footpath straight ahead (east) through woods. Trail soon enters dense rhododendron and laurel and skirts broad shoulder of Flattop Mountain at nearly constant elevation.

9.5   In saddle, cross end of wildlife management-area road.

9.6   Reach Oglesby Branch (named for the founder of the TERC Hiking Club, who was the first member to fall into it). Make sharp right, and descend with stream, crossing it several times.

10.0   Stream bears away to left; descend straight ahead through woods and rhododendron.

10.1   Leave well-defined trail, and make sharp right. In a short distance, turn left, downhill, then turn left onto dirt road. After about 50 yards, turn right from road, and descend through woods.

10.2   Descend stone steps to U.S. 19W, and cross highway to North Carolina Highway Department A.T. sign on southern side of highway and end of section. (To right, west along highway, it is 0.3 mile to Spivey Gap and 1.5 miles to Tennessee line.) To continue on A.T., proceed left, east, along side of highway for 50 yards, and descend bank into woods.

Trail Description, South to North

| Miles | Data |

0.0   From North Carolina Highway Department A.T. sign on southern side of U.S. 19W, proceed straight across highway, climb bank on stone steps, and turn left, ascending on Trail through woods. In a short distance, reach dirt road. Turn left onto road, and proceed about 50 yards; turn right from road onto trail, and ascend through woods. Then, descend to Oglesby Branch (named for the founder of the TERC Hiking Club, who was the first member to fall into the previously unnamed branch.) Ascend along stream.

0.4   Side trail forks uphill, to right; keep left, and follow left branch of stream.

0.6   Turn back sharply left, and climb steeply on log steps, directly away from stream.

0.7   Cross end of wildlife management-area road, and soon reach saddle, 3,800 feet. (Avoid broad trail leading slightly to left down hollow.) Proceed straight ahead through hardwood forest at nearly constant elevation, skirting along broad shoulder of Flattop Mountain. Trail soon passes through dense laurel and rhododendron.

1.4   Reach dirt wildlife management-area road in gap. (Back to left, road leads to Spivey Gap. To right, road forks; right fork circles around wildlife opening and continues east along side of Flattop Mountain; left fork descends northwest.) Cross road, and descend steeply into hollow, following Bear Woods Trail (west). After 400 feet, Trail skirts to left around hillside.

1.6   Reach crest in small gap. Bear right, and descend ridgecrest through dense rhododendron.

1.8   Leave Flattop Wildlife Management Area, and cross state line into Tennessee. Side trail leads downhill to left.

1.9   Reach old logging road through Devils Creek Gap, 3,400 feet. (To left, road descends to Kan Lot and U.S. 19W; to right, it descends into Devils Creek watershed and ends.) Follow trail along crest directly across road. After short distance, bear right, and follow graded trail. (For next 2.5 miles, Trail skirts eastern slope of No Business Knob, making numerous sharp switchbacks. Direction is generally north. Along route are several vistas of Flattop Mountain to east the over Devils Creek drainage. Unaka Mountain can occasionally be seen in the distance to the northeast, beyond Nolichucky River.)

3.4   Cross small stream.

3.7   Cross small creek.

4.3   Cross small creek; 50 feet beyond, in hemlock grove, is spring beside Trail on left. Continue up draw toward gap.

4.5   Reach broad crest (3,180 feet). On left is **No Business Knob Shelter** (nearest water is spring that was passed 400 yards back on Trail).

4.6   Reach trail junction. (Unblazed trail straight ahead, north, descends 0.5 mile to end of gravel USFS road, passable by car in dry weather; road leads 5.0 miles to Unaka Springs, Tenn., 1.0 mile from end of this section.) Turn back sharply left (west), and continue on graded trail, which skirts well below summit of No Business Knob (4,160 feet). Next 1.5 miles have practically no change in elevation.

6.6   Bear left around shoulder of ridge; ahead is impressive view of Temple Hill Knob. Descend steadily.

6.9   Enter old logging road that enters uphill from right. (This road, impassable by car, descends via Mine Flat to Unaka Springs at 2.1 miles and Nolichucky River Bridge at 3.0 miles.) Keep left, and follow road uphill about 50 yards to Temple Hill Gap, 2,850 feet. Turn right, away from logging road, and ascend steadily on former access road, skirting right side of Temple Hill.

7.7   Reach crest of Temple Ridge (3,220 feet). Trail leaves access road, which switches back to left and continues 0.5 mile to summit of Temple Hill (3,710 feet); no view. Follow crest trail north along Temple Ridge.

8.6   In saddle, old graded trail (obscure) leads to left down side ridge. Ascend slightly over knoll; then resume steady descent. Trail is graded in places and makes numerous switch-backs.

9.0   Reach overlook; Unaka Springs can be seen almost directly below. From here, follow lightly wooded (predominantly pine and laurel) crest of Cliff Ridge, which has many fine views of Nolichucky River and surrounding area.

9.7   Reach saddle and, bearing left from crest, avoid side trail downhill to right. Descend steep hillside by switchbacks through dense rhododendron.

10.0   At last switchback to right, Trail levels somewhat and circles end of ridge for 0.2 mile. Descend steps to road beside river. Turn left (to right, road leads 0.8 mile to Unaka Springs).

10.2   Reach paved road (former U.S. 19W and 23, as shown on 1939 edition of TVA Chestoa quadrangle) at western end of bridge (1,700 feet) and end of section. (Paved road to left, northwest, leads through several turns 0.9 mile to U.S. 23, and beyond, left, southwest, an additional 0.7 mile to a restaurant, and service station/grocery with limited selection of supplies.)

Spivey Gap (U.S. 19W), North Carolina, to Sams Gap, Tennessee-North Carolina (U.S. 23)
Section Eleven
12.7 Miles

Brief Description of Section

The Trail route in this section combines interesting forests and high farming country with extraordinary views. From the northern end of the section, near Spivey Gap, the Trail ascends through a superb white-pine and hemlock stand and then through hardwoods. Rewarding views are available from High Rocks, a promontory looking north over the Trail route and west, where Sections 12 and 13 in the Pisgah National Forest are visible. The Trail descends along the crest of the Bald Mountain Range to Whistling Gap and then ascends to the wooded summit of Little Bald. It then descends along the ridge to the base of Big Bald and climbs across extensive meadows to the summit, a superb example of the true "bald" of the southern Appalachians, with a magnificent panoramic view.

Beyond Big Bald, the Trail descends along the main crest to Street Gap, where a dirt road crosses the ridge. From Street Gap the Trail ascends across extensive open pastures and follows the ridgecrest until it reaches the final sharp descent into Sams Gap. *Note:* Relocations planned in the Sams Gap area to improve treadway and scenic quality may be open in 1993.

The maintenance of the Trail from here south to Davenport Gap is under the jurisdiction of the Carolina Mountain Club, Asheville, N.C.

Points of Interest

The summit of High Rocks, 50 feet off the Trail, has splendid views of Little Bald, Temple Hill, and No Business Knob.

Big Bald's summit offers one of the finest panoramic views in the southern Appalachians. Mt. Mitchell in the Black Mountain range, the highest peak east of the Mississippi, bears 145 degrees and is 20 miles distant. Mt. LeConte in the Great Smokies bears 240 degrees and is 60 miles distant. Between these two ranges, the Nantahalas lie to the southwest. Coldspring Mountain with its two peaks, Camp Creek Bald and Big Butt, is close to the northwest. The Unaka Mountains are to the northeast.

The summit of Big Bald and ridgeline to Little Bald were acquired by the USFS from the Big Bald Development Corporation in 1977, with the corporation retaining the right to maintain and use its dirt road to Big Stamp and a spur road to the summit. This road leads back into North Carolina to a locked entrance gate and beyond to a complex of summer homes, a golf course, restaurant, lodge, and ski resort on the eastern and southern slopes of the mountain range. South of the summit, where the A.T. becomes level for several hundred feet, the developer's road is out of sight on the crest 200 feet to the east, leading 1.5 miles to the restaurant and lodge.

Road Approaches

The northern end of this section is on U.S. 19W, 0.3 mile south of Spivey Gap. On U.S. 19W, it is 7.0 miles to U.S. 23 at Ernestville (8.0 miles north to Erwin, Tenn.) and 43 miles south to Asheville. South on U.S. 19W, then east on U.S. 19E, it is 42 miles to Spruce Pine and 27 miles to Burnsville, N.C.

At Street Gap, a dirt road crosses the ridge. To the north into Tennessee from Flag Pond via Higgins Creek, the road is steep but passable by cars with good traction. To the south into North Carolina, a Jeep road leads 0.5 mile to the first inhabited house on Puncheon Fork Road—good route for 30 miles via U.S. 23 to Asheville

The southern end of the section is at U.S. 23 in Sams Gap. To the south, it is 12 miles to Mars Hill and 31 miles to Asheville. To the north, it is 6.0 miles to Flag Pond and 2.0 miles farther to Rocky Fork (where Tenn. 352 leads west 4.4 miles to Devil Fork Gap), 13 miles to U.S. 19W at Ernestville, and 20 miles to Erwin.

Maps

Refer to ATC Tennessee-North Carolina Map Two for route navigation. For additional area detail, refer to TVA Chestoa, Tennessee-North Carolina; Bald Creek, North Carolina-Tennessee; and Sams Gap, North Carolina-Tennessee, quadrangles. A good self-guiding map with descriptive text is *100 Favorite Trails of the Great Smokies and the Carolina Blue Ridge*, compiled by the Carolina Mountain Club and Smoky Mountains Hiking Club and available from the clubs or ATC. The USFS map covering the Toecane Ranger District of the Pisgah National Forest is also a valuable guide.

Shelters, Campsites, and Water

This section has one shelter:

Bald Mountain Shelter: Built in 1988 by Carolina Mountain Club; 5.6 miles from the northern end of the section on a 0.1 mile side trail; accommodates 10; water available from spring 50 feet on side trail.

Next shelter: north 9.6 miles (No Business Knob Shelter); south 9.3 miles (Hogback Ridge Shelter).

Good campsites are available near the springs at Whistling Gap, the head of Tumbling Creek, Higgins Creek, and Low Gap. Water also is available at eight other springs along the route.

At U.S. 19W, it is 0.3 mile up the highway to Spivey Gap, where a dirt road leads 0.2 mile to USFS Spivey Gap Picnic Area (spring, picnic tables, fireplaces, and toilets, but no shelters). North Carolina wildlife checking station is at campground entrance.

Public Accommodations and Supplies

At the northern end of the section, the closest accommodations are in Erwin, Tenn., which has several motels, restaurants, and grocery stores. Ample accommodations and supplies are also available in Asheville. A restaurant and lodge are accessible 1.5 miles from the Trail on Big Bald.

From Sams Gap on U.S. 23, it is 2.8 miles south into North Carolina to a cafe and 3.2 miles to a grocery store and gas station.

History

Near the summit of Big Bald is Greer Rock, site of "Greer House," the home of David Greer in the early 1800s. Spurned by his sweetheart when living in South Carolina, he came to Big Bald to live as a hermit. Legend has it that he dug a 12-foot room under the rock, lined the walls with clay, and used a stone for a front door. He kept livestock there and dug a moat to keep the animals confined. He lived much as his animals did and was known as "Old Hog Greer." He lived on Big Bald off and on from 1802 to 1834. His violent temper kept him from holding jobs very long and caused arguments with his neighbors and law-enforcement officers. He killed one man in an argument and eventually was killed in one himself. His home under the rock is no longer evident, but the remains of the moat can still be traced.

Precautions

The traverse of this section from north to south involves steep climbing from Spivey Gap to High Rocks, from Whistling Gap to Little Bald, and from Big Stamp to Big Bald. The summit of Big Bald (5,516 feet) is 2,316 feet higher than the Trail crossing of the highway in Spivey Gap. Traverse from south to north is less difficult, because Sams Gap is 600 feet higher than Spivey Gap.

Heavy annual growth may make portions of the route difficult to follow during summer months.

Near Spivey Gap on both sides of U.S. 19W are sections of North Carolina's Flattop Wildlife Management Area, where dogs and guns are not allowed without a permit.

Caution should be observed on Big Bald. Marking across the bald summit is accomplished by blazes on short posts and rocks, making the route obvious in clear weather. In foggy or stormy weather, the hiker easily can become disoriented and lose the Trail. In bad weather, the blue-blazed bypass trail around the bald should be taken. On Big Bald, it can be windy, rainy, and cold any time of year. To avoid hypothermia, hikers and Trail campers should be well-prepared with warm clothes, sleeping gear, and tents. (See "First Aid," page 13.)

Trail Description, North to South

Miles   **Data**

Note: Watch for relocations due to highway construction, in the Sams Gap area, which may be open in 1993; follow the white blazes.

0.0   From junction of A.T. with U.S. 19W (3,200 feet) 0.3 mile east of Spivey Gap, descend southern bank of highway, cross Big

Creek, and ascend southwest. Enter white-pine grove after 100 yards, following winding route through woods.

0.2   Pass to left of deer browse field. Above field in dense hemlock and white-pine stand, enter old roadway, continuing uphill.

0.5   Beyond top of log steps, stream lies to left; area has been used for **campsite**. Continue ascent steeply to right. (Watch for relocation in 1993 or 1994. Follow white blazes.)

0.6   Turn left, and cross stream. Soon turn sharp right and ascend by graded trail.

1.4   Reach broad saddle. At far end, ascend by northern ridge of High Rocks. (Note wildlife management-area boundary markings on left.) Steep climb is eased by switchbacks and log steps. Near summit, Trail passes to left over ridge and then bears right on steep, eastern slope for 250 feet. Note safety cable.

1.6   Reach junction with blue-blazed trail, which continues ahead around rocky summit of High Rocks (4,280 feet) and descends to rejoin A.T. at 1.2 miles. A.T. ascends to right 15 feet to small notch with peak of High Rocks to left. Descending, it skirts below rocky cliffs.

2.0   Reach sag in ridge.

2.3   Reach small clearing and good **campsite** in Whistling Gap. (To right, a trail leads north 0.1 mile to spring; beyond, an old trail continues to U.S. 19W at North Carolina-Tennessee line.) Continue across broad sag, and ascend, slightly at first.

2.8   Pass an upright rock blazed with A.T. symbol on right. Trail crosses knob into sag and continues ascent of Little Bald. (Watch for switchback to south in 1993 or 1994. Follow white blazes.

3.3   Trail veers to right off crest.

3.5   Pass spring to right below Trail. Trail now ascends more steeply up northern slope of Little Bald with several switchbacks and stone steps. Near summit, find vista on right (to north, Temple Hill and No Business Knob are prominent).

4.2   Reach top of Little Bald (5,185 feet). Summit is wooded and has no summer view. Here, Trail joins North Carolina-Tennessee state line and descends to southwest on narrow ridge through beech woods.

4.5 Where grade becomes more level, reach turnaround at end of old road. Trail alternates frequently between old road and woods trail.

5.2 On old road, reach sign on tree for water. To right, blue-blazed trail leads down into Big Bald Creek; good **tent camping** on ridgecrest; good spring is 0.2 mile down this trail at head of Tumbling Creek. Ahead, old road continues with old A.T. route on left and present A.T. proceeding slightly to right, on right slope of ridge. Pass spring on left side of Trail.

5.4 Beyond spring, in 200 feet, cross small stream. Continue through woods on right slope with moderate climb. Cross dirt road, climb bank, and soon bear left, still ascending.

5.6 Side trail heading north goes 0.1 mile to **Bald Mountain Shelter** (spring is 50 feet down a side trail that begins halfway between shelter and A.T.). The areas around the spring and shelter are *too fragile for camping*. See mile 5.2 for a good **camping** spot.

5.9 Leaving birch woods, enter open meadows. Behind is view of Little Bald.

6.1 Pass over small rise with sparse growth of trees among large boulders. Ahead is close-up view of Big Bald summit. Descend moderately along open ridgecrest.

6.5 Descend to Big Stamp, treeless saddle at northern base of Big Bald, where Big Bald development road from Wolf Laurel crosses sag. (To right, road leads onto summit of Big Bald, and a fork to right leads 0.3 mile to double springs; possible **campsite**. To left, blue-blazed trail follows road 0.3 mile and via graded trail continues around southeastern side of the bald to rejoin A.T. In inclement weather, this trail provides a good alternate route and should be strongly considered during periods of poor visibility or severe weather. Navigation across open balds is difficult when visibility is limited.) In Big Stamp, A.T. crosses dirt road and steeply ascends open northeastern slope of Big Bald.

6.7 Reach summit of Big Bald (5,516 feet). From summit, Trail goes south 100 feet and, bearing right, begins winding descent toward Slipper Spur, which extends to southeast. As you leave grassy bald, pass through small shrubs and trees.

7.0 Trail bears left, leaving Slipper Spur, and descends steeply through rhododendron with switchbacks.

7.2   Cross small streams; grade is more gentle.

7.4   Reach junction with blue-blazed trail from left. (This is alternate trail leading around southeastern side of Big Bald to Big Stamp at 6.0 miles. Back 150 feet left on this trail is sign for water, with spring 10 feet to right.) Trail continues down slight grade.

7.5   Reach blue-blazed trail on right, which leads 100 yards down slope to spring.

8.0   Trail crests side ridge extending to northwest, and then descends.

8.5   Pass ruins on right below Trail. (Fifty yards above to left on ridge road, where powerline crosses ridge, are good views to south over Wolf Laurel development.)

8.9   Pass spring on Trail. Continue on northern slope of state-line ridge with descent through mature hardwood forest. Early spring wildflowers are striking.

9.5   Reach dirt-track crossing, 50 yards below Low Gap on Tennessee side. (The dirt track comes up from Higgins Creek to dirt road above on ridgeline. To right, just below Trail, find good spring.) Trail soon bears left, following the ridge, and ascends diagonally to left.

9.6   Blue-blazed trail on right leads 20 yards to spring.

9.7   Reach state-line ridge and old road in sag. Follow road to right, climbing steeply.

9.8   At top of rise, turn left onto graded trail. Rejoin old road in one-quarter mile, bearing left.

10.8   Reach Street Gap (about 4,100 feet). (To right, road leads to Flag Pond via Higgins Creek. To left, road leads 0.6 mile to paved road and the first inhabited house on Puncheon Fork Road, which is good route for 30 miles via U.S. 23 to Asheville.) From Street Gap, bear right on graded trail. Ascend through old Christmas-tree farm.

11.0   Cross steep old road and ridgeline; enter pasture.

11.1   Trail switches back to right when it approaches fence. When Trail rejoins fence, follow it to summit, entering trees. (Behind, Big Bald is prominent to northeast.)

11.3   Cross fence line, and descend steeply.

11.6   Pass around left edge of abandoned talc mine. After 100 yards, pass dirt road on right, which leads down to U.S. 23 in Tennessee.

11.7   In slight sag, intermittent spring can be found 10 yards to right across fence. Continue along series of knobs and sags to left of fence.

12.4   Pass through intersecting wire fence. Trail ascends, crossing to right of fence. At top of knob, Trail turns right and descends steeply to left of ridgeline. Reach embankment above highway and turn left, descending ramp.

12.7   Reach U.S. 23, 50 yards south of road crest in Sams Gap (3,800 feet).

Trail Description, South to North

Note: Watch for relocations due to highway construction, in the Sams Gap area, which may be open during 1993; follow the white blazes.

Miles   **Data**

0.0   Fifty yards south of road crest in Sams Gap (3,800 feet), ascend ramp, and follow eastern embankment 50 yards. Turn right, ascending through woods to right of ridgecrest. Soon, climb more steeply to top of wooded knob at 0.3 mile.

0.3   Pass through intersecting wire fence, and continue to right of fence along crest.

1.0   In slight sag, intermittent spring lies 10 yards to left, across fence. After 200 feet, pass dirt road, which leads down to left to reach U.S. 23 in Tennessee.

1.1   Pass to right of abandoned talc mine, and continue ascent to right of barbed-wire fence.

1.4   At top of knob (about 4,440 feet), emerge from woods into open meadows. (Big Bald is prominent to northeast.) Descend across meadow to left of fence.

1.6   Follow fence as it bears to right, skirt small knob to left, then switch back to left where A.T. again approaches fence. Continue across field.

1.9   Leave field, cross ridgecrest and descend through old Christmas-tree farm to Street Gap.

2.1   Reach road in Street Gap. (To left, road leads to Flag Pond via Higgins Creek. To right, road leads 0.6 mile to paved road and first inhabited house on Puncheon Fork Road, which is good route for 30 miles via U.S. 23 to Asheville.) At far side of road, follow dirt road through fence, ascending ridgecrest with superb views of summit of Big Bald ahead to left. (Dirt road follows Trail for 1.1 miles and then continues along ridgeline for 2.7 miles to Wolf Laurel Road.)

2.7   Bear right (south) of ridge where old road goes straight up ridge. Follow graded trail; switch back to left.

2.9   Reach ridgecrest and turn right. Descend steeply; enter Cherokee National Forest.

3.0   Trail leaves dirt road and ridgeline by descending diagonally to left and then following left (Tennessee) slope of ridge.

3.1   Blue-blazed trail leads left 20 yards to spring.

3.2   Reach Low Gap 50 yards down on Tennessee side. Good spring lies just below Trail. To continue, cross dirt track (which enters from Higgins Creek to reach dirt road above on ridgeline), and ascend through mature hardwoods (maple, cherry, buckeye, and beech). For next mile, Trail continues with little change in elevation through spring-wildflower garden.

3.8   Pass spring on Trail.

4.2   Pass ruins to left below Trail. (Fifty yards to right, above on ridge road where powerline crosses ridge, are good views to south over Wolf Laurel development.) Trail continues skirting left slope of ridge and then climbs gradually.

5.2   About 500 feet after beginning gentle ascent, reach blue-blazed trail on left that leads 100 yards down slope to spring.

5.3   Reach trail junction. (Blue-blazed trail bears right and leads 150 feet to good spring. This trail passes around southeastern side of Big Bald on graded trail and turns left on Wolf Laurel Road to rejoin A.T. at 6.2 miles in Big Stamp. In inclement weather, this trail provides good alternate route and should be strongly considered during periods of poor visibility or severe weather. Navigation across open balds is difficult when visibility is limited.) From junction, A.T. continues to left and begins ascent of Big Bald.

5.5   Ascend fairly steep and rocky slope, and cross small streams. In 500 feet, enter rhododendron area, ascending.

5.7   Reaching more level ground, Trail swings to right and continues generally east up slope of Big Bald. Trail passes through area of scattered small trees and shrubs (mountain ash, serviceberry, and hawthorn) and enters open, grassy bald. Follow blazes and pathway cut in sod; turn north.

6.0   Reach highest point on Big Bald (marked by post at 5,516 feet). From summit of Big Bald, descend steep, northeastern slope to Big Stamp, a treeless saddle.

6.2   Reach junction with blue-blazed alternate trail, which skirts summit from 5.3 miles, entering from right on Wolf Laurel Road. (Continuation of road to left to grassed-over parking lot leads onto summit and, by another fork, right, leads 0.3 mile to double springs. This area is possible **campsite**.) Ascend moderately, and follow ridgecrest generally northeast over extensive meadows, with wide views.

6.6   Pass over small rise with sparse growth of trees among large boulders. A close-up view of Big Bald summit is to the southwest.

6.8   Descend from open meadow with view of Little Bald ahead. Enter birch woods, and soon cross dirt road. Trail passes through mature woods on left slope.

7.1   Side trail heading north goes 0.1 mile to **Bald Mountain Shelter** (spring 50 feet down a side trail that begins halfway between shelter and A.T.). This shelter is one of the highest on the A.T. and the area around it is *too fragile for camping*. See mile 7.5 for good camping spot.

7.3   Cross small stream, and, in 200 feet, pass spring to right.

7.5   Blue-blazed trail on left enters from Big Bald Creek; good **tent camping** on ridge; good spring is 0.2 mile down this trail at head of Tumbling Creek. Along this section, Trail is alternately in woods and on old road.

8.2   Reach end of old road. Trail ascends narrow ridge along left side of fence through beech grove.

8.5   Reach top of Little Bald (5,185 feet). Summit is wooded and offers no summer view. Trail leaves state line and continues in North Carolina to end of section. From Little Bald, Trail bears left of ridgecrest, descending. After 150 feet, a vista to left looks north (No Business Knob and Temple Hill are prominent). Trail continues rather steep descent on northern slope of mountain, with several switchbacks and steps.

9.2   Pass spring to left below Trail in more level section.

9.4   At this point, former route of A.T. from summit of Little Bald enters from right. (Watch for new switchback to south in 1993 or 1994.) Continue descent on ridge, with barbed-wire fence approaching on right. Continue through sag with faint trail to left.

9.9 After ascent of slight rise, pass upright rock to left of Trail, which is blazed with A.T. symbol. After 0.3 mile, Trail enters broad sag.

10.4 Reach Whistling Gap (over 3,840 feet). Far end of gap is used as **campsite**. On left, trail leads 0.1 mile to spring. (Beyond spring, old A.T. continues to U.S. 19W at North Carolina-Tennessee line west of Spivey Gap. Continue ahead on crest, ascending. Cross small knob.

10.7 From sag, ascend toward High Rocks. Near summit, reach junction with blue-blazed trail. (Alternate route to right leads steeply to high point from which peak of High Rocks, 4,280 feet, can be reached. From this high point, cross ridge, and circle beneath northern rim of High Rocks, and rejoin A.T. at 11.1 miles.) From start of blue-blazed route, Trail bears left and skirts base of rocky cliff. Ascend to small saddle with peak of High Rocks to right.

11.1 Blue-blazed trail joins Trail, which continues to left on steep, eastern slope about 250 feet. Note safety cable. Turn left across northern ridge of High Rocks, and begin steep descent with steps and switchbacks. Wildlife management-area boundary markings are on right as Trail becomes less steep.

11.3 Leave far end of saddle on graded trail, which bears to the right.

11.5 Trail descends over rock ledge and switches back to the right. Continue descent on graded trail.

12.0 Turn sharp left onto steep trail, and descend.

12.1 Cross stream, and turn right to continue downward.

12.2 Pass area used as **campsite** with stream on right. Descend log steps, and continue downward less steeply on old road. Enter dense hemlock and white-pine stand.

12.5 Pass to right of deer browse field, and follow winding route through woods. Cross Big Creek, and ascend bank of highway.

12.7 Reach end of section at U.S. 19W (elevation 3,200 feet). To continue north on A.T., ascend northern bank of highway.

Sams Gap to Davenport Gap
77.9 Miles

Brief Description of Section

This part of the A.T. extends from Sams Gap (U.S. 23) to Davenport Gap, the eastern boundary of the Great Smoky Mountains National Park.

Except where the Trail descends from the ridge to cross the French Broad River at Hot Springs, N.C., and where it makes the descent to the Pigeon River near Waterville, the route is generally along the state line between North Carolina and Tennessee. This range is known as the Bald Mountains.

The state line is circuitous at the beginning, proceeding 4.0 miles west from Sams Gap, and then forming an enormous projection north for the next 10.0 miles to Big Butt on Coldspring Mountain. Some of this is a cleared ridgecrest, which has magnificent views. The fire towers on Camp Creek Bald and Rich Mountain also permit expansive views. West of Hot Springs, the Trail route is particularly outstanding. The widespread views from Walnut, Max Patch, and Snowbird mountains are unsurpassed. A feature of the region is the luxuriant rhododendron growth. The Trail on Big Firescald Knob is virtually a tunnel through dense thickets of this shrub. The cascades of State Line Branch come into view as one approaches the Smokies.

This section of Trail is marked throughout by white paint blazes and standard metal A.T. markers. Some distances along the main route and side trails are indicated by USFS signs.

The quadrangle maps covering this part of the Trail are Sams Gap, Flag Pond, Greystone, Davy Crockett Lake, Hot Springs, Spring Creek, Lemon Gap, and Waterville. These maps are may be obtained from TVA. A good self-guiding map with descriptive text is *100 Favorite Trails of the Great Smokies and the Carolina Blue Ridge*, compiled by the Carolina Mountain Club and the Smoky Mountains Hiking Club. It is available from those clubs and ATC.

The Trail here is mainly on national-forest lands. The North Carolina side is in the Pisgah National Forest; on the Tennessee side, it is in the Cherokee National Forest. The A.T. here is managed cooperatively by these two forests and the Carolina Mountain Club (CMC).

Additional information about the Pisgah National Forest may be obtained from the forest supervisor, National Forests in North Carolina, or the district ranger, French Broad Ranger District. Information about the Cherokee National Forest may be obtained from the supervisor, Cherokee National Forest, or the district ranger, Nolichucky Ranger District. Addresses may be found on pages 245-246.

Long-distance travel over this part of the Trail is facilitated by a well-spaced chain of eight shelters, four of which were originally built from 1938 to 1940 by the Civilian Conservation Corps (CCC) under the direction of the district forest ranger at Hot Springs. Each shelter has wood flooring with adequate room for at least five people. Springs are nearby. CMC began a section-wide shelter-renovation/replacement project in 1988. USFS shelters, together with those in the Smokies, make a complete shelter chain from Sams Gap to the Little Tennessee River at Fontana Dam, a distance of 149 miles.

Sams Gap (U.S. 23) to
Devil Fork Gap (N.C. 212)
Section Twelve
8.2 Miles

Brief Description of Section

From north to south, the general route of the Trail in this section is west from Sams Gap through Rice Gap to Big Flat and then north to Boone Cove Gap and Devil Fork Gap. This northern portion, following the circuitous route of the state line, produces the curious situation in which Tennessee is east of North Carolina and the hiker is actually traveling north, although heading south along the Trail toward Springer Mountain, Georgia.

From Sams Gap, the Trail ascends steeply at first to the crest of the Bald Mountains along the state line and then traverses a series of knobs through cutover and mature forests, interspersed with high farm lands for 3.0 miles to Rice Gap, where a road, passable by truck, crosses the crest. Beyond the gap, the Trail reaches Big Flat and swings abruptly north, passing over Frozen Knob (Lick Rock, 4,579 feet) slightly east of its summit. The route turns downhill and to the right of Sugarloaf Gap before reaching Sugarloaf Knob and crosses the upper portion of Boone Cove to regain the state line on the ridge beyond. The Trail descends the ridgecrest to the highway in Devil Fork Gap to join an excellent USFS trail through the Pisgah National Forest.

Points of Interest

Most of the route is wooded, but it has a number of rewarding views, notably from the sag north of Frozen Knob (Lick Rock).

Road Approaches

The northern end of the section is on U.S. 23 at Sams Gap on the Tennessee-North Carolina state line, 20 miles south of Erwin, Tenn., via Ernestville, 13 miles distant, and Flag Pond, 6.0 miles distant. The gap is also 31 miles north of Asheville.

The southern end of this section is at Devil Fork Gap, also on the Tennessee-North Carolina state line. From Erwin, it is southwest on U.S. 23 for 12 miles to Rocky Fork to the junction with Tenn. 352 (U.S. 23 bears left, south), then west on Tenn. 352 for 4.2 miles to Devil Fork Gap. From North Carolina, the gap may be reached from Hot Springs, N.C., by taking U.S. 25W and 70 east 6.0 miles, then N.C. 208 north 3.0 miles, and N.C. 212 northeast 15 miles.

A midpoint of the section at Rice Gap can be reached from Flag Pond (on U. S. 23) by proceeding southwest on a steep, gravel road along Rice Creek for 6.0 miles.

Maps

Refer to ATC Tennessee-North Carolina Map Three for route navigation. For additional area detail, refer to TVA Sams Gap, North Carolina-Tennessee, and Flag Pond, Tennessee-North Carolina, quadrangles.

Shelters, Campsites, and Water

This section has one shelter:

Hogback Ridge Shelter: Located 2.2 miles from the northern end of section, 0.1 mile from A.T.; water available at spring 440 yards west from shelter; latrine located in opposite direction 300 feet.

Next shelter: north 9.3 miles (Bald Mountain Shelter); south 8.7 miles (Flint Mountain Shelter).

A farmhouse in the Flag Pond area sometimes offers overnight accommodations. A fair campsite is available in Big Flat. Water is available at the campsite and two other places in this section.

Public Accommodations and Supplies

At the northern end of the section, the closest accommodations are in Erwin, Tenn., which has several motels, restaurants, and grocery stores. Ample accommodations and supplies are also available in Asheville. A restaurant and lodge are accessible 1.5 miles from the Trail on Big Bald.

From Sams Gap, south on U.S. 23, it is 2.8 miles to a cafe and 3.2 miles to a grocery store and gas station.

Precautions

Because of the numerous steep grades and the possibility that travel will be retarded by heavy annual growth, a liberal time allowance should be made for this section.

Trail Description, North to South

Miles   **Data**

0.0 One hundred fifty feet south of U.S. 23 crest at Sams Gap (3,800 feet), enter wide path, and ascend. Bear right, and pass cemetery gate 300 feet in from trailhead. Ascend steeply through woods.

0.2 Cross fence, and bear to left. Steps are 180 feet from fence crossing. Trail continues ascent.

0.3 Reach first stile; trail levels out here. Reach second stile in 0.1 mile. After passing stile, follow fenceline to right; descend.

0.6 Reach sag, then ascend.

0.8 Reach top of first knob; fence still to right. Trail bears somewhat to the west.

1.1 Cross fence (fence is now to your left). In 0.2 mile, cross fence again, putting fence to right.

1.7 Reach High Rock (4,460 feet). Trail bears west. (Intersecting fence and faint trail to right lead 150 feet to rocks with view of valley, obscured by trees in summer.) Reach second, higher summit in about 400 feet; descend on narrow ridge.

2.0 Reach sag. Trail joins gravel road. Soon, crest slight rise, and begin steady descent to Rice Gap.

2.2 Blue-blazed trail to the left leads to **Hogback Ridge Shelter**, 0.1 mile from the A.T. Spring is 440 yards from shelter on trail to the west; latrine is in the opposite direction, about 300 feet.

3.3 Reach Rice Gap (3,800 feet). Ascend old road through woods along fence. After 0.3 mile, pass through fence to woods to the right, and ascend by switchbacks to Big Flat.

3.7 Begin steeper ascent by switchbacks, crisscrossing former A.T. route, through open woods and blackberry growth. Ascent moderates after 0.2 mile.

4.3 Reach level area and a fair **campsite**, called Big Flat, after traversing a minor rise. Rock formations to the right.

4.9   Reach summit of Frozen Knob, passing old, unused stile while ascending moderately.

5.2   Traverse first rise past Frozen Knob.

5.7   Cross forest road, and bear to northeast. Enter open area, and cross road again in 0.1 mile. Trail begins descent.

6.1   Reach corner of old fence, with open areas to the right and left. Trail nearly level with slight descent, turning left.

6.4   Reach Sugarloaf Gap (4,000 feet). Sugarloaf Knob (4,560 feet) is to the left.

6.8   Cross stream as trail descends. After 0.3 mile, cross stream again and a woods road.

7.4   After passing small, fenced cemetery and descending steps, cross stream again, with barn close at right. Descent slackens after a moderate-to-steep downhill grade.

7.6   Cross old forest road; Trail nearly level.

7.7   Reach and cross Boone Cove Road (2,960 feet), after passing through level, open area with house to the right and crossing small footbridge over stream. Cross road directly to ascending trail, with wide switchbacks through wooded area.

8.0   Reach high point of small ridge. Then, cross stile in 300 feet and a second stile in another 300 feet. Enter meadow.

8.2   After descending through meadow with one switchback, cross a third stile to N.C. 212 (Tenn. 352) at Devil Fork Gap, end of section, just west of summit of Devil Fork.

Trail Description, South to North

Miles   **Data**

0.0   From N.C. 212 (Tenn. 352) just west of summit of Devil Fork, cross stile, and ascend through meadow with one switchback.

0.2   Reach high point of small ridge, after entering wooded area and crossing two more stiles 300 feet apart, the second being 300 feet from high point.

0.5   After descending trail with wide switchbacks in wooded area, reach Boone Cove Road (2,960 feet). Cross road directly, and cross small footbridge over stream into level, open area with house to left.

0.6   Cross old forest road, and begin ascent, gently at first.

0.8   Cross stream with barn close to trail at left, then ascend steps, and pass small fenced cemetery. Trail ascends moderately to steeply.

1.1   Cross stream again and woods road, with another stream crossing 0.3 mile farther. Trail continues ascent.

1.8   Reach Sugarloaf Gap (4,000 feet). Sugarloaf Knob (4,560 feet) is to right. Trail turns to right and becomes nearly level.

2.1   Reach corner of old fence with open areas to right and left. Trail again begins to ascend.

2.4   After ascent, cross forest road, and enter open area, bearing to south-southwest. Cross forest road again in 0.1 mile.

3.0   Traverse last rise before Frozen Knob.

3.3   Reach summit of Frozen Knob.

3.9   Reach level area called Big Flat, after passing old, unused stile to left while descending moderately; fair **campsite** at this location. Rock formations to left.

4.3   Begin steeper descent by switchbacks, crisscrossing former A.T. route through open woods and blackberry growth. Descent moderates after 0.2 mile.

4.9   Reach Rice Gap (3,800 feet). A.T. begins fairly steep climb out of Rice Gap on dirt road. Trail bears left on ridge, passing over small elevations and reaching a sag in 0.5 mile. Ascent then becomes steeper along narrow ridge. After passing over knob, there is short descent to sag, the end of vehicular use from Rice Gap.

6.0   Blue-blazed trail to right leads to **Hogback Ridge Shelter**, 0.1 mile from the AT. Spring is 440 yards from shelter on trail to west; latrine is in opposite direction, about 300 feet.

6.2   Trail narrows and ascends with swichbacks.

6.5   Reach High Rock (4,460 feet). (Intersecting fence and faint trail to left lead 150 feet to rocks, with view of valley obscured by trees in summer.) Descend alongside fence.

7.1   Cross fence, and follow fence line (fence is to right). In 0.2 mile, cross fence again, putting it to left of trail.

7.4   Reach top of last knob before Sams Gap, fence still to left. Trail bears somewhat to east.

7.6   Reach sag after descent; ascend. Fenceline continues to left.

7.8   Reach first stile. Trail levels out; reach second stile in 0.1 mile, and begin descent.

8.0   Descend steps, and cross fence in 180 feet. Descend steeply through wooded, open area until passing cemetery gate 450 yards from fence crossing.

8.2   Reach U.S. 23, 300 feet from cemetery and 150 feet south of highway crest. To continue north on A.T., cross U.S. 23 directly, and ascend through small field, bearing left.

Devil Fork Gap (N.C. 212) to Allen Gap (N.C. 208-Tenn. 70)
Section Thirteen
20.2 Miles

Brief Description of Section

The route of this section follows the USFS "State Line Trail," which is quite circuitous. Proceeding from north to south, the Trail trends northwest to Big Butt and then turns abruptly southwest. In this direction, there is little steep climbing, except at the beginning and from Flint Gap to the crest of Coldspring Mountain.

Points of Interest

From Green Ridge to Camp Creek Bald, the route is along a partially cleared ridgecrest, with extensive views, especially at the Ball Ground and Blackstack Cliffs.

Camp Creek Bald firetower (0.15 mile by side trail from A.T.) has a magnificent view. The rhododendron thickets at Bearwallow Gap are exceptionally dense.

USFS trail signs indicate mileages to points on intersecting trails.

Road Approaches

The northern end of the section is at Devil Fork Gap, on the Tennessee-North Carolina state line. The gap may be reached from Erwin, by taking U.S. 23 south for 12 miles to the community of Rocky Fork and then Tenn. 352 for 4.2 miles to Devil Fork Gap. From Hot Springs, N.C., the gap may be reached by taking U.S. 25W and 70 east 6.0 miles, then N.C. 208 north 3.0 miles, and N.C. 212 northeast 15 miles.

The southern end of the section is at Allen Gap, also on the Tennessee-North Carolina state line, 25 miles south of Greeneville, Tenn., on Tenn. 70. It may also be reached from Hot Springs by taking U.S. 25W and 70 east 6.0 miles and then N.C. 208 north 9.0 miles.

Camp Creek Bald, which the Trail skirts 7.0 miles north of the southern end of the section, can be reached by a gravel USFS fire road. This road begins on Tenn. 70 at a point 0.5 mile west of Allen Gap, proceeds northeast along Paint Creek, and reaches Camp Creek Bald after 9.0 miles.

Maps

Refer to ATC Tennessee-North Carolina Map Three for route navigation. For additional area detail, refer to TVA Flag Pond, Tennessee-North Carolina; Greystone, Tennessee-North Carolina; Davy Crockett Lake, Tennessee-North Carolina; and Hot Springs, North Carolina-Tennessee, quadrangles.

Shelters, Campsites, and Water

This section has three shelters:

Flint Mountain Shelter: Rebuilt by CMC in 1988; 2.7 miles from northern end of section; accommodates 8; water available at spring; latrine located 75 feet to west.

Next shelter: north 8.7 miles (Hogback Ridge Shelter); south 5.9 miles (Jerry Cabin Shelter).

Jerry Cabin Shelter: Stone shelter built in 1968 by USFS; located at Chestnut Log Gap, 8.6 miles from northern end of section; inside fireplace available; water available at side trail 100 yards to west.

Next shelter: north 5.9 miles (Flint Mountain Shelter); south 6.7 miles (Little Laurel Shelter).

Little Laurel Shelter: Stone shelter rebuilt in 1967; located 15.3 miles from northern end of section; accommodates 5; water available at boxed spring on side trail 100 yards to right.

Next shelter: north 6.7 miles (Jerry Cabin Shelter); south 8.6 miles (Spring Mountain Shelter).

Camping is available at Horse Creek Campground, along Middle Spring Ridge (see mile 6.7 southbound). Water is available at the shelters, at six other springs along the Trail, and at Allen Gap.

Public Accommodations and Supplies

Accommodations are available in Erwin, which has several motels, restaurants, and grocery stores. Ample accommodations and supplies are also available in Asheville. A restaurant and lodge are accessible 1.5 miles from the Trail on Big Bald at several motels. Camping gear and accommodations are also available at Asheville.

A service station is located in Allen Gap with a limited stock of groceries, running water, and a telephone, but no public accommodations. Rocky Fork has a restaurant.

History

On the high, open ridgecrest (4,500 feet) of Coldspring Mountain, just north of Green Ridge, is a single grave with government tombstones at each end for William and David Shelton. This simple grave portrays the tragedy of divided families during the Civil War in this remote area of the southern Appalachians, where Union men were usually the mountaineer owners of small farms and the Confederates were the townspeople and owners of farms in the lowlands. David Shelton and his young nephew, William, left their mountain farms and families in the remote Shelton Laurel section of North Carolina and enlisted (probably in Kentucky) in North Carolina companies with other men from their state who were backing the Union cause. When the Sheltons returned for a rendezvous with their families in a crude mountain cabin on Coldspring Mountain, they and a boy lookout were ambushed and killed by Confederates. All three were buried by their families at the site in a single grave. Two preachers acquired the markers from the federal government and, around 1915, hauled them up the mountain on an ox sled and erected them. As the stones were furnished from federal funds, and he was not a soldier, the lookout was not mentioned.

North of Camp Creek Bald, the A.T. was located prior to 1967 across Jones Meadow, along the state-line ridge that separates private, grassy land on the Tennessee side from land of the national forests in North Carolina on the east. To avoid private-resort development, the A.T. was relocated within forest land for 2.0 miles north from Camp Creek Bald firetower. The present Trail is accessible by a side trail leading 100 yards to the firetower road, about 100 yards above the road junction with the state line at Jones Meadow. After an initial receivership, the development changed hands several times and, in 1979, was maintained as the Viking Mountain Private Club. At the end of 1980, the elaborate lodge and most other structures stood vacant except for a caretaker's home beside the fire road.

Precautions

Game-management areas border on the crest of the ridgeline. The Trail enters these areas at times; care should be taken to observe regulations regarding dogs and firearms.

Trail Description, North to South

Miles	Data
0.0	From the road (N.C. 212) in Devil Fork Gap (3,107 feet), climb steps on northern side of road, and turn right in field. Ascend with switchback to left, and reach ridge in woods.
0.1	Turn right, and, in 50 yards, pass through fence. Trail goes through slight sag and then follows left slope for about 0.3 mile. Cross small ridge, and descend steps onto old railroad grade.
0.6	After 200 feet on railroad grade, reach vista. (View extends from Camp Creek Bald to the west along Bald Mountains to Green Ridge Knob to the north.) Continue on railroad grade, gradually descending about 0.6 mile. Then, climb diagonally up slope to right.
1.4	Reach ridge trail (to right is former A.T. route from Devil Fork Gap). Proceed on ridgecrest.
1.8	The site of old Locust Ridge Shelter (removed in 1982) has a possible **campsite**. Water is down left side in ravine. Beyond next rise, Trail skirts western side of Flint Mountain.
2.7	Pass spring, and cross two branches. After an additional 100 feet, reach **Flint Mountain Shelter** (latrine is 75 feet west).
3.1	Cross ridge, and descend right slope, first on narrow Trail, and then more steeply on old logging road.
3.5	Reach Flint Gap (3,425 feet). (Old logging railroad grade crosses Flint Gap and leads to right down to Flint Creek to Rocky Fork, Tenn.) Ascend graded trail.

3.9   Turn right on dirt road approaching from Mill Creek, N.C., and, after 200 feet, turn left on ridge, ascending. Dirt road, which Trail follows about 3.0 miles, ascends steeply on ridgecrest. In about 1,000 feet, Trail leaves ridgecrest to left, continuing ascent.

4.5   Back on crest where old road enters from right, bear left, and ascend steeply, skirting left slope of Coldspring Mountain.

4.7   At top of rise, with Green Ridge Knob above on left, cross crest of ridge on Coldspring Mountain, and descend into woods. Follow worn road, and enter stand of 40-year-old white pines.

5.2   At far end of this field, pass single grave on left with head-stones at each end for "Wm. Shelton, Co. E, 2 N.C. Inf." and "David Shelton, Co. C, 3 N.C. Mtd. Inf." killed here during Civil War; gravestones were erected about 1915. Continue along crest in alternating woods and overgrown fields.

5.4   Reach blue-blazed dirt road to left, which leads 125 yards downhill to spring.

5.5   Where road curves to left in dip in overgrown area, there is a good spring 100 yards to right in ravine. Pass to left of summit of Gravel Knob, and skirt low summit on right.

6.7   Trail reaches its northernmost limit for this section and turns abruptly southwest. In 100 feet, Trail leaves left side of road to enter dense woods. (From opposite side of road, the blue-blazed Squibb Creek Trail leads east through the Ball Ground on ridge of Rich Mountain and then along Middle Spring Ridge to **Horse Creek Campground**, 4.5 miles, in Cherokee National Forest. In 250 feet, reach side trail on right leading 100 feet to rocky promontory, Big Rock, 4,838 feet, with panoramic views of valley to north and west. Camp Creek Bald lies at 250 degrees, Big Bald at 120 degrees, and Gravel Knob at 140 degrees.) Continue on rocky Trail in mixed hardwood forest, and descend massive rock steps.

7.0   Cross dirt road, and, in 500 feet, reach a small, grassy knoll with cleared vista to north and west. (On right side of Trail is a small stone memorial to Howard E. Bassett of Connecticut, a 1968 thru-hiker whose ashes were scattered nearby on April 27, 1988. He died six months earlier, at age 83.) Cross the road again.

7.2   Pass huge boulder to left of Trail. After 0.25 mile, reach cleared field, and skirt its left side.

7.8   Leave field to enter woods, turn left, and descend North Carolina side on switchbacks.

8.6   Trail rejoins road in Chestnut Log Gap (4,150 feet) and, in 100 yards, reaches **Jerry Cabin Shelter**. Side trail opposite shelter leads northwest 100 yards to good spring on wooded northern slope of knob.

8.8   Fork Ridge Trail (Big Creek Trail on quad map) enters from left. (Down this trail, Big Creek Road is 2.0 miles. Carmen, N.C., is 4.0 miles south on this road.) A.T. continues along crest on dirt road.

9.6   Dirt road that Trail has been following for most of last 3.0 miles turns down to right, leading 3.0 miles to Round Knob Spring and into **Round Knob Campground** Road. Continue along ridgecrest on graded trail. Skirt right side of Big Firescald Knob.

11.1   Pass spring on left bank above Trail. Enter dense growth of rhododendron.

11.8   Reach Bearwallow Gap in rhododendron thicket. (USFS Whiteoak Flats Trail leads left 2.5 miles to Hickey Fork Road.) From Bearwallow Gap, continue through rhododendron growth.

12.0   Wide trail to right leads approximately 200 feet to Blackstack Cliffs, offering outstanding views north and west in Tennessee; 200 feet beyond, Trail takes left fork. Continue through dense rhododendron.

12.2   Side trail to left leads 50 feet to fine views from rocky promontory (White Rock Cliffs), including Black Mountain Range with Mt. Mitchell (6,684 feet), highest peak in eastern United States. Begin short descent on switchbacks, with extensive views to south and east.

12.3   Pass spring on left below Trail. Continue ahead on level path through mature hardwood forest and stands of mountain laurel and rhododendron, skirting southern slope below developed area of Jones Meadow.

13.2   Reach old lumber road. (To right, in 100 yards, old road connects with Camp Creek Bald fire road, opposite microwave tower. Fire road ascends left about 0.8 mile to summit and firetower; to right, it is 100 yards to Jones Meadows, where fire road turns left from state line crest and descends along Paint Creek to Tenn. 70 near Allen Gap.) Straight ahead are buildings of former Viking Mountain Private Club. Turn left, down lumber road.

13.3   In 50 feet, turn right uphill from road, and reach spring to right of Trail. Continue to left, ascending eastern ridge of Camp Creek Bald. Circle south of summit in dense stand of rhododendron about 100 yards below Camp Creek Bald firetower (not visible).

14.0   Reach trail junction. (Trail to left leads down Seng Ridge to Pounding Mill Trail, Whiteoak Flats Trail, and Shelton Laurel Road at 6.2 miles. Trail to right ascends 0.2 mile to Camp Creek Bald firetower, 4,844 feet, with magnificent view of Great Smokies to southwest.) Continue straight ahead, descending slightly along crest. Private ownership on Tennessee side ends after 0.3 mile. Continue descent of ridge with national-forest lands on both sides of Trail.

15.3   Reach **Little Laurel Shelter** on left. (Blue-blazed side trail on right bears back diagonally for 100 yards to boxed spring. Trail to spring is beginning of Dixon Trail, leading 1.5 miles to Camp Creek Bald fire road along Paint Creek.) A.T. descends steadily near ridgecrest.

18.3   Reach fork; A.T. bears left, south of crest. Straight ahead is former A.T. route.

18.6   In stand of white pine, about 200 yards from crest on southern slope, cross Old Hayesville Road in gap. Ascend, and switch back left around hill on graded trail.

18.8   Pass blocked trail on right, descending around left slope.

19.2   Return to crest in sag, and cross old dirt road. Go uphill immediately on right fork of graded trail.

19.3   Turn left into trail coming up ridge, and continue ascent.

19.6   Avoiding trail ahead (A.T. before 1974), turn right from ridgeline, and proceed on right slope of ridge.

20.2   Reach end of section at Tenn. 70, about 0.1 mile north of ridgeline (state line) in Allen Gap (2,234 feet). A.T. continues across Tenn. 70.

Trail Description, South to North

Miles   **Data**

0.0   From Tenn. 70, directly opposite end of previous section and
       0.1 mile north of state line in Allen Gap (2,234 feet), ascend left
       to ridge, then bear east.

0.6   Turn left along level crest. (Trail to right was A.T. to Allen
       Gap before 1974.)

1.0   In sag, cross old woods road, and bear right. (Ahead, gravel
       road from left can be seen ascending ridge.) Trail continues
       on right slope of ridge.

1.4   Pass blocked trail on left.

1.6   Reach Old Hayesville Road 200 yards south of crest. Cross
       road, and ascend through stand of white pines.

1.9   Rejoin crest where old (1968) A.T. route enters from left. Bear
       right, and continue ascent on crest.

4.9   Reach **Little Laurel Shelter** on right. (Blue-blazed trail bears
       diagonally left 100 yards to boxed spring. Trail to spring is
       beginning of Dixon Trail, leading 1.5 miles to Camp Creek
       Bald fire road along Paint Creek. Continue ascent of ridge
       with national-forest land on both sides, for first mile, after
       which private ownership begins on Tennessee side.

6.2   Reach trail junction. (To left, trail ascends 0.2 mile to fire-
       tower, 4,844 feet, with magnificent view of Great Smokies to
       southwest. To right, down Seng Ridge, trail leads to Pound-
       ing Mill Trail, Whiteoak Flats Trail, and Shelton Laurel Road
       at 6.2 miles.) Continue straight ahead 300 feet below Camp
       Creek Bald firetower (not visible), circling southern side of
       summit, and enter dense stand of rhododendron. Descend
       eastern ridge of Camp Creek Bald through woods.

6.9   Pass spring on left, and reach old lumber road 50 feet farther
       ahead. Follow road to left, slightly uphill.

7.0   A.T. turns right. (Old road ascends for 100 yards to connect
       with Camp Creek Bald fire road with tower opposite. Fire
       road ascends left about 0.8 mile to summit and USFS lookout
       tower; to right, it is 100 yards to Jones Meadow, where fire
       road turns left from crest and descends along Paint Creek to
       Tenn. 70 near Allen Gap. Straight ahead are buildings of
       former Viking Mountain Private Club.) Trail descends gradu-

ally through woods 100 yards below Jones Meadow along southern slope, passing through stands of laurel and rhododendron.

7.9   Pass spring on right below Trail. In open area, ascend switchbacks with extensive views to the south and east.

8.0   Side trail to right leads 50 feet to White Rock Cliffs, with views of Black Mountain Range, including Mt. Mitchell (6,684 feet), highest peak in eastern United States. Continue to left on level path in dense rhododendron approximately 0.1 mile to junction with state-line trail and former A.T. from Jones Meadow.

8.2   Wide trail to left leads approximately 200 feet to Blackstack Cliffs, with outstanding views to north and west in Tennessee.

8.4   Reach Bearwallow Gap. (USFS Whiteoak Flats Trail leads right 2.5 miles to Hickey Fork Road.) From Bearwallow Gap, continue through dense rhododendron, skirting left side of Big Firescald Knob.

9.1   Pass spring on right bank above trail.

10.6 Dirt road enters from left (leads down 3.0 miles to Round Knob Spring on Round Knob Campground Road). Trail follows dirt road ahead along crest.

11.4 Fork Ridge Trail (Big Creek Trail on quad map) enters from right. (Leads to Big Creek Road in 2.0 miles and Carmen, N.C., in 2.0 additional miles.)

11.6 Reach **Jerry Cabin Shelter** (side trail opposite shelter leads diagonally northwest 100 yards to good spring on wooded, northern slope of knob). Reach Chestnut Log Gap (4,150 feet) in 100 yards. Trail veers right from dirt road to follow graded trail ascending North Carolina side of ridge with switchbacks and steps.

12.4 Trail skirts right side of ridge, with extensive views into Tennessee Valley and (to rear) of Camp Creek Bald.

13.0 Pass huge boulder to right of Trail. Ascend in woods, cross dirt road, and reach a small bald knob with a cleared vista. (To left of Trail is a small stone memorial to Howard E. Bassett of Connecticut, a 1968 thru-hiker who died at age 83 in 1987. His ashes were scattered nearby in April 1988.) Recross dirt road in woods.

13.4   Enter boulder field, and descend on steps into ravine. Climb out over massive stones in hardwoods.

13.5   Side trail to left leads 100 feet to rocky promontory, Big Rock (4,838 feet), with views of Tennessee Valley, Camp Creek Bald at 250 degrees, Big Bald at 120 degrees, and Gravel Knob at 140 degrees. In 250 feet, winding trail reaches dirt road, which A.T. will follow for approximately 3.0 miles. (Directly opposite is blue-blazed Squibb Creek Trail leading northeast through Ball Ground on ridge of Rich Mountain, and then along Middle Spring Ridge to **Horse Creek Campground**, 4.5 miles, in Cherokee National Forest.) Trail turns right onto road, and, 100 feet beyond, road and Trail both turn 90 degrees right, passing along eastern side of low summit. Trail bears southwest along ridgecrest, then passes to right of Gravel Knob.

14.7   Reach once-open area now overgrown with briars. (To left 100 yards is a spring in ravine.) Avoid dirt road to left, and bear right, descending.

14.8   Reach blue-blazed dirt road on right, leading downhill to spring (125 yards). Continue along crest on old road through woods and enter stand of 40-year-old white pines.

15.0   Pass a single grave on right with headstones at each end for "Wm. Shelton, Co. E, 2 N.C. Inf." and "David Shelton, Co. C, 3 N.C. Mtd. Inf." Both men were killed here during Civil War; gravestones were erected about 1915. Road continues on crest and climbs, with Green Knob Ridge above on right.

15.5   Reach end of ridge; Trail breaks sharply left, descending.

15.7   Bear right along eroded roadway (avoiding better road straight ahead). Descend along ridge.

16.3   In 200 feet after sharp right, turn off ridge. Trail switches back left (leaving dirt road, which proceeds ahead down to Mill Creek) and continues down graded trail.

16.7   Reach Flint Gap (3,425 feet). (Old logging-railroad grade crosses this gap; trail to left along grade leads down Flint Creek to Rocky Fork, Tenn.) From Flint Gap, ascend, following logging road.

17.1   Cross ridge, and continue on graded Trail on right slope.

17.5   Pass **Flint Mountain Shelter** on right (latrine is 75 feet west). Soon, cross two small branches, with spring on left immediately beyond.

18.8   A.T. leaves ridgecrest, descending to right to reach old railway grade in 250 yards. Trail follows railway grade to left.

19.6   Reach vista to right. (Views to north and west extend from Camp Creek Bald along Bald Mountains to Green Ridge Knob.) Trail turns left and, after 200 feet, leaves railway grade. Climb steep slope to left. Trail is on right slope for about 0.3 mile.

20.2   Reach N.C. 212 in Devil Fork Gap (3,107 feet). A.T. crosses road and continues directly opposite up hill.

Allen Gap (N.C. 208-Tenn. 70) to Hot Springs, North Carolina
Section Fourteen
14.7 Miles

Brief Description of Section

North to south in this section, the Trail ascends steadily from Allen Gap along Spring Mountain toward Rich Mountain, crosses the Rich Mountain fire road in Hurricane Gap, and, shortly thereafter, ascends steeply up the northern slope of Rich Mountain. The Trail turns left from the state-line ridge short of the summit, descends south 0.5 mile to Roundtop Ridge, then turns southeast to Tanyard Gap. It follows an old logging grade to Mill Ridge, crosses its extensive scenic meadows just south of wooded summit, and descends past a small pond and two springs, skirting ridge knobs on the eastern slope en route to Pump Gap. From there, the Trail ascends Lovers Leap Ridge, before descending by switchbacks to the French Broad River.

The route is primarily graded USFS trail, most of which is on protected right-of-way, although the extensive work on Lovers Leap from Pump Gap to the French Broad River was done in 1988-91 by ATC Konnarock-crew and Carolina Mountain Club volunteers.

The elevation of Allen Gap is 2,234 feet, Rich Mountain is 3,670 feet, Tanyard Gap is 2,278 feet, Mill Ridge near the Trail is 2,800 feet, Pump Gap is about 2,100 feet, Lovers Leap is about 1,800 feet, and Hot Springs is 1,326 feet.

From north to south, this route requires three steady climbs from Allen, Hurricane, and Tanyard gaps. The grade is gradual and involves no difficulty. Traveled in this direction, there is 900 feet less climbing than from south to north. In case of serious flooding of the French Broad River at Hot Springs, the hiker could cut up the northern slope to U.S. 25 and 70 from Silvermine Creek, where it approaches the river.

From south to north, the initial climb to Lovers Leap Ridge is 1,000 feet, from Pump Gap to Mill Ridge is 600 feet, from Tanyard Gap to Rich Mountain is 1,300 feet, and from Hurricane Gap to Spring

Mountain is 600 feet. The grade, other than the initial ascent to Lovers Leap Rock, is gradual and presents no difficulty.

Points of Interest

Except for the scenic open meadows at Mill Ridge, most of the route is along forested ridges, with many outstanding views in winter. The best views are from the Rich Mountain firetower, from which one can look to the southwest directly down the main ridge of the Great Smokies from Mt. Cammerer to Mt. Guyot. The Black Mountains, including Mt. Mitchell (6,684 feet), the highest mountain east of the Mississippi River, are prominent 30 to 35 miles to the southeast.

Lovers Leap Rock on Lovers Leap Ridge drops about 500 feet to the eastern bank of river below. From the rock ledges, one has outstanding views of Hot Springs below and the French Broad River Valley as far as Paint Rock.

One hundred yards north of Hurricane Gap is a 1983 memorial stone to Rex R. Pulford, who died of a heart attack there while on a thru-hike. His daughter, who completed a thru-hike earlier, and her husband operate the Walasi-yi Center at Neels Gap on the Georgia A.T.

An A.T. hikers' registration box, formerly at USFS ranger headquarters, is maintained in the lobby of the Hot Springs post office. The headquarters of the French Broad Ranger District (National Forests in North Carolina), is on Bridge Street in Hot Springs, 400 feet east of the southern end of the section. Information and A.T. shelter permits for Great Smoky Mountains National Park may be obtained here during office hours.

Road Approaches

The northern end of the section is at Allen Gap on the Tennessee-North Carolina state line, 25 miles south of Greeneville, Tenn., on Tenn. 70. It may also be reached from Hot Springs, by taking U.S. 25 and 70 east 6.0 miles and then N.C. 208 north 9.0 miles.

The southern end of the section is in Hot Springs, at the intersection of N.C. 209 and U.S. 25 and 70, 26 miles east of Newport, Tenn., 17 miles northwest of Marshall, N.C., and 39 miles northwest of Asheville.

At Tanyard Gap, 8.9 miles from the northern end of the section, the Trail crosses over U.S. 25 and 70. This point is 4.0 miles east of Hot Springs and 36 miles northwest of Asheville.

Another intermediate point on this section, Hurricane Gap, may also be reached by car. From Hot Springs, take U.S. 25 and 70 east 5.0 miles and then USFS 467 north for 4.0 miles. This point may also be reached from Greeneville, Tenn., by taking Tenn. 70 south for 15 miles, then Tenn. 107 south for 3.0 miles, and an unpaved rural road south for 7.0 miles.

Maps

Refer to ATC Tennessee-North Carolina Map Three for route navigation. For additional area detail, refer to TVA Hot Springs, North Carolina-Tennessee, quadrangle.

Shelters, Campsites, and Water

This section has one shelter:
Spring Mountain Shelter: Built by CCC in 1938; 3.7 miles from northern end of section; accommodates 5; water available at spring 75 yards down North Carolina side, opposite shelter.

Next shelter: north 8.6 miles (Little Laurel Shelter); south 14.2 miles (Deer Park Shelter).

Good campsites are available 2.7 and 6.1 miles south of the shelter. Water is available from springs at these and six other places along the Trail.

Public Accommodations and Supplies

Hot Springs has a hostel, maintained for hikers by the Jesuit Residence. For details, see Section Fifteen. Motel accommodations, stores, restaurant, barber shop, and laundromat are also available in Hot Springs.

Accommodations are not available in Allen Gap. A service station in the gap has a limited stock of groceries; running water available here.

History

Lovers Leap, a huge rock face above the French Broad River visible from Hot Springs, was supposedly named by the Cherokee Indians when a maiden of their tribe, Mist-on-the-Mountain, threw herself from the crag after her northern lover, Magwa, was killed by a jealous rival, Lone Wolf. The Cherokee shared this area between the Great Smokies and Big Bald with the Creek Indians as a neutral hunting ground.

At the beginning of the nineteenth century, travel from eastern Tennessee to Asheville was by a turnpike extending through Paint Rock and Hot Springs along the river and then up Silvermine Creek through Tanyard Gap, down Hurricane Creek and the Laurel River, and across the French Broad River on a ferry. Bishop Francis Asbury used this route almost annually from 1800 until his final trip through Hot Springs in 1815, after having traveled by horseback a quarter of a million miles for Methodism.

In 1778, two Indian scouts searching for stolen horses discovered the springs at Hot Springs, where a hotel was built in 1782. A road to Tennessee was built in 1795, providing access to the Warm Springs Spa.

During the 1890s, Warm Springs was renamed Hot Springs, and the Mountain Park Hotel was built there. It was a handsome, rambling structure and could accommodate 1,000 guests. Nearby were the famed springs, which contained many mineral elements. A springhouse for drinking water and a bathhouse were built in the springs themselves. During the years when health-seekers believed in the efficacy of mineral waters, Hot Springs was one of the most popular resorts in western North Carolina.

After the United States entered World War I, as many as 2,800 German prisoners were interned in the hotel. They performed band concerts and enjoyed their stay in the beautiful surroundings. On one occasion, when it was rumored that they were to be transferred, some of them poisoned the drinking water, hoping to be made ill enough to prevent being removed. Unfortunately, they used too much poison, and, as a result, some of the prisoners died.

After medical opinion developed that the benefits derived from the waters of the springs resulted from hydrotherapy and that the treatment could be given in any medical institution, the decline in the numbers of persons who came to Hot Springs resulted in the closing of the famous hotel.

At its height, Hot Springs numbered more than 1,200 persons, but, in 1979, its population was about 330.

The springs were reopened in the early 1990s, and ATC's Trust for Appalachian Trail Lands is working with town officials on long-range planning.

Trail Description, North to South

Miles   Data

0.0   From Tenn. 70, 0.1 mile west of Allen Gap, bear left in woods along foot of slope with rhododendron stand above Trail on right. Spring is to left of Trail at 200 feet.

0.1   Cross logging road leading back to left to Allen Gap. In 100 feet, switch back right above road, ascending steadily in woods to ridge. Proceed along ridge.

2.0   Reach Deep Gap.

2.2   Pass spring 10 feet to right in ravine. Beyond, skirt ridge slope of Spring Mountain.

3.7   Reach **Spring Mountain Shelter**, 3,300 feet (spring is 75 yards down North Carolina side, opposite shelter). Trail continues along ridgeline.

5.4   Reach Hurricane Gap. (Fire road entering from left leads from U.S. 25 and 70 to Rich Mountain firetower.) Trail follows fire road 70 feet uphill, leaves right side of road to swing around ridge, then returns to road in 1,000 feet.

5.6   Cross road, and, where gated USFS road forks to left, ascend bank into woods. Pass spring on right in 0.3 mile.

6.2   Short of summit of Rich Mountain, turn left from ridgeline.

6.4   Cross head of ravine with good spring on right and good **campsite**. (Side trail 200 feet beyond on right comes out 0.1 mile from Rich Mountain firetower, 3,643 feet, from which are magnificent panoramic views.) Descend around eastern slope of Rich Mountain.

6.9   Take left fork downhill, following former USFS Rich Mountain telephone line right-of-way for 100 feet. Then, bear right into woods.

7.0   Reach road, bear right for 50 feet, and ascend log steps to continue on Trail.

7.4   Cross footlog below good spring.

8.4   Trail turns sharply to right, then left, descending.

8.5   Turn right, continuing descent.

8.8   Descend log steps steeply to old roadbed above highway. Turn left, and follow old roadway. Descend bank by log steps to cross old U.S. 25 and 70 (no longer used) at Tanyard Gap (2,278 feet). Then, follow gravel path to concrete overpass of new U.S. 25 and 70.

8.9   After concrete overpass, A.T. bears right along gravel logging road, then turns and ascends by log steps to old woods road, which Trail follows above gravel road for next 0.5 mile. Reach old homestead site, and descend former driveway, turning left onto gravel road.

9.6   Trail crosses crest of open meadows on southern slope of wooded Mill Ridge, with sweeping views. Pass USFS road to right with gate. (Piped spring is 50 feet beyond gate.) Continue on woods road south 100 yards.

9.8   In saddle, Trail turns right downhill through grassy field to pond. Pass above boxed spring and along pond (excellent **campsite**) to dam. Descend log steps. Trail follows left slope of ridge in woods for next 1.5 miles, at first above ravine in rhododendron thicket, and crosses a number of trails and roads.

10.5   On right, blue-blazed trail leads back to ridgecrest, where lumber road lies 50 yards above Trail. A.T. joins blue-blazed trail for 50 feet (blue-blazed trail descends ridge to left). A.T. turns right, continuing descent of eastern slope of Mill Ridge.

11.4   Reach Pump Gap. (In Pump Gap, blue-blazed trail crosses A.T. To right, it leads 2.0 miles to Silvermine Creek Valley and rejoins A.T., serving as alternate route, avoiding Lovers Leap Ridge.) From Pump Gap, ascend 80 yards, then bear right, ascending on graded trail around right slope of Lovers Leap Ridge.

12.1   Reach ridgecrest, and bear right along ridgeline with French Broad River gorge 1,000 feet below on left. There are occasional views ahead to left of Bluff Mountain and to right of Rich Mountain.

13.0   Outstanding views looking west over French Broad River, 600 feet below, and narrow valley at Hot Springs. (Side trail to left leads 40 feet back to prominent crag, offering remarkable vista.)

13.3   Reach sharp edge of crest. Lovers Leap Rock extends straight ahead to northwest, dropping 500 feet to eastern bank of river below. Views are superb a few feet out on rock ledge. Trail signs indicate Silver Mine Trail (old A.T.) and #308 Lovers Leap trailheads. Trail turns to left and descends by switchbacks cut in the steep rock face. **Caution** is advised for safe footing on possible loose gravel and rock fragments on trail.

13.5　Reach another prominent overlook, again offering excellent views of river and town. Trail continues descent by switchbacks.

13.8　Trail finishes descent and parallels river edge, heading downstream.

14.2　Trail reaches small road bridge, leaving immediate vicinity of river. Nantahala Outdoor Center is at right. Approach nearby U.S. 25 and 70 highway bridge, ascending steep bank at underpass.

14.3　From eastern end of highway bridge, follow U.S. 25 and 70 over French Broad River. On right, pass road to former Warm Springs Spa, large mineral springs resort in 1800s. Pass cafe and Southern Railway station on right. Cross Spring Creek.

14.6　Hot Springs post office, with A.T. hikers' registration book in lobby, is on right. Beyond, on left, is USFS ranger district headquarters.

14.7　Reach end of section at junction of U.S. 25 and 70 with N.C. 209. (To continue on A.T., follow N.C. 209 south 0.3 mile. Turn right from highway for 30 feet, and ascend old roadbed to right. Climb steep bank to left, and cross road. Beside Trail to right is hostel maintained for hikers by Jesuit Residence.)

Trail Description, South to North

Miles　　　　　　　　　　　**Data**

0.0　This section commences in Hot Springs at junction of U.S. 25 and 70 with N.C. 209. Follow U.S. 25 and 70 east.

0.1　On right is USFS ranger district headquarters. Fifty feet beyond on left is Hot Springs post office, with A.T. registration book for hikers in lobby. Cross Spring Creek just beyond, and pass Southern Railway station on left. In 200 feet on left is road to former Warm Springs Spa, large mineral springs resort in 1800s. Cross French Broad River.

0.4   At eastern end of bridge, descend right bank of highway to paved Silvermine Creek Road along riverbank. Road bears left in front of outfitters for river float trips and passes several houses. Cross small road bridge.

0.5   After crossing this bridge, trail approaches and parallels river's edge, heading upstream. Nantahala Outdoor Center is at left.

0.9   Trail leaves river's edge, ascending the steep slope of Lovers Leap Ridge by a series of switchbacks.

1.2   Reach first prominent overlook, affording spectacular views of river and town. Trail continues ascent by switchbacks cut in the steep rock face. **Caution** is advised for safe footing on possible loose gravel and rock fragments on trail.

1.4   Reach Lovers Leap Rock on sharp edge of ridgecrest, which drops northwest to river's edge 500 feet below. Views are superb a few feet out on rock ledge. Trail signs indicate the Silver Mine Trail (old A.T.) and #308 Lovers Leap trailheads. Trail turns to right past the rock and leaves the edge of steep slope.

1.7   At this point on crest, side trail leads right 40 feet to prominent crag, with outstanding views to the west of Bluff Mountain and, down French Broad Valley, of Meadow Creek Mountains in Tennessee. Continue ascending. (There are occasional winter views of river and railway 1,000 feet below.)

2.6   Trail bears left off ridge and descends around northern slope of Lovers Leap Ridge for 0.7 mile. On steep trail coming down ridge, turn left in 80 yards into Pump Gap.

3.3   In Pump Gap, blue-blazed trail crosses A.T. to left, leading back down to Silvermine Creek and A.T. at mile 0.9 of this section. From Pump Gap, ascend on graded trail up Mill Ridge.

4.2   Trail meets blue-blazed trail approaching side ridge from right. At 50 feet beyond junction, A.T. bears to right away from blue-blazed trail, which ascends to ridgecrest where lumber road lies 50 yards above A.T. (Old family cemetery with several headstones is on eastern side of lumber road.) Trail continues on eastern slope of ridge and crosses a number of old roads and trails. It passes through rhododendron thicket above ravine and reaches foot of concrete dam.

Ascend steps to left of dam and pass along bank of pond (excellent **campsite**). Pass above boxed spring to right, and ascend steeply across meadow to road.

4.9   Turn left into gravel road leading north across open meadows on wooded Mill Ridge. At 100 yards, pass gated USFS road to left. (Piped spring is 50 feet beyond gate.)

5.1   Where road turns left to continue 0.7 mile to Tanyard Gap, A.T. leaves road and ascends former driveway to pass around house foundation and descend to old woods roadbed. Follow woods road for next 0.5 mile. Cross new U.S. 25 and 70 via concrete overpass, then follow gravel path to cross old, unused U.S. 25 and 70 at Tanyard Gap (2278 feet).

5.8   From Tanyard Gap (2,278 feet), climb log steps on northern side of highway to old roadway that curves back to left.

5.9   Ascend log steps up bank to Trail, which ascends left slope of ridge in woods and rhododendron.

6.2   Trail turns left, descending gently. After switchbacks to right and left, it ascends on left slope of ridge.

7.3   Trail crosses log footbridge below good spring on right. Continue ascent around several ridges. Descend log steps to road, and bear right 50 feet.

7.7   Leave road on left, and continue through woods. Reach former USFS Rich Mountain telephone line right-of-way, and follow to left 100 feet.

7.8   From junction with Roundtop Ridge Trail on left (former route of A.T. from Hot Springs), ascend around eastern slope of Rich Mountain. Near summit, reach cross trail where A.T. turns right and former A.T. continues ahead to ridge. (To left 0.1 mile is Rich Mountain firetower, 3,643 feet, which has panoramic views.) A.T. descends from trail junction 200 feet to right and reaches good spring in ravine. Nearby is good **campsite**.

8.2   From spring, ascend steeply, then bear left around ridge to reach crest.

8.4   Turn right onto ridgecrest, and descend steadily down northern slope of Rich Mountain, passing spring on left in 0.3 mile. Descend through rhododendron to reach fire road 100 yards above fork.

9.1   Trail crosses fire road from Rich Mountain firetower, swings around ridge, and, after 1,000 feet, returns to the road 70 feet from road junction in Hurricane Gap.

9.3   Reach Hurricane Gap. Ascend; generally follow ridgeline.

11.0 **Spring Mountain Shelter** (3,300 feet) is directly on Trail (spring is 75 yards down on eastern side opposite shelter). Continue ascent along ridgeline, passing below high points of Spring Mountain, and descend.

12.5 Pass spring 10 feet to left in ravine.

12.7 Reach Deep Gap. Ascend Buzzard Roost Ridge, follow along ridge, and descend steadily. Trail bears left from main ridgeline, descending small side ridge in Tennessee.

14.6 Cross logging road that leads right to Allen Gap. Trail continues through woods, passing spring on right. Descend through rhododendron.

14.7 Reach paved highway, Tenn. 70, 0.1 mile west of Allen Gap. To continue north on A.T., cross highway, and enter woods, ascending on graded trail.

Hot Springs, North Carolina, to Max Patch Road (N.C. 1182)
Section Fifteen
20.2 Miles

Brief Description of Section

From Hot Springs, N.C., to Lemon Gap, the A.T. was constructed in 1936 by the Civilian Conservation Corps (CCC) under the direction of the Pisgah National Forest. Proceeding from the northern end of the section at Hot Springs, the Trail mostly ascends for the first 10.3 miles, until it reaches Bluff Mountain. The Trail beyond Bluff Mountain generally follows the state line. From Lemon Gap to the end of this section, the Trail follows a 1983-1984 relocation that takes it over the broad, grassy summit of Max Patch (4,629 feet), the southernmost point on the A.T. being retained as a typical open, grassy bald. The view from Max Patch is magnificent, with the highest peaks in the East (Mt. Mitchell in the Blacks and many peaks in the Smokies) visible on a clear day.

From north to south, the traverse of this section requires considerable exertion. There is a steady climb from Hot Springs to the crest of the ridge; beyond, to Garenflo Gap, the route is somewhat gradual; from this gap for 3.5 miles, there is an ascent of 2,186 feet to the summit of Bluff Mountain. The net gain in elevation from Hot Springs is 3,360 feet. Beyond, the Trail descends to Kale Gap and then ascends 600 feet to the summit of Walnut Mountain. The climb is 1,079 feet from Lemon Gap to the summit of Max Patch. The total amount of climbing for this section, north to south, is 5,800 feet.

From south to north on this section, there is a climb of 400 feet to the Max Patch summit, a climb of 730 feet from Lemon Gap (3,550 feet) to Walnut Mountain, and a descent of 600 feet to Kale Gap; from Kale Gap, there is a climb of 986 feet to Bluff Mountain and a descent of 3,360 feet to Hot Springs (1,326 feet) on the French Broad River. Thus, the section is much more easily traversed in the south-to-north direction, with a total amount of climbing of only 1,800 feet.

Max Patch Mountain was purchased by the USFS in 1982 for protection of the Appalachian Trail, which formerly passed by it on a

3.8-mile roadwalk. A new 6.2-mile route was opened to take the A.T. over the summit. The ATC Konnarock Crew started digging the long sidehill relocation in 1983. A group from the Carolina Mountain Club, retired from "work," completed the longer portion of the Trail on weekly trips, opening it in 1984.

Points of Interest

This section of the Trail has been located to offer extraordinary views. The terrain presents an extremely jumbled and rugged appearance. The features of the route are Bluff Mountain (4,686 feet), Walnut Mountain (4,280 feet), and Max Patch Mountain (4,629 feet). The summit of Tennessee Bluff (4,600 feet), on the state line west of Bluff Mountain, is not on the A.T.

The finest views are from the completely open, grassy summit of Max Patch Mountain (4,629 feet). The bald summit at one time was used as a landing strip for small planes, and sheep and cattle have been pastured there. Extraordinary views of the surrounding mountains are available, including Mt. Mitchell (6,684 feet) and the Black Mountain Range to the east. Westward, there is a close-up vista of the Great Smoky Mountains.

A registration book for A.T. hikers is located in the lobby of the Hot Springs post office, on Bridge Street, 0.1 mile east of the northern end of this section.

Road Approaches

The northern end of this section is in Hot Springs, at the intersection of N.C. 209 and U.S. 25 and 70, 26 miles east of Newport, Tenn., 17 miles northwest of Marshall, N.C., and 39 miles northwest of Asheville.

The southern end of the section is on the dirt Max Patch Road (N.C. 1182) on the Tennessee-North Carolina state line. An intermediate point, Lemon Gap, is also on N.C. 1182 at the Tennessee-North Carolina state line. Lemon Gap may be reached from Newport, by following U.S. 25 and 70 for 12 miles to Del Rio, Tenn., and Tenn. 107 from there south for 14 miles to the gap.

A midpoint of the section, Garenflo Gap, is accessible by car from Hot Springs by taking N.C. 209 for 7.0 miles south to the community of Bluff, N.C., and a dirt road 1.6 miles north to the gap.

Maps

Refer to ATC Tennessee-North Carolina Map Three for route navigation. For additional area detail, refer to TVA Hot Springs, North Carolina-Tennessee; Spring Creek, North Carolina; and Lemon Gap, North Carolina-Tennessee, quadrangles.

Shelters, Campsites, and Water

This section has three shelters:

Deer Park Mountain Shelter: Built in 1938 by CCC; located 3.2 miles from northern end of section; accommodates 5; water available at spring.

Next shelter: north 14.2 miles (Spring Mountain Shelter); south 9.5 miles (Walnut Mountain Shelter).

Walnut Mountain Shelter: Built in 1938 by CCC; located 12.7 miles from northern end of section; accommodates 5; water available at fenced-in spring 75 yards north of shelter.

Next shelter: north 9.5 miles (Deer Park Mountain Shelter); south 1.8 miles (Roaring Fork Shelter).

Roaring Fork Shelter: Log shelter built by CMC; accommodates 10; water available.

Next shelter: north 1.8 miles (Walnut Mountain Shelter); south 11.3 miles (Groundhog Creek Shelter).

Water is also available at springs or streams at nine other places along the Trail.

Public Accommodations and Supplies

Hot Springs has motel accommodations, inns, stores, a restaurant, and a laundromat. Also in Hot Springs, opposite the Forest Service Work Center, is a hostel maintained for hikers by the Jesuit Residence. It has one building with a kitchen and provides cooking and refrigeration facilities and a combination lounge and eating room. Thru-hikers may stay more than one night. The parking area near the hostel will accommodate ten cars.

Trail Description, North to South

Miles	Data

0.0   From junction with U.S. 25 and 70, follow N.C. 209. In 0.3 mile, turn right from highway for 30 feet, follow old roadbed to right, and climb steep bank to left.

0.3   Reach road that leads left to the work center of the French Broad Ranger District and right to hostel for hikers maintained by Jesuit Residence. Trail crosses parking area and begins ascent of Deer Park Mountain. Switchbacks at first are followed by steady climb.

1.2   Fine views of French Broad River and town of Hot Springs. Climb steeply.

1.5   Reach crest of ridge along Deer Park Mountain. Beyond, ascend along ridge.

3.2   On right, pass gravestones beside Trail, and immediately reach Gragg Gap. To left, 75 yards, is **Deer Park Mountain Shelter** (on trail halfway to shelter, spring is on the right; generally requires cleaning out because of slow flow). To right 200 yards, a small stream (head of Blood River) at former farmstead offers alternate source of water. From Gragg Gap, ascend slowly along series of knobs.

3.8   Skirt left side of prominent knob, with deep gorge of Little Bottom Branch below to left.

4.5   Reach Little Bottom Branch Gap. After 0.3 mile, ascend Lamb Knob. Views of Bluff Mountain are to the west.

5.5   Bear right, downhill from trail ahead (former A.T. through John Taylor Hollow Gap, it rejoins present A.T. in 0.6 mile). Continue along western slope of Long Mountain.

6.6   After emerging from woods and passing under powerline, descend steps to Garenflo Gap, 2,500 feet. (USFS road is gated to right and leads to Bluff to left.) Trail turns right into sunken roadway. (Another yellow-blazed USFS road descends to Middle Fork of Shut In Creek.) Trail ascends gradually to left, in woods, passing under telephone line in 250 feet.

7.5   Cross old road grade and USFS road from Garenflo Gap. Continue to ascend.

8.0   Cross two small brooks. Continue ascent, bearing northwest with winter vistas to right of Bald Mountain Range.

8.4   Cross road. Trail continues ascent.

8.6   Reach old road. Ascend steep bank beyond by steps. Pass below huge boulder, cross intermittent stream, and ascend to right, passing above rock ledges.

8.7   Cross old road. A.T. ascends ridge by steps and switchbacks, after passing below tremendous rock.

8.9   Big Rock Spring is 50 yards ahead in ravine. Trail ascends by log steps and continues ascent. After reaching old road, follow it to right 75 yards. Leave road, pass spring to right of Trail, and, 200 feet beyond, cross another road.

9.5   Pass through USFS boundary fence, and pass excellent spring 80 yards below to right (no blue-blazed trail).

9.7   Ascend log steps, and make sharp left. (Former A.T. enters from right.) Trail climbs steadily through splendid hardwoods.

10.3   Reach top of Bluff Mountain (4,686 feet). The Bluff is easternmost of four dominating peaks along the state line between the French Broad and Pigeon rivers. Its wooded summit affords no outlooks. From summit of Bluff Mountain, descend around southern slope of Tennessee Bluff, the summit of which is on the state line north of A.T.

11.0   Cross brooks, and continue descent around Tennessee Bluff.

11.2   Pass Catpen Gap to left, which has good views. (Max Patch Mountain is at 210 degrees.)

11.7   Join woods road, entering from right. Follow road into Kale Gap (3,700 feet), with white-pine plantation to right.

11.9   From low point of Kale Gap, cross fence and field. Enter woods, and ascend steeply up Walnut Mountain.

12.4   On crest of ridge, turn sharp right through fence. Ascent is more gradual.

12.7   Reach **Walnut Mountain Shelter** (fenced-in spring is 75 yards north, behind and below shelter). Continue ascent for 250 feet, to the pass just to right of summit of Walnut Mountain (4,280 feet). Descend gradually through fields and woods.

13.3   Cross two branches of stream about 150 feet apart. Trail descends to left of stream through rhododendron. Pass white-pine plantation on right.

14.0   Reach small clearing in Lemon Gap (about 3,550 feet) adjacent to N.C. 1182, which here enters Tennessee as Tenn. 107 to Del Rio. Across the clearing, A.T. reenters woods, descending to left.

14.2   Trail crosses stream and woods road. For more than 3.0 miles, A.T. goes generally southwest up the western side of Roaring Fork Valley, crossing numerous small tributaries. In just 100 yards, reach first log footbridge.

14.5   Side trail leads 100 yards to left to **Roaring Fork Shelter** (spring and outhouse).

15.1   Trail passes below a large rock on right.

15.4   Cross footbridge.

15.7   Cross old woods road, and ascend ramp. The next half-mile has several stream crossings.

16.5   Descend ramp, and cross old road, which leads right to N.C. 1182. In 25 yards, cross footbridge. Trail now enters a beautiful area with some very large hemlocks and ascends above a stream.

16.6   With beautiful cascades to left, Trail switches back sharply to right and continues ascent among hemlocks. A sweeping curve to the left brings Trail back to a generally southern course in 0.2 mile.

17.2   Footbridges located at this location.

17.4   Descend ramp, and make sharp left. After crossing stream, the Trail follows old railroad grade about 0.3 mile, gradually ascending.

17.7   Leave grade by climbing steps to right.

18.0   Cross stream, and ascend bank on steps. Enter area of dense rhododendron and hemlocks.

18.1   Ascend ramp to cross a road grade, and proceed to right on old road for 100 yards.

18.2   Pass through stile to emerge in open meadow on western slope of Buckeye Ridge, with Max Patch Mountain ahead on right.

18.3   Trail leaves ridge on grassy roadbed to right through attractive clumps of rhododendron. Bear right from road, descending in field to enter woods.

19.0   Trail passes through stile onto open meadows of Max Patch.

19.2   To right, a trail leaves the A.T. and leads to a parking lot on N.C. 1182. A.T. follows eastern rim of bald, ascending on graded trail. Black Mountain Range, including Mt. Mitchell, can be seen to the east.

19.4 On bending to right, Trail crosses open summit of Max Patch (4,629 feet), marked by benchmark (1933). Trail then veers south on western brow of the bald. (To the southwest are expansive views of the Smokies. Nearer, in morning light, the white aerial-navigation tower on Snowbird Mountain is visible.)

19.7 Trail leaves summit by steps on steep ridge and skirts southern slope of Max Patch Mountain.

19.8 Cross gravel road leading right to N.C. 1182, and enter woods, descending.

20.1 Cross small stream (head of West Fork of Little Creek, which flows into Meadow Fork), and ascend through rhododendron.

20.2 A.T. passes through stile and reaches end of section at Max Patch Road, N.C. 1182. A.T. continues directly opposite the crossing.

Trail Description, South to North

Miles   **Data**

0.0 From N.C. 1182 (Max Patch Road), directly opposite the end of Section Sixteen, A.T. passes through a stile, enters woods, and descends to left, through rhododendron.

0.1 Cross small stream (head of West Fork of Little Creek), and ascend gradually in woods.

0.4 Leaving woods, cross gravel road (to N.C. 1182) to right, onto southern slope of Max Patch Mountain.

0.5 Trail turns left up ridge on steps and then bears to west on open bald, which has wide views of the Smokies to the southwest. The white aerial-navigation tower on Snowbird Mountain is visible in morning light. Trail follows western brow of the bald northward.

0.8 A.T. crosses summit of Max Patch (4,629 feet), marked by benchmark (1933), and swings north again, gradually descending. Trail is marked with blazed posts on the open balds. Views to the east reveal Mt. Mitchell in the Black Mountains.

1.1 Beyond an intersecting fenceline, a trail from N.C. 1182 joins A.T. from the left.

1.2 Trail passes through stile and enters woods, descending to right.

1.4 Between two stiles, Trail passes a piped spring.

1.6 Trail emerges from woods, bears left, and begins slight climb in meadow on slope of Buckeye Ridge to a grassy road grade. Clumps of rhododendron are notable.

2.0 A.T. passes another stile and enters woods on old road grade to right. Cross intersecting road grade on right in 100 yards, and descend on Trail to left through heavy rhododendron growth under hemlocks.

2.2 Descend steps to stream crossing, and follow Trail west of Roaring Fork Valley.

2.4 By steps and ramp, descend to old railroad grade, which continues about 0.3 mile.

2.8 Beyond stream crossing, a road grade leads to left to N.C. 1182. Trail turns sharply right and proceeds on steep hillside with Roaring Fork below. Cross footbridges at this location. Descend, eventually coming to fine views of cascading stream. Continue descent above stream in dense hemlock woods.

3.7 Cross bridge. Rough roadway leads left to N.C. 1182. Ascend ramp, and continue on steep slope in more open woods, with the first of three stream crossings.

4.5 Descend ramp to cross old woods road.

4.8 Cross footbridge.

5.1 Trail passes below large rock on left. Cross footbridges over small streams.

5.8 Side trail leads right 100 yards to **Roaring Fork Shelter** (spring and outhouse).

6.0 Cross log bridge, and then cross stream in another 100 yards. Climb gradually to right of stream.

6.2 Trail enters a small clearing at Lemon Gap (3,550 feet). On left, N.C. 1182 continues northward into Tennessee as Tenn. 107. A.T. does not cross road but crosses clearing and ascends to right on graded trail, reentering hardwoods. Follow on right of stream, through rhododendron.

6.9 Cross first branch of stream and second branch 150 feet beyond. Ascend steadily, climbing Walnut Mountain.

7.3   Emerge from woods into overgrown field, and bear right. Cross crest just left of summit of Walnut Mountain (4,280 feet).

7.5   Reach **Walnut Mountain Shelter** (fenced-in spring is 75 yards north, behind and below shelter). Continue beyond shelter, descending steadily.

7.8   Pass white-pine plantation on right. Make sharp left on crest of ridge through fence, and descend eastern slope of Walnut Mountain. Emerge from woods, and bear left across open fields with view to right.

8.3   Reach sag in Kale Gap (3,700 feet). From gap, enter woods, following old road for 0.2 miles.

8.5   Bear right above road. Ascend steadily, and skirt southern side of Tennessee Bluff for next 1.5 miles, to summit of Bluff Mountain. (Summit of Tennessee Bluff is not on A.T.)

9.0   Pass Catpen Gap to right, from which good views open up. Max Patch Mountain is at 210 degrees.

9.2   Cross brook and second water course 200 yards beyond.

9.9   Reach summit of Bluff Mountain (4,686 feet). The Bluff is easternmost of four dominating peaks along state line between the French Broad and Pigeon rivers. Its wooded top has no outlook. Beyond, begin steady descent for next 3.5 miles to Garenflo Gap through splendid hardwoods.

10.5   Leave trail ahead (former A.T.), turning sharp right after descending log steps. In about 0.1 mile, pass spring 80 yards below to left (no blue-blazed trail).

10.7   Continue along ridge through USFS boundary fence.

11.0   After crossing road in 200 feet, pass spring to left of Trail. Continue descent, and reach road, which Trail follows to right 75 yards, then descend diagonally below road.

11.3   Reach log steps. At foot of steps, Big Rock Spring lies to right in ravine. Pass below tremendous rock, and continue descent.

11.5   Cross old road. Pass above rock ledge 100 feet farther, cross intermittent stream, and pass below huge boulder.

11.6   Descend log stairs steeply to old road.

11.8   Cross another road, and continue downhill, with winter vistas of Bald Mountain range to left.

12.2   Cross small brook and another 200 yards beyond. Continue descent through rhododendron corridor.

12.7   Cross USFS road. (Road to right leads 0.8 mile to Garenflo Gap.) Descend, and, in 100 yards, cross old road grade, and continue downhill under rhododendrons.

13.1   Cross ridge. (A blue-blazed trail leads right to a vista and returns to the A.T. in 0.1 mile.) A.T. descends and follows left slope of ridge to Garenflo Gap (2,500 feet).

13.6   Reach Garenflo Gap with USFS road above on right. Turn left, ascend steps, cross bottom of field, and walk under powerline. Make sharp right, and descend, entering woods. For next 2.0 miles, Trail circles western slopes of Long Mountain (3,120 feet) and Lamb Knob (3,204 feet) through hardwood forests, with frequent views in winter of Bluff Mountain and Round Mountain (with tower) to west.

14.1   Take left fork (avoiding former A.T. to right, which ascends to John Taylor Hollow Gap). Trail descends, soon crosses two small footbridges, and ascends.

14.7   Former A.T. enters from right and joins present A.T.

15.7   Reach Little Bottom Branch Gap. Trail turns right along steep slope of Canebrake Ridge above deep gorge of Little Bottom Branch to right.

17.0   Reach Gragg Gap. To left 200 yards is small stream, head of Blood River. To right 75 yards is **Deer Park Mountain Shelter** (on trail halfway to shelter is spring, which usually requires cleaning because of slow flow). Leaving Gragg Gap, pass gravestones on left of Trail, and ascend Deer Park Mountain, generally following its crest.

19.0   Fine views of French Broad River and town of Hot Springs.

19.9   On left, pass hostel maintained for hikers by Jesuit Residence, cross parking area, and reach USFS entrance road. (To right 200 yards lies work center of French Broad Ranger District.) Cross road, descend steep bank, and follow old roadbed to reach paved road (N.C. 209). Turn left on N.C. 209 toward Hot Springs, and follow Bridge Street.

20.2   Reach junction of N.C. 209 and U.S. 25 and 70. This is end of section. A.T. passes through Hot Springs on U.S. 25 and 70 (Dixie Highway).

Max Patch Road (N.C. 1182) to Davenport Gap (Tenn. 32-N.C. 284)
Section Sixteen
15.2 Miles

Brief Description of Section

The route here is graded USFS trail, much of it constructed by the CCC between 1936 and 1938.

This section is the southernmost in the Pisgah National Forest. From Max Patch Road, which follows the Newfound Mountains along the border of Madison and Haywood counties, the southbound A.T. follows the state-line crest with slight changes in elevation until it drops steeply into Brown Gap. It then climbs steeply to a saddle between the high points of Harmon Den Mountain and descends gradually toward Deep Gap.

From the crest of the divide in Deep Gap, the Trail ascends steadily to Turkey Gap, generally following the state line. From Turkey Gap, the Trail ascends steeply up the eastern slope of Snowbird Mountain to Wildcat Top and crosses a sag to the West Peak. The Trail then descends steadily through sparse timber along an old road to Spanish Oak Gap. Here, the A.T. bears left, southwest from the state line, and descends along Painter Creek.

The Trail crosses the ridge into Tennessee, crosses the Waterville School Road, and follows above it on a wooded hillside, returning to the road near the Waterville interchange of I-40. It continues on the road under I-40 and over the Pigeon River on concrete Browns Bridge, near the mouth of Tobes Creek, and ends at Davenport Gap, the eastern boundary of Great Smoky Mountains National Park.

Elevation at the beginning of the section on Max Patch Road is 4,280 feet; at Deep Gap, about 3,000 feet; at Snowbird Mountain (West Peak), 4,263 feet; at Pigeon River, 1,400 feet; and at Davenport Gap, 1,975 feet. The section north to south has a net descent of about 2,300 feet. Traverse of this section is therefore easier in the north-to-south direction.

Points of Interest

Outstanding views of the eastern Smokies can be observed from the FAA tower building erected in 1964 on the western peak of Snowbird Mountain. The summit is cleared for 500 feet on all sides of the tower. In spring, a short stretch (1.2 miles) from the northern end of the Trail section provides outstanding wildflower displays. Approaching the Smokies, there are fine views of the scenic cascades by State Line Branch. A state-line marker dated 1899 is located at Davenport Gap.

Road Approaches

The northern end of the section is on Max Patch Road (N.C. 1182) on the Tennessee-North Carolina state line. This point can be reached by car from Lemon Gap, also on the state line, by following Max Patch Road for 3.8 miles south. Lemon Gap may be reached from Newport, Tenn., by following U.S. 25 and 70 for 12 miles to Del Rio, Tenn., and Tenn. 107 south from there for 14 miles to the gap.

The southern end of the section at Davenport Gap on the Tennessee-North Carolina state line is most easily reached by car by taking the Waterville, Tenn., exit (No. 451) from I-40 and several secondary roads for 2.0 miles across the Pigeon River and through the villages of Waterville and Mount Sterling.

Access is available at an intermediate point where the A.T. crosses I-40 and the Pigeon River, 1.0 mile downstream (northwest into Tennessee) from the Tennessee-North Carolina state line. This point on I-40 is 60 miles southeast of Knoxville, Tenn., 15 miles southeast of Newport, and 47 miles northwest of Asheville.

Another intermediate access point is located at Brown Gap, which may be reached from the Harmon Den exit (No. 7) of I-40 in North Carolina by taking gravel Cold Springs USFS 148 for 3.0 miles east and then USFS 148A for 1.2 miles north to the gap.

Davenport Gap has no public transportation.

Because of vandalism, it is not advisable to leave cars overnight at Davenport Gap or on Waterville School Road. Park at the Big Creek Ranger Station in the park near Mount Sterling, 1.0 mile south of the gap on N.C. 284, during seasons when rangers are present.

Maps

Refer to ATC Tennessee-North Carolina Map Three for route navigation. For additional area detail, refer to TVA Lemon Gap, North Carolina-Tennessee, and Waterville, Tennessee-North Carolina, quadrangles.

Shelters, Campsites, and Water

This section has one shelter:

Groundhog Creek Shelter: Stone structure with raised floor; 5.6 miles from northern end of section; accommodates 6; water available at stream 100 yards from shelter.

Next shelter: north 11.3 miles (Roaring Fork Shelter); south 10.5 miles (Davenport Gap Shelter).

Excellent campsites are located at Brown Gap, Snowbird Mountain, Painter Branch, and State Line Branch. Water is available at these campsites, as well as three other springs on the Trail.

Public Accommodations and Supplies

Except for a limited supply of groceries in Mount Sterling, no public accommodations or supplies are readily available at either end of this section. In Tennessee, at Newport (ZIP Code 37821), Cosby (ZIP Code 37722), and Gatlinburg (ZIP Code 37738), stores, post offices, restaurants, and lodging are available.

Trail Description, North to South

Miles	Data
0.0	From Max Patch Road (N.C. 1182) about 0.5 mile southwest of summit of Max Patch Mountain (4,629 feet), where road bears southeast along crest of Newfound Mountains, follow Trail west through woods along ridge. (Avoid lumber roads leading right, downhill, into Tennessee.)
0.2	Make sharp right, uphill, leaving old roadbed, which continues ahead as Cherry Creek Trail with yellow blazes. Continue along ridgecrest through fine hardwood forest.

2.1   At this point, spring can be found 100 yards to right in ravine.

2.3   Old road leads around ridge to right, away from Trail. Trail ahead descends steeply.

2.7   Reach Brown Gap (3,500 feet), which has a campsite. To right, in Tennessee, spring is 100 yards down right leg of dirt road from Max Patch Road (4.0 miles). Left leg leads to Deep Gap. From Brown Gap, Trail ascends steps and swings left on graded trail, ascending.

3.3   Reach saddle of ridge, Harmon Den Mountain, 3,840 feet, with faint trail to summit on left. Descend, skirting left slope of ridge.

3.8   Descending steep bank, enter lumber road, which is gated 200 feet above on right. Follow road to right 100 feet, then leave it by descending left bank into trail. Follow crest of Flat Ridge.

5.6   In Deep Gap, also known as Groundhog Creek Gap (about 2,900 feet), trail to left down old road in North Carolina leads 0.2 mile to Groundhog Creek Shelter (beyond shelter, trail leads 100 yards to good water in stream). Trail bears right and, 100 feet farther, turns left where dirt road from Deep Gap Creek in Tennessee ends (passable by four-wheel-drive vehicle). With white-pine plantation on left, ascend steeply on graded trail.

6.4   Vista to south (prominent peak to southeast is Crabtree Bald in Newfound Mountains). After reaching ridgecrest, ascend more gradually.

6.9   Reach Turkey Gap (slight sag). Trail bears left, ascending eastern peak of Snowbird Mountain, also called Wildcat Top (4,201 feet).

7.4   Pass 25 feet below spring, and, in 200 yards, cross crest of Wildcat Top, about 400 feet south of actual summit.

7.6   Beyond Wildcat Top, descend to sag between peaks of Snowbird Mountain. (To left in sag, 250 yards down wide trail, are spring and campsite.) From sag, A.T. was widened for use as service road for FAA tower on western peak of Snowbird.

8.1   Trail passes side trail to white FAA tower building, enclosed by fence, on summit of western peak of Snowbird (4,263 feet), with wonderful views in all directions, especially of Smokies to southwest. (Road to tower leads 11.0 miles to I-40 at

Hartford, Tenn., via Grassy Fork.) Trail bears left in woods and joins old woods road from tower. It follows descending ridge of Snowbird Mountain for more than 0.5 mile.

9.6   Just before Spanish Oak Gap, A.T. turns sharply left from ridgeline onto graded trail, descending steadily. (Road continues ahead to Cates Creek and Grassy Fork in Tennessee.)

10.1 Trail turns right from ridge, descending gradually along developing Painter Branch, passing in 1,000 feet a good **campsite** to left near stream.

10.5 Cross small creek. (Blue-blazed trail to left crosses Painter Branch and leads to excellent **campsite** and good spring.) Trail bears right, away from Painter Branch, and skirts southern slope of Snowbird Mountain.

10.9 Bear left from old roadway, resuming descent.

11.8 To right on slight ridge, pass old wire fence.

12.6 Descend steps, and turn right onto old woods road.

12.8 Reach gravel Waterville School Road. Turn right for 200 feet up road, cross stream on left, and turn left downstream on graded Trail.

13.3 Descend steps in rock cut, and turn right on Waterville School Road to pass under I-40 down to Pigeon River. Cross concrete bridge over river.

13.7 From southern end of bridge, follow hard-surfaced road until it turns left in 35 yards (gravel road goes straight ahead, uphill). Cross culvert over Tobes Creek, and immediately turn right, uphill, onto Trail beside creek. After four short switchbacks, pass prominent rock formation on left.

13.9 At foot of cascades, cross State Line Branch, and, in 25 yards, make sharp left to ascend steeply above scenic cascades. Cross and recross State Line Branch before skirting hillside to right. Reach blue-blazed trail, which leads to right 60 yards to good springhouse. Ahead on right across small stream are ruins of small cabin. Possible **campsite**.

14.4 Make sharp right along ascending ridge.

14.5 Pass under powerline in cleared strip. Reenter woods, and ascend steeply. Skirt right slope of ridge for 0.2 mile.

14.7 Cross woods road.

14.9 Skirt right side of ridge for 0.1 mile, then skirt left side of knob. Descend to ramp to N.C. 284 in Davenport Gap.

15.2   End of section at Davenport Gap, N.C. 284, which becomes
        Tenn. 32 at the state line just to the west. To continue on A.T.,
        follow graded Trail ahead. **Davenport Gap Shelter** is 0.9
        mile farther.

Trail Description, South to North

Miles   **Data**

0.0   From intersection of Trail from Newfound Gap with N.C. 284
        (Tenn. 32), follow highway 20 yards to right. Cross road, and
        take Trail up ramp. Make sharp left, and, in 25 yards, make
        sharp right, and continue uphill. Trail veers to right to pass
        around knob, then passes to left of second knob.

0.3   Turn left onto ridge trail, descend to sag, then pass over rise
        to woods road. Cross road, and skirt left side of ridge, then
        descend on ridgeline.

0.7   Pass under powerline in cleared strip with view of Snowbird
        Mountain across Pigeon River Gorge.

0.8   Turn sharply left, downhill. Cross State Line Branch, and
        turn right, downstream.

1.1   Pass ruins of cabin, cross small stream, and reach blue-blazed
        trail leading left 60 yards to spring in springhouse. **Campsite**
        here. Trail skirts hillside to left, descends steeply, crosses, and
        recrosses State Line Branch. Continue 0.1 mile above scenic
        cascades.

1.3   After sharp right turn, cross stream below cascades, and
        continue descent on right bank. Pass prominent rock forma-
        tion on right. After four switchbacks, reach hard-surfaced
        road. (To right, Waterville is 1.0 mile.) Turn left on road, cross
        culvert over Tobes Creek (gravel road enters from left), and
        turn right.

1.5   Cross concrete road bridge over Pigeon River, turn right, and
        pass under I-40. Follow gravel Waterville School Road, bear-
        ing right. After 500 feet, ascend bank by steps on left side of
        road.

1.9   Proceed above road on wooded hillside for next half-mile,
        then descend to cross stream; turn right on Waterville School
        Road for 200 feet.

2.4   Turn left from gravel road, and ascend on old dirt road.

2.6   Where roadway crosses sag in ridge, ascend steps up left bank, and enter woods. Soon, pass under high-tension powerline, where opening gives good views of Mount Sterling 5.0 miles to the south. Turn left above powerline, and ascend with several long switchbacks to state-line ridge.

3.5   Circle around ridge, entering Pisgah National Forest and North Carolina Wildlife Management Area.

4.3   Old road (now wide trail) enters from left. Follow it for next 0.3 mile. Trail reaches Painter Branch and bears left above stream. (Blue-blazed trail to right crosses Painter Branch, leading to excellent **campsite** and good spring.)

4.7   Cross small creek (excellent **campsites** just below here and 1,000 feet farther). Trail continues ascent to left of Painter Branch as stream becomes smaller.

5.1   Turn left, uphill, on ridge. Graded trail ascends steadily and climbs to right 200 feet before Spanish Oak Gap on ridge, not reaching gap. (Worn road on ridge leads left down to Cates Creek and Grassy Fork in Tennessee.)

6.4   On main ridge of Snowbird Mountain, Trail continues ascent on old road for more than 0.5 mile. Near summit, Trail on old road bears right in woods and joins a dirt road.

7.0   Side trail to left leads to white FAA tower on peak of Snowbird Mountain (4,263 feet). (From summit, traveler gets grandstand view of eastern Smokies. Road to tower climbs 11.0 miles from Hartford, Tenn., exit of I-40.) Follow old road.

7.6   Reach second and lower sag between two peaks of Snowbird Mountain. (To right is old trail leading 250 yards down to spring and good **campsite**.) Ascend, and cross crest of Wildcat Top (4,201 feet), eastern peak of Snowbird, bearing right about 400 feet south of actual summit. Begin descent on North Carolina slope of ridge.

7.8   Trail passes 25 feet below Wildcat Spring (good spring).

8.3   Reach slight sag (Turkey Gap), continuing descent.

8.8   Reach vista to south. (Prominent peak to southeast is Crabtree Bald in Newfound Mountains.) Descend more steeply toward Deep Gap.

9.6   After passing white-pine plantation on right, reach Deep Gap (about 2,900 feet) on crest of divide with dirt road to left (passable by four-wheel-drive vehicle from Deep Gap Creek in Tennessee). (Road to right leads 0.2 mile in North Carolina to **Groundhog Creek Shelter**. Beyond shelter, trail leads 100 yards to good water in stream.) Turn right on old road for 100 feet and then left on graded trail, ascending. Trail ascends steadily up Flat Ridge.

11.4 Trail enters lumber road on left (road is gated 100 feet above) and follows it for 100 feet. Leave road by ascending left bank into trail.

11.9 Reach saddle of ridge (Harmon Den Mountain, 3,840 feet) with faint trail to summit to right.

12.5 Reach Brown Gap (3,500 feet), with **campsite**. To left, spring is 100 yards down right leg of dirt road in Tennessee from Max Patch Road (4.0 miles); left leg leads to Deep Gap. To right of gap, gravel road passable by automobile descends steeply 1.5 miles to Cold Springs USFS road, connection between I-40 at Harmon Den exit and Max Patch Road. From Brown Gap, Trail ascends steeply.

12.9 Old road to left leads away from Trail.

13.1 Spring can be found 100 yards to left in ravine.

15.0 Descend steep bank, and turn left on old road leading to Max Patch Road.

15.2 Reach Max Patch Road, N.C. 1182 (about 4,250 feet), and end of section. Trail crosses road and enters woods through a stile.

Great Smoky Mountains National Park
70.5 Miles

Most of the 72.1 miles of the A.T. between the Pigeon River and the Little Tennessee River lie within the Great Smoky Mountains National Park, along the crest of the Great Smokies, the master chain of the southern Appalachians. With the exception of the Black Mountains in North Carolina, the Smokies are the loftiest and most rugged mountains in the East. The trails within the park are maintained primarily by the National Park Service (NPS). The A.T. in the park is managed cooperatively by the NPS and the Smoky Mountains Hiking Club, based in Knoxville, Tenn.

Although the first serious proposal to establish a national park in the Smoky Mountains was made before 1900, the efforts that were ultimately successful began in 1923. Private and public efforts to acquire land began in 1925. In 1928, John D. Rockefeller, Jr., contributed five million dollars to match contributions of states and private citizens, and purchasing of land began in earnest. By 1930, 158,000 acres had been bought; by 1935, 400,000 acres. The park was formally dedicated in 1940 by President Franklin D. Roosevelt.

Visitors can gain information from the park visitors center or by mail.

Other Trails in the Smokies

A folder, *100 Favorite Trails of the Great Smokies and the Carolina Blue Ridge*, complete with maps and descriptions, is available from the Carolina Mountain Club and ATC.

More information may be obtained from the park visitors center at Gatlinburg, Tenn., and from the Smoky Mountains Hiking Club, P.O. Box 1454, Knoxville, Tenn. 37901.

Maps

Trails Illustrated's Great Smoky Mountains National Park map, included with this guide, details topography, trails, shelters and campsite locations, as well as other park facilities. For more detailed topography, see the following quadrangles: USGS Waterville, Tennessee-North Carolina; Hartford, Tennessee-North Carolina; Luftee Knob, North Carolina-Tennessee; Mt. Guyot, Tennessee-North Carolina; LeConte, Tennessee-North Carolina; Clingmans Dome, North Carolina-Tennessee; Silers Bald, North Carolina-Tennessee; Thunderhead Mountain, North Carolina-Tennessee; Cades Cove, Tennessee-North Carolina; and Fontana Dam, North Carolina-Tennessee. These maps are available from U.S. Geological Survey, Branch Distribution (see page 246).

Campfires

Firewood is so scarce in the Smokies that hikers are advised to carry stoves. Stoves have the added advantage of providing cooking facilities in wet weather, which frequently occurs in the Smokies.

Water

A canteen, preferably two, is indispensable. Water sources have been indicated in the Trail data. In dry seasons, it is often necessary at many of the springs to go farther down the mountain. Water may also be located on the slopes of other gaps, in addition to those specifically mentioned.

Bears

The protection given to all forms of wildlife within the Great Smoky Mountains National Park has resulted in a problem with bears.

Bears are numerous at parking places and are attracted by food at shelters. Do not feed bears or leave food at shelters where bears can get it. Bears will steal food if it is not protected. Most shelters in the park have wire grills across the open front so that food may be safely stored in them. Some have separate food caches. If such storage places are not available, suspend food and packs from a rope or wire stretched high between two trees. Food left in automobiles may attract bears and result in damage to the car. Packs and tents may be similarly damaged. Excess food should be burned or carried out, not buried or left in the open. Tin cans and nonburnable refuse should also be carried out. Give bears a wide berth, particularly if they have cubs with them. It is dangerous to feed, tease, frighten, or molest them in any way.

Pets and firearms are not permitted on any park trails.

Shelters

The park has a chain of 13 shelters along the A.T., five in the eastern part and eight in the western part. These shelters were specially built by the NPS for Trail use and are located at intervals of an easy day's travel. Use of each structure is limited to one night. Users are expected to carry out all nonburnable refuse. Shelters in the park are listed in the introduction to each section. Fires are permissible only in the fireplace or at iron grills outside each shelter.

Camping Permits

Permits are required by the NPS for both camping and use of the shelters and approved campsites along the A.T. This is not a requirement on most other parts of the Trail. It is a violation of Park Service regulations, punishable by fine, for overnight hikers to travel in the Great Smoky Mountains National Park without a (free) camping permit. A.T. shelter permits for thru-hikers may be obtained at ranger stations and visitors centers in the park or at the USFS French Broad Ranger District Headquarters in Hot Springs, N.C., located across from the post office on the main street in town. Northbound thru-hikers may get permits at the TVA Fontana Dam Visitors Center. Advance reservations are required for shelter permits.

To prevent overcrowding at shelters and the deterioration of the Trail environment, the Park Service issues for a given night only as many camping permits as the capacity of the shelter. Between April 1 and June 15, three bunk spaces are reserved at each A.T. shelter in the park for thru-hikers. Camping adjacent to the shelters, as well as at unauthorized places along the trails, is forbidden. Hikers planning trips of more than one day should write to or phone Great Smoky Mountains National Park, Gatlinburg, Tenn. 37738, for regulations on shelter use and camping.

Trail Location

The original route of the A.T. extended the length of the Great Smokies to Deals Gap. Beyond, the Trail traversed 3.3 miles of privately owned land to Tapoco, where it crossed the Little Tennessee and Cheoah rivers on a highway bridge and then led back east along the crest of the Yellow Creek Mountains. This route was necessary because there was no other crossing of the Little Tennessee River.

The building of the TVA dam at Fontana on the Little Tennessee River made possible a Trail relocation that not only eliminated a difficult and circuitous route but added several unusual features to the Trail system: Fontana Dam, which serves as a crossing of the Little Tennessee; a 29-mile-long lake that forms the southern boundary of the Great Smokies; and Fontana Village, a recreational center. At the suggestion of the Smoky Mountains Hiking Club, the Trail was relocated in 1946 and 1947 to leave the crest of the Smokies at Doe Knob, the point of most direct access to Fontana Dam.

From here, the route to Fontana Dam was constructed by NPS. Shuckstack, just off the route of the Trail, gives an outstanding view of the southern Appalachians. The relocation ascends from the dam to the original route on the crest of Yellow Creek Mountain near High Top. The relocations shortened the route by 11.7 miles.

This change in route eliminated from the Trail two outstanding features, Gregory Bald and Parson Bald. Since the establishment of the park and the suspension of grazing, most of these balds have become overgrown and their open features, which were their outstanding attraction, are rapidly disappearing. Gregory and Andrews balds are being kept open by cutting of woody growth, however.

A portion of the original route has been officially designated as Gregory Bald Trail and continued as a side trail.

Fontana Dam and Fontana Village

Fontana Dam, part of the TVA system, was constructed on the Little Tennessee River during World War II to furnish hydroelectric power. The dam is 480 feet high, the highest in the East and the sixth highest in the United States. The powerhouse and penstock are at the bottom near the center of the river channel.

In May 1946, Fontana Village, which had been constructed at Welch Cove to house TVA construction workers, was leased for operation as a public recreation area. The village is some three miles from the dam and at an elevation of 1,800 feet, immediately at the base of the Yellow Creek Mountains. Extensive facilities are available here, including a lodge, cafeteria, drug store, grocery store, post office, laundry, and medical center, and some 300 houses.

The area has an extensive recreation program under the direction of a recreational supervisor. Hiking, fishing, horseback trips, and flower walks are featured.

The area is covered by the USGS Fontana Dam, N.C., quadrangle. Booklets on Fontana and a map may be obtained by writing Fontana Village Resort, Fontana Dam, N.C. 28733, or by calling (800) 849-2258.

The dam, in creating the lake with a normal shoreline at an elevation of about 1,710 feet, flooded out N.C. 288 from Deals Gap to Bryson City. A hard-surfaced road, N.C. 28, leads from U.S. 129 to Fontana Dam (9.5 miles from Deals Gap) and continues to a junction with U.S. 19, nine miles south of Bryson City.

Geology of the Appalachian Trail through the Great Smoky Mountains

The geologic evolution of North America's eastern continental margin is complex, involving at least three periods in which mountains were raised by tectonic forces in the Earth's crust and culminating with the opening of the Atlantic Ocean and building of the Appalachian Mountain chain some 300 million years ago. During these mountain-building events, bedrock was exposed to intense pressure and heat, which altered rock texture and mineral composition in a process known as metamorphism. Bedrock that underlies the Blue Ridge Mountains of the southern Appalachians ranges in age from about 600 million to 1 billion years. The bedrock illustrates varying degrees of metamorphism, which is evidenced by the rock types present (slate, which forms from shaley sediments; marble, which forms from limestones; quartzites, which form from sandstones; and gneiss, which can form from a variety of parent rock types) and minerals present (mica, garnets, and staurolite in more highly metamorphic rocks). In general, the bedrock along the Trail is older and more highly metamorphic in Georgia and North Carolina south of the Nantahala River than that in the Smokies. The following description of geology along the A.T. between Springer Mountain and the Big Pigeon River is excerpted from *Underfoot: A Geologic Guide to the Appalachian Trail*, by Collins Chew (1988, Appalachian Trail Conference).

Most of the Appalachian Trail in Georgia rises and falls along the peaks and gaps of the eastern ridge of the Blue Ridge. The ridgeline generally separates streams flowing northwest to the Mississippi River from those flowing south to the Gulf of Mexico or the Atlantic Ocean. The Trail passes over several of the higher mountains in the state. Distant views to the southeast from the A.T. in Georgia are of the Piedmont Plateau–farmland, woodland, and a few scattered mountains. To the northwest are views of mountains and valleys of the interior of the Blue Ridge and of vast, unbroken forests, which are unusual south of Maine.

The rocks beneath the Trail in Georgia are roughly uniform and coarsely crystalline. There is little obvious relationship between rock type and topography, since mountain and valley are underlain by similar rock. The first gold rush in the United States was centered in Dahlonega, Ga., 15 miles southeast of Springer Mountain, in the 1830s, and former gold mines and prospects are scattered throughout the area.

At 4,461 feet, Blood Mountain is the highest point of the Appalachians in Georgia and the second highest in the state. Massive gneiss makes up the summit area of Blood Mountain. After a stretch through the Nantahala Mountains of North Carolina, the A.T. closely follows the North Carolina-Tennessee state line and traverses many complex landforms, some related to the nature of the underlying rocks.

The Trail northbound leaves the eastern ridge of the Blue Ridge near Carter Gap, turns north, and crosses the Nantahala and Little Tennessee rivers. Then, it climbs to the western ridge of the Blue Ridge at the crest of the Great Smoky Mountains and the Tennessee state line.

Ten miles north of the Georgia line, the northbound A.T. hiker climbs above 5,000 feet for the first time, at Standing Indian Mountain (5,498 feet). In this part of North Carolina, as along the Trail in Georgia, the topography has no obvious relation to the underlying rocks. These rocks are coarsely crystalline and, in many places, show bands of light and dark minerals. The light minerals are generally quartz and feldspar; the dark minerals are micas and hornblende.

Just past Carter Gap, The Trail leaves the Blue Ridge Divide and follows the ridge that separates streams flowing into the Nantahala River and those flowing more directly to the Little Tennessee River. On this cross ridge, peaks above 5,000 feet are commonplace. Albert Mountain (5,250) is particularly steep and impressive. A cliff at the top of Albert Mountain has vivid examples of the contorted bands of light and dark rock typical of coarse-grained gneiss. Farther north, Wayah Bald boasts three continuous miles of A.T. above 5,000 feet. Its rocks are stained a distinct orange by the weathered oxides of iron, which are not washed away by water. East of Wayah Bald is the Cowee Valley near Franklin, N.C., where mines provide gravel for tourists to wash for rubies and a few semiprecious gems.

North of Wesser Bald along the A.T. are the first really significant changes in the rocks and topography. Slate, a fine-grained rock that breaks into sheets, is the first sign of change. Slate forms jaggy, craggy outcrops. The sparkling mineral mica, formed by the gentle heating of slate, is abundant in places.

A big event for the northbound hiker is the 2,700-foot descent to the Nantahala River, the first river crossing the A.T. and the lowest point so far along the Trail. The Nantahala River cuts its valley for about ten miles along a belt of easily eroded rock. The belt is much longer than the Nantahala River Gorge and forms a new low area to, and west of, the A.T. all the way from Springer Mountain. This band of rock, composed largely of marble and mica, is a bed of rock folded down into the older gneiss common in the area. The marble is slightly soluble in water and washes away. Erosion appears to have formed a long valley through the mountains, but, rather than being one stream valley, it includes several streams that cross or follow the lowland belt. The northbound hiker must climb out of the deep gorge and make the first 3,000-foot climb of the A.T. to reach Swim Bald and then, a 700-foot climb to Cheoah Bald. The ridge just south of Cheoah Bald is a knife-edge outcrop of slate.

As the A.T. nears the crest of the Smokies, rocks along the way no longer show the shiny minerals seen to the south. They appear more like the sediments from which they were formed: slate from mud, siltstone from bedded silts, and sandstone from sand. These sedimentary rocks underlie the A.T. throughout the Great Smoky Mountains National Park and almost to Max Patch Mountain. The Trail passes a type of rock found under the A.T. only in the western Smokies: a gray, massive rock called graywacke, containing pebbles of blue quartz slate and the white mineral feldspar, all in a fine-grained gray matrix.

From the main ridge of the Smokies, the view to the north reveals the much lower valley and ridge area beyond the outlying lower ridge of the Blue Ridge. Between Doe Knob and Thunderhead Mountain, the view of the first valley to the north reveals the open, low farmland area of Cades Cove, an isolated patch of the younger valley and ridge rock surrounded by Blue Ridge rock. Thunderhead Mountain provides expansive views of the area. Its summit is one of several grassy balds in the area that has probably existed since precolonial times.

Between Buckeye Gap and Silers Bald, the A.T. rises above 5,000 feet and remains at least that high for 34 miles, the longest length of the Trail above 5,000 feet. Clingmans Dome (6,643 feet) was named for General Thomas L. Clingman, soldier, statesman, scientist, and explorer, who was the first to write about the Carolina mountains and the first to measure the dome's elevation. Charlies Bunion shows the slate that makes much of the ridge in the Smokies. A severe fire following logging operations in 1925 allowed all the soil to erode, leaving the area bare. The Sawteeth, farther north on the A.T., are also made up of slate.

On its descent from the high country, the A.T. passes the trail to the spectacular, tilted rock ledges of Mt. Cammerer, then drops to 1,500 feet and crosses the Big Pigeon River, where it cuts through the ridge in a deep gorge.

The following comment on the geological structure of the Great Smoky Mountains, which is exposed at Newfound Gap, is quoted from *Nature Notes* (October 1939):

Great Smoky Mountains Expose Oldest Rock Strata in East

Motorists in the Great Smoky Mountains National Park who travel over the highway from Gatlinburg, Tennessee, to the Continental Divide, at Newfound Gap, and thence down to the village of Cherokee, North Carolina, may view one of the finest geological sections exposed in the entire East.

Along this scenic drive, which mounts to over 5,000 feet above sea level, rock layers of slate, quartzite and conglomerate, tilted at astonishing angles, confirm the account given by geologists of how these very ancient mountains were brought forth. The Appalachians, which probably have been much higher in past eons than now, have been elevated and worn down not once but several times. Originally some of the strata laid down in prehistoric seas as muds and sands contained fossil. These fossil-bearing rocks either have been worn away or so layered by heat and pressure that few evidences of the life that existed during their formation have been found up to the present time.

Davenport Gap (Tenn. 32-N.C. 284) to Newfound Gap (U.S. 441)
Section Seventeen
31.3 miles

Brief Description of Section

This section traverses the wildest, and at one time the most difficult, portion of the Great Smokies. From Davenport Gap (1,975 feet), it is a long, continuous climb of 3,025 feet over a distance of 5.2 miles to the crest of the state line, west of Mt. Cammerer, the eastern beginning of the Great Smokies.

Beyond are many deep gaps and high peaks, with 11 major climbs and the same number of descents. After passing over Cosby Knob, the Trail swings around Mt. Guyot, a short distance from its 6,621-foot summit. The next peaks are Tri-Corner Knob, Mt. Chapman, Mt. Sequoyah, Pecks Corner, Porters Mountain, and Charlies Bunion. After passing Mt. Kephart, the Trail descends 955 feet to Newfound Gap. The route through the section is graded, with a grade of no more than 15 percent. The Trail is maintained so that hikers can enjoy the succession of panoramic views without constant attention to the footway.

The route is indicated by white-paint blazes as well as by dug footway. Board signs mark intersections with side trails.

Because much of the Trail is on or near the state line, the slopes have been designated in the Trail data as North Carolina or Tennessee.

Points of Interest

Much of the Trail in this section passes through high-elevation spruce-fir forests. The spruce-fir forests of the Great Smokies are in a period of decline because of insect attack by the balsam wooly aphid, killer of mature fir trees. Overstory canopy trees in the spruce-fir forests have died, allowing sunlight to reach the understory, thus resulting in massive blackberry growth. At times, this growth nearly blocks the Trail. Unlike the broader crest south and west of Newfound

Gap the crest here is narrow, particularly in the section known as the Sawteeth, where one may stand astride the state line. The outstanding peaks are Mt. Kephart, named for Horace Kephart, an early A.T. planner, distinguished authority on the region, and author of *Our Southern Highlands*; the Jump-Off, which allows a magnificent view north of the entire range as far as Mt. Guyot; Mt. Chapman, named in honor of Colonel David C. Chapman, who was instrumental in establishing the park; and Mt. Guyot, named for Arnold Guyot, whose explorations prior to the Civil War and manuscript map constitute invaluable source material for a study of the region.

The eastern beginning of the Great Smokies is Mt. Cammerer, formerly White Rock, which was renamed to commemorate the outstanding services to the Great Smoky Mountains National Park by former NPS Director Arno B. Cammerer. The stone tower (5,025 feet) on Mt. Cammerer gives a 360-degree view of the Smokies. This is one of the most spectacular views along the Trail. Between Mt. Cammerer and Mt. Guyot is a section known as Hell Ridge, named so because of the devastation caused by forest fires on the North Carolina side and because it was difficult to travel.

The highest point in the section is about 6,360 feet, where the Trail swings around the Tennessee side of Mt. Guyot, a short distance below the 6,621-foot summit.

Views from Charlies Bunion are extraordinary. To the west are the Jump-Off and Mt. Kephart, to the northwest is Mt. LeConte, to the north are gorges on headwaters of Porters Creek, slightly to the northeast is Greenbrier Pinnacle, and to the east is the jagged knifelike section of the state line known as the Sawteeth Range. This spectacular formation on a densely forested ridgecrest was said to have been created by a fire on the North Carolina slope, following timbering operations; afterwards, the vegetation was washed away by severe storms, resulting in the present-day, recovering young forest.

Road Approaches

From Davenport Gap north via Tenn. 32, it is 26.5 miles to Newport, from which, via I-40 or U.S. 70, it is 45.4 miles to Knoxville (71.9 miles from Davenport Gap); via Tenn. 32 and U.S. 321, it is 30.6 miles to Gatlinburg. South via N.C. 284 and 276, it is 29 miles to Dellwood, N.C., and U.S. 19, which leads to Asheville, a total of 60 miles from Davenport Gap. A shorter route to Newport (19 miles north) and to Asheville (57 miles southeast) follows N.C. 284 to Mount Sterling village (Big Creek Ranger Station and primitive campground a short distance upstream): Turn left on gravel road beside Big Creek, and continue through Waterville and across Browns Bridge to I-40. N.C. 284, while narrow and steep, has extraordinary views of the eastern end of the Great Smoky Mountains National Park.

Public transportation is not available in Davenport Gap. Because of vandalism, it is not advisable to leave cars overnight near Davenport Gap. Park at the Big Creek Ranger Station in seasons when rangers are present.

The southern end of the section at Newfound Gap is reached from U.S. 441, the highway that crosses the Great Smoky Mountains at Newfound Gap. From this highway, it is 16 miles to Gatlinburg and 55 miles to Knoxville, both northwest in Tennessee, and 20 miles southeast to Cherokee, N.C.

Maps

Refer to ATC Great Smoky Mountains National Park Map for route navigation. For additional area detail, refer to USGS Clingmans Dome, North Carolina-Tennessee; Mt. LeConte, Tennessee-North Carolina; Mt. Guyot, Tennessee-North Carolina; Luftee Knob, North Carolina-Tennessee; Hartford, Tennessee-North Carolina; and Waterville, Tennessee-North Carolina quadrangles.

Shelters, Campsites, and Water

This section has five shelters and 15 water sources. The shelters are listed below.

Miles from Davenport Gap	Shelter
0.9	Davenport Gap
8.0	Cosby Knob
15.7	Tri-Corner Knob
20.9	Pecks Corner (0.4 mile from A.T.)
28.3	Icewater Spring

Public Accommodations and Supplies

Public accommodations and supplies are not available on or near the Trail at either end of this section. Stores, post offices, restaurants, and lodging are available at Newport, Cosby, Gatlinburg, and Cherokee.

Precautions

The many deep gaps and high peaks in this section involve considerably more climbing than a casual inspection of the route would indicate. Allow for extra time and exertion.

The section is easier to hike southwest to northeast, from Newfound Gap (5,045 feet) to Davenport Gap (1,975 feet), than in the reverse direction. In traversing the section from southwest to northeast, the climbing totals 4,608 feet and the downhill travel, 7,678 feet.

See information in the immediately preceding section, "Great Smoky Mountains National Park," for advice about firewood, water sources and scarcity, wildlife protection, bears, and camping permits.

Trail Description, North to South

Miles	Data
0.0	From Davenport Gap (1,975 feet), at Tenn. 32 and N.C. 284, follow graded trail west, and cross small clearing.
0.2	Water can be found in field below and to left of Trail.
0.9	**Davenport Gap Shelter** (built-in bunks accommodate 12) is located 100 yards to right of Trail, with spring nearby. Ascend steadily.
1.9	Chestnut Branch Trail leads 2.0 miles to Big Creek Ranger Station and **campground**.
2.8	Reach lower Mt. Cammerer Trail, leading 7.8 miles to **Cosby Campground** on Tennessee side.
3.1	Reach side trail on left leading 50 yards to spring.
3.2	Cross spur on North Carolina side, ascend, and skirt southern slope of Mt. Cammerer. Note spectacular trail construction.

4.4   Pass through gap in spur off side of Mt. Cammerer, and ascend slope of mountain.

4.7   Reach small uphill site used as a camp by CCC in construction of Mt. Cammerer tower; just beyond is spring on right.

5.2   Graded side trail on right leads 0.6 mile to Mt. Cammerer tower. Beyond side trail, route ascends.

5.4   Cross high point (about 5,000 feet); then cross spur on Tennessee side of Sunup Knob (5,050 feet), with good views.

6.7   Cross crest of Rocky Face Mountain, a spur on Tennessee side.

7.3   Descend to Low Gap (4,242 feet). Trails lead from here to Walnut Bottoms (North Carolina side), following Low Gap Branch, and to **Cosby Campground** (Tennessee side), following Cosby Creek 2.5 miles. From Low Gap, climb 785 feet to Cosby Knob.

7.9   Water crosses Trail.

8.0   **Cosby Knob Shelter** is 150 feet to left; built-in bunks accommodate 12; spring nearby. Trail enters the four-mile Hell Ridge.

8.6   Cross spur on Tennessee side after swinging around North Carolina side of Cosby Knob (5,145 feet).

9.0   Cross spur, and pass around forested side of Ross Knob (5,025 feet), on Tennessee side.

9.5   Reach Camel Gap (4,645 feet). Camel Gap Trail leads to Big Creek and Walnut Bottoms from here. Ascend, swinging to Tennessee side.

10.5 Reach wooded side of Camel Hump Knob (5,250 feet).

11.9 Reach Snake Den Ridge Trail, which joins A.T. from Tennessee side. This trail goes by Maddron Bald and down Snake Den Mountain to **Cosby Campground**. Spring is about 0.8 mile down this trail. Follow A.T. around slope of Inadu Knob (5,941 feet). "Inadu" means "snake" in Cherokee and refers to snake dens on the mountainside.

12.2 Reach Yellow Creek Gap.

12.8 Reach Deer Creek Gap (6,020 feet). Fantastic views of Mt. Guyot, Luftee Knob, Balsam Corner, and Mt. Sterling can be seen from here.

13.0 Leave burned-over section, and enter virgin balsam-fir and red-spruce forest.

13.3 Good view of English Mountain, Tennessee. Trail ascends.

13.4   Cross Pinnacle Lead, spur off Tennessee side of Old Black. Pinnacle Lead forms boundary between Sevier and Cocke counties of Tennessee.

13.6   Reach gap between Mt. Guyot and Old Black.

13.8   Reach faint trail, obstructed by blowdowns, leading up north slope of Mt. Guyot. Climb requires about one hour to reach top of second-highest peak in Great Smokies.

13.9   Pass Guyot Spring.

14.5   Cross Guyot Spur (6,360 feet), highest point on A.T. in eastern Smokies.

15.1   Reach sharp-ridged gap between Tri-Corner Knob and Mt. Guyot; then climb along Tennessee side of Tri-Corner Knob (6,100 feet). Balsam Mountain, leading from Tri-Corner Knob, forms boundary between Swain and Haywood counties of North Carolina. Tri-Corner Knob is junction of two major ranges, the Smoky and the Balsam, and was given its name by geographer Arnold Guyot.

15.5   Balsam Mountain Trail enters from left. **Laurel Gap Shelter** is 7.0 miles via this trail; accommodates 14; spring nearby.

15.7   Come to trail junction. A.T. bears right. Left fork leads 100 yards to **Tri-Corner Knob Shelter** on North Carolina side. Built-in bunks accommodate 12; spring nearby.

15.8   Reach Big Cove Gap (5,825 feet). Ascend, following state line between north and middle peaks of Mt. Chapman.

16.7   Reach high point of Trail on Mt. Chapman.

17.5   Reach Chapman Gap (5,650 feet).

18.2   Reach high point of Mt. Sequoyah (6,000 feet).

18.9   Cross Old Troublesome, a spur off Tennessee side of Mt. Sequoyah.

19.2   Reach Copper Gap (5,650 feet), then climb 250 feet to Eagle Rocks.

19.9   Find water 800 feet down North Carolina side on northern end of Eagle Rocks.

20.0   Reach spectacular view of precipitous slopes and sharp gorges caused by headwaters of Eagle Rocks Creek.

20.4   Swing around western peak of Eagle Rocks (5,900 feet) and then around North Carolina side of Pecks Corner, junction of Hughes Ridge and state line.

20.9   Reach Hughes Ridge Trail on left. (This trail leads to **Pecks Corner Shelter**, formerly Hughes Ridge. Built-in bunks accommodate 12 persons; spring nearby. To reach shelter, follow graded Hughes Ridge Trail south for 0.4 mile to gap and then turn left, downhill, 100 yards in beech woods.) About 100 feet beyond junction of Hughes Ridge Trail is intermittent spring on right side of A.T.

21.1   Cross Hughes Ridge.

22.2   Reach Bradleys View on state line, with unusually fine views into deep-cut gorge of Bradley Fork and over mountains in North Carolina.

23.5   Cross Woolly Tops Lead.

23.8   Pass around side of Laurel Top (5,865 feet).

24.8   Reach False Gap (5,400 feet). Site of the original Porters Gap has been the subject of considerable controversy; the conflicting sites are Porters Gap and False Gap. Porters Gap, beyond on Trail, is at extremely high elevation, which worked against its acceptance as the true gap. The name False Gap was applied to contrast to Porters Gap. From False Gap, Trail ascends 100 feet to Porters Mountain.

25.5   Reach Porters Gap (5,500 feet), on state line, near junction of Porters Mountain and state-line ridge. Trail leads along crest of jagged range, known as the Sawteeth.

26.9   Reach 0.8-mile section that was swept by fire following timbering operations in 1925. Spectacular views.

27.1   Pass Dry Sluice Gap Trail, formerly Richland Mountain Trail, which enters at left from **Smokemont Campground**, 8.5 miles distant. Via this trail and Grassy Branch Trail, it is 3.8 miles to **Kephart Shelter**: accommodates 14; creek water.

27.2   Reach Dry Sluice Gap (5,375 feet). Water may be found about 400 feet down North Carolina side. Beyond, ascend along fire-scarred ridge.

27.4   Pass around higher peak of Charlies Bunion and then around right side of precipitous western (lower) peak of the Bunion. Lower or western peak is sometimes called Fodder Stack; higher peak is called Charlies Bunion.

27.7   Pass from the fire-scarred area into virgin forest.

28.2   Pass spring on right.

28.3   Reach **Icewater Spring Shelter** on the left. Bunks can accommodate 12.

28.6   Boulevard Trail enters on right. On Boulevard Trail, it is 5.3 miles to **LeConte Lodge and Shelter**. Accommodations are available at lodge from late March to early November. Shelter accommodates 12. About 100 yards from A.T., spur trail off Boulevard Trail leads 0.8 mile to Mt. Kephart (6,150 feet) and the Jump-Off (6,100 feet). The Jump-Off has spectacular views.

28.9   Reach elevation of about 6,000 feet, and begin gradual descent to Newfound Gap.

29.4   Fine views of Clingmans Dome (6,643 feet), highest point in park, to southwest and of Thomas Ridge and Oconaluftee River gorge to south.

29.6   Reach Sweat Heifer Creek Trail, on state line, which leads down Kephart Prong on North Carolina side. The name Sweat Heifer probably came from driving cattle up this steep trail to high, grassy pastures. **Kephart Shelter** is 3.7 miles down this trail; accommodates 14; creek water.

31.3   Reach U.S. 441 in Newfound Gap (5,045 feet).

Trail Description, South to North

Miles   **Data**

0.0   From crest of U.S. 441 at Newfound Gap (5,045 feet), at northeast corner of parking area, follow graded Trail northeast along North Carolina side. The hardwoods are mainly yellow birch. The conifers are red spruce and Fraser fir, locally called balsam. This section lies in Swain County, North Carolina.

1.7   Pass graded Sweat Heifer Creek Trail leading down Kephart Prong. The name Sweat Heifer probably came from driving cattle up this steep trail to high, grassy pastures. On North Carolina side via this trail, **Kephart Shelter** is 3.7 miles; accommodates 14; creek water.

2.0   Fine views to southwest of Clingmans Dome (6,643 feet), highest point in park, and of Thomas Ridge and Oconaluftee River gorge to south.

2.4   On state line, begin descent from elevation of about 6,000 feet.

2.7   At trail junction, take right fork. Left is Boulevard Trail. On Boulevard Trail, it is 5.3 miles to **LeConte Lodge and Shelter.** Accommodations are available at lodge from late March to early November. Shelter accommodates 12. About 100 yards from A.T., spur trail off Boulevard Trail leads 0.8 mile to Mt. Kephart (6,150 feet) and the Jump-Off (6,100 feet), which has spectacular views. From junction with Boulevard Trail, swing around North Carolina side of Mt. Kephart.

3.0   Reach **Icewater Spring Shelter**. Built-in bunks accommodate 12 persons. Spring is 75 yards farther on trail. Beyond, descend.

3.6   Enter 0.8-mile section that was swept by fire after timbering operations in 1925. Spectacular views.

3.8   Pass around left side of precipitous western (lower) peak of Charlies Bunion.

3.9   Pass around higher peak of Charlies Bunion. Lower (western) peak is sometimes called Fodder Stack; higher (eastern) peak is Charlies Bunion.

4.1   Descend to Dry Sluice Gap (5,375 feet). Water may be found about 400 feet down North Carolina side.

4.2   Reach junction with Dry Sluice Gap Trail, formerly Richland Mountain Trail. Take left fork. Right leads 8.5 miles to **Smokemont Campground**; via this trail and Grassy Branch Trail, it is 3.8 miles to **Kephart Shelter**: accommodates 14; creek water.

4.4   Pass out of fire scar, and follow along sharp crest of Sawteeth Range.

5.8   Pass through Porters Gap (5,500 feet), near junction of Porters Mountain and state-line ridge.

5.9   Cross crest of Porters Mountain on Tennessee side.

6.1   Cross spur of ridge on Tennessee side, and continue descent.

6.5   After drop of 100 feet from Porters Mountain, reach False Gap (5,400 feet). Ascend steeply for 0.3 mile, and then more gradually.

7.5   Pass around side of Laurel Top (5,865 feet).

7.8   Cross Woolly Tops Lead. Descend again, after having gained 400 feet in elevation since leaving False Gap.

9.1   On state line is Bradleys View, with unusually fine views into deep-cut gorge of Bradley Fork and over mountains in North Carolina.

9.6   Commence ascent around Pecks Corner. Come to junction of Hughes Ridge and state-line range. Behind are good views of

Laurel Top and the Sawteeth Range, with Mt. LeConte visible through False Gap.

9.9   Cross unnamed ridge on North Carolina side.

10.2   Cross Hughes Ridge.

10.4   Keep straight ahead at junction with graded Hughes Ridge Trail. Hughes Ridge Trail goes to **Pecks Corner Shelter**, formerly Hughes Ridge Shelter. Built-in bunks accommodate 12; spring nearby. To reach shelter, follow graded Hughes Ridge Trail south for 0.4 mile to gap, and then turn left, downhill, 100 yards in beech woods. Beyond, Hughes Ridge Trail continues to **Smokemont Campground**.

10.6   Follow state line with good views of Eagle Rocks and Mounts Sequoyah, Chapman, and Guyot.

10.9   Swing to North Carolina side around western peak of Eagle Rocks (5,900 feet).

11.3   Reach spectacular view of precipitous Tennessee slope and sharp gorges carved out by headwaters of Eagle Rocks Creek. Trail has ascended 500 feet from gap just west of Pecks Corner and Hughes Ridge.

11.4   At northern end of Eagle Rocks, water can be found about 800 feet down North Carolina side.

12.1   Enter Copper Gap (5,650 feet).

12.4   Cross Old Troublesome, a spur off Tennessee side of Mt. Sequoyah.

13.1   Cross high point of Mt. Sequoyah (6,000 feet).

13.8   Reach Chapman Gap (5,650 feet). From Chapman Gap, follow North Carolina side.

14.6   Reach high point of Trail on Mt. Chapman, having climbed 600 feet from Chapman Gap.

15.5   Reach Big Cove Gap (5,825 feet). Ascend Tri-Corner Knob.

15.6   Reach trail junction. To follow A.T., bear left. Right leads 100 yards to **Tri-Corner Knob Shelter** on North Carolina side. Built-in bunks accommodate 12; spring nearby.

15.8   Reach junction with side trail. A.T. turns left. To right is graded Balsam Mountain Trail to Hyatt Ridge. **Laurel Gap Shelter** is 7.0 miles via this trail; accommodates 14; spring nearby. Swing to Tennessee side, and climb around side of 6,100-foot Tri-Corner Knob. Tri-Corner Knob is at junction of two major ranges, the Smoky and the Balsam, and was given its name by geographer Arnold Guyot. Balsam Mountain, leading off from knob, forms boundary between Swain and Haywood counties of North Carolina.

16.2   Follow state line through sharp-ridged gap between Tri-Corner Knob and Mt. Guyot, with fine views into North Carolina, particularly of Mt. Sterling and North Carolina side of Hell Ridge. Follow Tennessee slope of Mt. Guyot.

16.8   Cross Guyot Spur. Elevation here is 6,360 feet, highest point on A.T. in eastern part of Great Smokies, but 261 feet below summit of Mt. Guyot. From last gap, there has been net ascent of 290 feet.

17.4   Reach Guyot Spring.

17.5   Faint, ungraded trail, badly obstructed by blowdowns, leads right, up northern slope of Mt. Guyot (6,621 feet). Climb about one hour to reach top of second-highest peak in Great Smokies. After dropping 130 feet from Guyot Spur, reach gap between Guyot and Old Black.

17.9   Cross Pinnacle Lead, a spur off Tennessee side of Old Black. Pinnacle Lead forms boundary between Sevier and Cocke counties of Tennessee. From here to Davenport Gap, in the main, Trail descends. Note pleasing view of English Mountain in Tennessee and of valley sections at foot of Great Smokies.

18.3   Enter Hell Ridge, so named because of devastation resulting from forest fire on North Carolina side along four-mile section of ridge, following timbering operations.

18.5   Follow state line through Deer Creek Gap (6,020 feet), with good views, particularly of Mt. Guyot, Luftee Knob, Balsam Corner, and Mt. Sterling, with their sharply defined ridges reaching down to Big Creek.

19.1   Reach Yellow Creek Gap. Swing around slope of Inadu Knob (5,941 feet). "Inadu" means "snake" in Cherokee and refers to snake dens on the mountainside.

19.4   Keep straight ahead at junction with Trail on Tennessee side. (Trail to left, Snake Den Ridge Trail, leads past Maddron Bald Trail and down Snake Den Mountain to **Cosby Campground**. A spring is about 0.8 mile down this trail; descent from A.T. to spring is gradual.) Swing to Tennessee side around wooded side of Camel Hump Knob (5,250 feet).

21.8   Reach Camel Gap (4,645 feet). Side trail on North Carolina side, Camel Gap Trail, leads down to Big Creek and Walnut

Bottoms. Pass around forested side of Ross Knob (5,025 feet), on Tennessee side.

22.5   Forest growth on Tennessee side changes from coniferous to deciduous, largely oaks, beeches, maples, and a few chestnuts that survived the blight.

22.8   Pass around North Carolina side of Cosby Knob (5,145 feet). Trail passes out of fire-denuded Hell Ridge and through virgin forests on both sides.

23.3   **Cosby Knob Shelter** is 150 feet to right. Built-in bunks accommodate 12; spring nearby.

23.4   Water crosses Trail.

24.0   Reach Low Gap (4,242 feet), having descended 758 feet from Cosby Knob. (From Low Gap, side trails lead down into both states. On North Carolina side, Walnut Bottoms Trail follows Low Gap Branch and then swings west near Walnut Bottoms; on Tennessee side, Cosby Trail follows Cosby Creek 2.5 miles to **Cosby Campground**.)

24.6   Cross crest of Rocky Face Mountain, spur on Tennessee side. In 0.5 mile, cross spur of Tennessee side of Sunup Knob (5,050 feet). Beyond are fine views in all directions.

25.9   After gaining 758 feet in ascent from Low Gap, cross high point (about 5,000 feet), and begin long descent toward Davenport Gap.

26.1   Where A.T. bears right, side trail continues ahead 0.6 mile along state line to historic tower on Mt. Cammerer, formerly White Rock, at eastern end of Great Smokies.

26.6   Pass spring. Just beyond, uphill, is small site used as a camp by CCC in constructing Mt. Cammerer tower.

28.1   Pass through gap in spur off North Carolina side of Mt. Cammerer. Descending along side of high rock cliff is spectacular trail construction.

28.2   Side trail leads right 50 yards to spring.

28.5   Lower Mt. Cammerer Trail from **Cosby Campground**, 7.8 miles distant, enters on Tennessee side.

29.4   Chestnut Branch Trail leads 2.0 miles to Big Creek Ranger Station and **campground**.

30.4   Pass trail leading 100 yards left to **Davenport Gap Shelter**. Built-in bunks accommodate 12; spring nearby.

31.1   Cross small clearing. Water is in field to right and below Trail.

31.3 Reach Davenport Gap (1,975 feet), at northeastern end of Great Smoky Mountains National Park, end of section. To continue on A.T., follow N.C. 284 (Tenn. 32), 20 yards to right, cross highway, and take Trail up ramp.

Newfound Gap (U.S. 441) to
Little Tennessee River (Fontana Dam)
Section Eighteen
39.2 miles

Brief Description of Section

This section of the Trail, from the northern end at Newfound Gap to Clingmans Dome (7.9 miles), was constructed by the CCC in 1939-40. This portion of the Trail generally follows the state line on the crest of the ridges and lies on the northern side of the highway that was constructed from Newfound Gap to the Forney Ridge parking area on the southern slope of Clingmans Dome. The highway is rarely visible from the Trail. This link replaces an earlier route that had become unsatisfactory after the road's construction.

From Clingmans Dome, the Trail follows the main crest of the Smokies to Silers Bald. West of Silers Bald, the Trail passes through several open gaps and bald knobs, the most prominent of which is Thunderhead. It was cleared as a fire trail by the NPS in 1931. Use of the Trail, even over the balds, has worn a footway that indicates the route. In addition, the route is marked with white-paint blazes.

Since the route generally follows the state line as far as Doe Knob, the slopes are designated as North Carolina and Tennessee.

After 31.7 miles from Newfound Gap, the Trail leaves the crest of the Great Smokies and turns south along a spur ridge, crossing Shuckstack to reach the Little Tennessee River at Fontana Dam.

Points of Interest

This section traverses the western half of the Great Smoky Mountains National Park and contains some of the finest peaks of the Great Smokies—the balds. Particularly impressive are Thunderhead and Spence Field. Views from the tower on Clingmans Dome, the highest peak in the Great Smokies (6,643 feet), from the balds, and from the firetower on Shuckstack are outstanding. Clingmans Dome is also the highest point on the whole A.T.

Beyond Clingmans Dome, in marked contrast to the coniferous forests of the eastern Great Smokies, the Trail passes through typical southern Appalachian hardwood forests. Some of the Trail is along a grass-grown ridge dotted with mature timber, affording delightful travel.

Situated in the center of a bowl of high surrounding mountains, Shuckstack has one of the most extraordinary outlooks in the southern Appalachians. The crest line of the Great Smokies from Thunderhead to Clingmans Dome is prominent. Hangover, southwest of the Great Smokies, is particularly impressive. To the south are the extensive high mountains of the Nantahala National Forest. Below is Fontana Lake.

Road Approaches

The northern end of the section is at Newfound Gap on the Tennessee-North Carolina state line. U.S. 441 crosses the gap 55 miles south of Knoxville, Tenn., 16 miles south of Gatlinburg, Tenn., and 20 miles north of Cherokee, N.C. No scheduled bus service is available through Newfound Gap.

The southern end of the section is at Fontana Dam on the Little Tennessee River. Fontana Village Resort, P. O. Box 68, Fontana Dam, N.C. 28733, is three miles from the southern end of this section, with stores, cafeteria, post office, and excellent accommodations available. The village is 39 miles west of Bryson City, N.C., by U.S. 19 for 14 miles and N.C. 28 for 25 miles. Fontana Village may also be reached by taking U.S. 129 south 37 miles to Deals Gap on the Tennessee-North Carolina state line and then N.C. 28 east for nine miles. No bus service is available to Fontana Village.

Maps

Refer to Trails Illustrated Great Smoky Mountains National Park Map, accompanying this guide, for route navigation. For additional area detail, refer to USGS Clingmans Dome, North Carolina-Tennessee; Silers Bald, North Carolina-Tennessee; Thunderhead, North Carolina-Tennessee; Cades Cove, North Carolina-Tennessee; and Fontana Dam, North Carolina, quadrangles.

Shelters, Campsites, and Water

This section has eight shelters (three on side trails) and 19 water sources. The shelters are:

Miles from Newfound Gap	Shelter
4.5	Mt. Collins
10.8	Double Spring Gap
12.5	Silers Bald
18.0	Derrick Knob
24.3	Spence Field
26.8	Russell Field
29.4	Mollies Ridge
34.0	Birch Spring

On the TVA Fontana Dam reservation, just south of the dam (the end of the section), is a shelter (constructed in 1980) that accommodates 20, has a picnic area, and, at the visitors center, showers.

Public Accommodations and Supplies

Only public restrooms are available at Newfound Gap. From the parking area at the crest of Newfound Gap, it is 16 miles to Gatlinburg, Tenn., which has motels, restaurants, and sources of supplies. The park headquarters is located two miles west of Gatlinburg.

Fontana Village (Fontana Dam, N.C. 28733) is three miles from the southern end of this section, with stores, cafeteria, post office, and accommodations.

History

At Indian Gap, trail-like remains of an old road built with Indian labor by Colonel William Thomas during the Civil War cross the Trail and the state line. This is the original transmountain road. It was built for obtaining saltpeter from Alum Cave Bluff, in an unsuccessful attempt to supply Confederate armies then under siege in eastern Virginia.

The correct location of Mt. Collins was once a subject of some controversy. An early USGS map had placed Mt. Collins east of Indian Gap (presently Mt. Kephart). Considering the peak between Indian Gap and Clingmans Dome as nameless, Asheville citizens sponsored a movement to name it Mt. Kephart in honor of Horace Kephart, noted authority on the southern Appalachians. A Guyot manuscript and map disclosed that this peak had been originally named Mt. Collins, and this name was restored. At the suggestion of the Tennessee Nomenclature Committee, the U.S. Geographic Board applied the name of Kephart to the prominent peak three miles east of Newfound Gap.

A spot about 0.2 mile west of the summit of Mt. Collins was once the site of Meigs Post. This was the starting point of Return J. Meigs' survey in 1802, the exact location of which, whether at this point or at Miry Ridge, was an issue in litigation involving the ownership of extensive timber lands.

Clingmans Dome formerly was known as Smoky Dome. It was renamed for Thomas Lanier Clingman, U.S. senator, mining prospector, and Civil War general who explored these mountains during the 1850s and extolled their virtues.

The Bote Mountain Trail is the old Anderson Road. The road derives its name from the founder and former president of Maryville College. Anderson promoted the construction of this road from Tuckaleechee Cove up Bote Mountain to the state line. The word "Bote" designates the ridge that the majority of the Cherokee Indian labor force building the road voted the route should follow. Having no "v" sound in their language, they indicated their choice by saying "bote."

Precautions

This section is only slightly more than 39 miles long, but, because of its many ascents and descents, allow at least three days for its traverse. The route is easier to hike north to south because of the large difference in elevation between the two ends of the section.

Across the balds, the route is unmistakable in clear weather, but, when it is cloudy, foggy, or dark, it is necessary to watch paint blazes.

Trail Description, North to South

Miles   Data

0.0   From junction of Newfound Gap Road and Trail from Davenport Gap, cross parking area to its western end, and descend through opening in guard wall at northwest side of parking area. Follow graded Trail, paralleling Clingmans Dome Road, which extends 7.6 miles to Forney Ridge parking area on southern slope of Clingmans Dome. Highway is to the left; pass rock retaining wall on left.

0.5   Continue straight ahead, where abandoned Thomas Ridge Trail leads left through tunnel under road. Ascend along Tennessee slope through beech and spruce forest.

0.9   At ridge top, old trail (former A.T.) enters on left. Beyond, ascend slope of Mt. Mingus with view of Mt. LeConte through balsam trees to right.

1.2   Reach crest of Mt. Mingus ridge; follow crest, and bear left. (Obscure trail to right leads to summit of Mt. Mingus, 5,802 feet.) From crest, descend North Carolina slope through balsam, with glimpse of road 100 feet to left.

1.6   Turn sharp left, after bearing right across state line.

1.7   Reach Indian Gap, and cross grassy open slope on Tennessee side. (Road from Newfound Gap to parking area on slope of Clingmans Dome, is on crest to left; fine view of North Carolina side. Old road crosses Trail here. On Tennessee side, old road is known as Road Prong Trail. It is 3.3 miles to Newfound Gap Road at Chimneys parking area.) At Indian Gap, enter woods on western slope and ascend Tennessee side, following graded Trail.

1.8   Turn sharp left onto state-line ridge.

1.9   Keep right; left is old trail along crest.

2.2   Reach Little Indian Gap. Follow state-line ridge for next 1.9 miles.

4.1   Trail leads left 35 yards to road and Fork Ridge Trail.

4.5   Take left fork. (Sugarland MountainTrail to right leads to **Mt. Collins Shelter** 0.5 mile down this trail. Built-in bunks accommodate 12; spring nearby.

5.0   Reach summit of Mt. Collins (6,188 feet). Descend gradually from Mt. Collins, then descend steeply.

5.6   Reach Collins Gap (5,886 feet). Trail on Tennessee slope skirts road, which is on state line.

6.7   Reach summit of Mt. Love (6,446 feet), then descend into gap (6,366 feet) at east base of Clingmans Dome. Beyond, ascend steeply to summit.

7.9   Reach Clingmans Dome (6,643 feet), highest point on A.T. Rare mountain cranberry is abundant here. (Side trail to left leads 50 yards to observation tower, providing a splendid view above red spruce and fir trees. From tower, paved path leads downhill 0.5 mile to Forney Ridge parking area at end of road, 7.6 miles from Newfound Gap.) Continue ahead, then descend slightly along narrow ridgecrest to gap at north base of Mt. Buckley, with fine view over East, or Main Prong of Little River on Tennessee side; Mt. LeConte is most prominent peak visible here.

8.3   Reach wide trail on left. This is Clingmans Dome Bypass Trail, leading 1.0 mile to Forney Ridge Trail, on which it is 1.5 miles to Andrews Bald and 11.5 miles to Fontana Lake; also leads to Forney Ridge parking area. Andrews Bald is one of two maintained balds that will remain grassy, open areas.

8.4   Ascend to summit of Mt. Buckley (6,582 feet). Descend steeply for 0.2 mile; then follow along ridge at head of Steel Trap Creek on North Carolina side (burned over in 1925).

8.8   Follow narrow ridgecrest.

10.2   Pass, on Tennessee side, junction of Goshen Prong Trail (leads to Goshen Prong of Little River and 10.0 miles to Elkmont). Descend slightly.

10.8   Reach Double Spring Gap (5,507 feet) and **Double Spring Gap Shelter.** (Built-in bunks for 12.) Gap is named for two springs, one on each slope, 15 yards from crest on North Carolina slope and 35 yards on Tennessee side. From gap, ascend through beech woods toward open knob east of Silers Bald. Beyond, vegetation changes: Spruce and fir growth becomes less dense and is succeeded by hardwoods, mainly beech.

11.3   Cross Jenkins Knob. Ahead is magnificent view of Silers Bald with Welch Ridge and High Rocks to left, Miry Ridge to right, and Thunderhead in background. Beyond this knob, few conifers are seen along Trail. Follow narrow, semiopen crest, crossing "The Narrows," where Trail has a devious course along ridgecrest, dropping a short distance down on Tennessee side to avoid ledges. Ascend through dense beech growth.

12.1   Take less-worn right fork uphill along backbone of ridge. (Left is graded Welch Ridge Trail, which leads 7.5 miles to High Rocks and 16.0 miles to Fontana Lake at Hazel Creek. Use care here.) Ascend on switchbacks through dense woods.

12.3   Reach open crest of Silers Bald (5,607 feet) and panoramic view. Silers Bald is named for Siler family, who pastured cattle on it in summer, driving them up Welch Ridge. From crest, bear slightly left along open slope, and then bear right, descending along path through narrow, open field.

12.5   At edge of woods, trail to right leads 100 yards to spring. Just beyond this trail, pass **Silers Bald Shelter** on right. (Built-in bunks accommodate 12.) Beyond shelter, follow ridgecrest through beech woods.

15.2   Descend steeply to Buckeye Gap (4,817 feet). Faint trails on both sides; water is 200 yards down North Carolina slope.

15.4   Reach graded Miry Ridge Trail on right, which leads 8.2 miles to public road at Elkmont, former summer resort. Keep on left fork.

16.0   Cross Cold Spring Knob (5,240 feet).

17.5   Skirt North Carolina slope of Mt. Davis, formerly known as Greenbrier Knob. Descend.

17.8   Reach Sams Gap (4,840 feet). Graded Greenbrier Ridge Trail enters from right, leading 8.3 miles to public road via Middle Prong Trail above Tremont Ranger Station. A good spring is 100 yards down and to left of Greenbrier Ridge Trail.

17.9   Cross spur of knob; then enter open field at far corner of Tennessee side.

18.0   Pass **Derrick Knob Shelter on right**. Built-in bunks accommodate 12; spring nearby. Shelter is located where herder's cabin once stood. Water is 50 yards to right on Tennessee slope. Cross overgrown field.

18.1   Enter woods at far corner of field. From Derrick Knob Shelter to Thunderhead, Trail is more strenuous.

18.3   Cross Chestnut Bald.

19.1   Reach Sugar Tree Gap (4,435 feet). (Note sugar maples.)

19.9 Enter Starkey Gap (4,500 feet). Now wooded, it was formerly grassy.

20.7 Bear left along North Carolina slope of wooded Brier Knob (5,215 feet), and descend.

20.8 Pass ledge, with view into North Carolina, into semiopen sag. Descend steeply along worn trail, skirting Tennessee slope of knob.

21.5 Enter Mineral Gap (5,030 feet).

22.2 Enter Beechnut Gap. Water is 75 yards down Tennessee slope.

22.5 Ascend through laurel and rhododendron toward eastern summit of Thunderhead. Reach summit of Thunderhead (5,527 feet). (Triangulation marker is here.) Shortly after, reach open ridge, and descend gradually with woods on left. Follow open ridgecrest. Trail leads for some two miles along open grass-grown crest, interspersed with wooded sections. Route on worn path is unmistakable in clear weather, but it is necessary to watch paint blazes on rocks when vision is restricted by fog or darkness. Views from Thunderhead are outstanding.

23.1 Cross Rocky Top (5,441 feet), which has views of Fontana Lake. Descend between jutting boulders, and bear right. Reach peak, and turn right down slope. Watch carefully for this turn, particularly in foggy or rainy weather.

23.9 In grassy sag, Jenkins Ridge Trail leads left 6.0 miles to the Lakeshore Trail at Pickens Gap. Follow right fork from intersection.

24.3 Pass Bote Mountain Trail on right, which is an excellent connection between Cades Cove and A.T. (At 0.2 mile below A.T., beside Bote Mountain Trail, is spring.) From junction with Bote Mountain Trail, bear left, and ascend field with splendid views. Spence Field is often considered the western end of Thunderhead. Almost immediately, pass Eagle Creek Trail, which leads left 8.0 miles to Fontana Lake. **Spence Field Shelter** is 250 yards down this trail on Spence Cabin Branch of Gunna Creek, tributary of Eagle Creek. Built-in bunks accommodate 12; spring nearby. Enter woods, and follow wide trail through sparse timber toward Little Bald. This section is very pleasant in which to travel.

25.4   Reach Little Bald. Turn left through meadow (splendid southern views), and, after 70 yards, turn right. Continue across meadow, and enter woods.

26.5   Enter open McCampbell Gap (4,328 feet), and, at edge of woods at far end of clearing, skirt North Carolina side of wooded McCampbell Knob.

26.8   Reach eastern end of Russell Field. (Graded Russell Field Trail to right leads 4.8 miles to Cades Cove Picnic Area via Anthony Creek Trail.) **Russell Field Shelter** is located at trail intersection. (Built-in bunks accommodate 14; spring is 150 yards down trail toward Cades Cove.) Skirt North Carolina side of Russell Field in woods.

27.3   Enter Big Abrams Gap (4,080 feet).

27.5   Reach top of knob; then descend steeply.

27.7   Enter Little Abrams Gap (4,120 feet). Ascend, switching back to grass-grown trail toward summit of Locust Knob.

29.1   Cross Devils Tater Patch (4,775 feet).

29.4   At Gant Lot, pass **Mollies Ridge Shelter.** (Built-in bunks accommodate 12; spring nearby.) Trail descends steadily for next mile.

30.3   Reach Ekaneetlee Gap (3,842 feet), through which passed an early Cherokee route from valley towns to overhill towns. Abandoned trail to right, Ekaneetlee Branch Trail, leads to Cades Cove in 5.8 miles. Water is found 100 yards down Tennessee slope. From gap, ascend toward Powell Knob on worn trail, bearing right.

31.1   Begin to skirt North Carolina side of Powell Knob (4,439 feet).

31.3   Reach Mud Gap (4,260 feet). Within 50 yards, leave gap, and ascend Doe Knob.

31.7   Reach summit of Doe Knob (4,520 feet). (Gregory's Bald Trail leads 3.1 mile to Gregory's Bald, passing Rich Gap and intersection with Gregory Ridge Trail at 2.0 miles.) Major change in route begins. Trail leaves crest of Great Smokies and turns south along spur ridge, crossing Shuckstack Mountain to reach Little Tennessee River at Fontana Dam. Original A.T. route continued west over Gregory and Parson balds to Deals Gap.

31.8   Begin descent along spur ridge with deep ravine on left. Beyond are outstanding views of crest line of Smokies from

Thunderhead to Clingmans Dome. Ahead, Greer Knob is prominent.

32.4   Begin skirting right (west) slope of Greer Knob.

33.1   Return to ridgecrest on south slope of Greer Knob, and descend for 250 feet.

33.2   Reach gap where water is located 100 yards down slope on right. From gap, follow narrow ridgecrest.

34.0   Reach Birch Spring Gap (3,834 feet). **Birch Spring Shelter** is 100 yards to right down slope. (Built-in bunks accommodate 12; spring nearby.) Ahead is view of Shuckstack Mountain firetower. From gap, ascend steeply for 400 feet, then follow ridgecrest and descend.

34.3   Reach Red Ridge Gap.

34.9   Reach Sassafras Gap (3,653 feet). To left, Lost Cove Trail leads 3.5 miles to Eagle Creek and the Lakeshore Trail. To right, gravel road leads to Twenty-mile Creek and to N.C. 28 at point 3.7 miles from Deals Gap on U.S. 129. (From Shuckstack to Little Tennessee River, terrain appears on USGS Fontana Dam quadrangle. This map, however, was prepared prior to construction of graded trail up Shuckstack Ridge and does not show present route of A.T. along ridge.) From Sassafras Gap, follow south toward prominent firetower on Shuckstack Mountain (4,020 feet).

35.2   Come onto ridgecrest. To left, old road leads 0.1 mile to firewarden's cabin and firetower on crest of Shuckstack. (Firetower, by virtue of location on high side spur, presents one of the most extraordinary panoramic views of southern Appalachians. Crest line of Great Smokies from Thunderhead to Clingmans Dome is prominent. Hangover to southeast and mountains to south in Nantahala National Forest are particularly impressive. Tower overlooks Fontana Lake. This view is feature of relocated trail.) Continue straight ahead, descending on trail constructed by NPS in 1963.

35.4   Turn sharp left. Fantastic views to south.

36.0   Reach gap between Shuckstack and Little Shuckstack. Skirt around west side of Little Shuckstack.

36.3   At bend in Trail, unreliable water source is a few yards to left.

36.4   Reach ridgecrest, and turn right, descending gradually.

38.3   Unreliable spring is ten yards to right.

38.6   Reach hard-surfaced road. Turn right along road, and almost immediately reach intersection with dirt road (abandoned N.C. 288). Continue through intersection, and follow hard-surfaced road along lakeshore for 0.6 mile to northern end of Fontana Dam.

39.2   Hard-surfaced road leads downstream 0.2 mile to parking overlook, which has spectacular view of dam and powerhouse. Trail crosses dam. Continue on road past visitors center (showers and toilets) to reach **Fontana Dam Shelter** on left at top of hill. *(See Appalachian Trail Guide to North Carolina-Georgia.)*

Trail Description, South to North

Miles   **Data**

0.0   From end of Fontana Dam on northern bank of Little Tennessee River, follow hard-surfaced road to right along lakeshore for 0.6 mile. (Hard-surfaced road from northern end of dam leads downstream 0.2 mile to parking overlook, which has spectacular view of dam and powerhouse.)

0.6   Reach intersection with dirt road (abandoned N.C. 288). On far side of intersection, turn left off hard-surfaced road, and enter woods. Graded trail, constructed by NPS in 1963, ascends Shuckstack Ridge gradually, crossing old A.T. several times.

0.9   Unreliable spring is ten yards to left. Ascend.

2.7   Shuckstack firetower is visible ahead.

2.8   Begin skirting west side of Little Shuckstack.

2.9   In bend of Trail, unreliable water is few yards to right.

3.3   Reach gap between Little Shuckstack and Shuckstack.

3.6   Excellent southern view.

3.8   Turn sharp right, ascending.

4.0   Reach ridgecrest. To right, road leads 0.1 mile to NPS cabin and firetower on Shuckstack, 4,020 feet. A.T. continues straight ahead.

4.3   Reach Sassafras Gap (3,653 feet). To right, Lost Cove Trail leads 3.5 miles to Eagle Creek and the Lakeshore Trail. To left, gravel road leads to N.C. 28 at a point 3.7 miles from Deals Gap on U.S. 129.

4.6   Come onto crest, and ascend, then descend for 0.2 mile.

4.9   Reach Red Ridge Gap, ascend, and follow ridgecrest.

5.2   Reach Birch Spring Gap (3,834 feet). To left, 100 yards down slope on worn trail, is **Birch Spring Shelter**. Built-in bunks accommodate 12; spring nearby.

6.1   Reach gap at southern base of Greer Knob. Spring is 100 yards to left down slope. From gap, ascend for 250 feet along crest.

6.2   Skirt western slope of Greer Knob for next 0.6 mile.

7.2   Reach sag at base of main crest of Great Smokies, and ascend steeply.

7.5   Reach crest of ridge. Turn sharp right, and reach Doe Knob in 400 feet. On Doe Knob (4,520 feet) is crest of Great Smokies. (Route turns right, east, and follows ridgecrest for 31.7 more miles to Newfound Gap. On left, Gregory Bald Trail comes in, 3.1 miles from Gregory Bald.) From Doe Knob, follow along level crest for 0.1 mile, then descend.

7.9   Reach Mud Gap (4,260 feet), then skirt North Carolina side of Powell Knob (4,439 feet).

8.1   Descend gradually for 0.7 mile.

8.9   Reach Ekaneetlee Gap (3,842 feet), through which passed an early Cherokee route from valley towns to overhill towns. Abandoned trail to left leads 5.8 miles to Cades Cove. Water is 100 yards down Tennessee slope. Ascend steeply from Ekaneetlee Gap for 0.3 mile on narrow trail. Beyond, ascend gradually along open ridge through sparse timber on wide trail.

9.8   Reach **Mollies Ridge Shelter**. Built-in bunks accommodate 12; spring nearby.

10.1   Cross Devils Tater Patch (4,775 feet), and follow open, grassy ridgecrest.

10.3   Cross Locust Knob.

11.5   Reach Little Abrams Gap (4,120 feet), and ascend steeply.

11.9   Reach Big Abrams Gap (4,080 feet), and ascend steadily.

11.8   Skirt North Carolina side of Russell Field in woods below edge of field.

12.4   At far end of Russell Field, bear right. Graded Russell Field Trail to left leads 4.8 miles to Cades Cove picnic area via Anthony Creek Trail. **Russell Field Shelter** is at trail intersection. Built-in bunks accommodate 14. Spring is 150 yards down trail to Cades Cove.

12.7   Reach grassy McCampbell Gap (4,328 feet).

13.8   Reach edge of meadow (Little Bald) with excellent southern views; turn left for 70 yards, and leave meadow. Turn right, and enter woods. Follow along flat crest through open woods, descending slightly, and enter grassy Spence Field, which is often considered the western end of Thunderhead. Splendid views.

14.9   Keep left. Eagle Creek Trail on right leads eight miles back to Fontana Lake. **Spence Field Shelter** is 250 yards down this trail on Spence Cabin Branch of Gunna Creek, tributary of Eagle Creek. (Built-in bunks accommodate 12; spring nearby.) On left, pass graded Bote Mountain Trail. (Makes connections to Cades Cove in 4.9 miles; Laurel Creek Road, 7.2 miles. A spring is 0.2 mile below A.T., beside Bote Mountain Trail.) Keep slightly to right in open Spence Field. Splendid views. Descend steeply.

15.3   Enter grassy sag. Jenkins Ridge Trail to right leads 6.0 miles to Lakeshore Trail at Pickens Gap. From Spence Field, Trail passes for two miles along Thunderhead. Route on worn path is unmistakable in clear weather, but watch paint blazes on rocks when vision is restricted by fog or darkness. From sag, ascend grassy and overgrown slope.

16.1   Reach summit of Rocky Top (5,441 feet), and ascend between jutting boulders. View of Fontana Lake.

16.7   Reach rhododendron-clad summit of Thunderhead (5,527 feet). Triangulation marker is here.

17.0   Reach Beechnut Gap. Water is 75 yards down Tennessee slope.

17.7   Reach Mineral Gap (5,030 feet).

18.4   Pass through semiopen sag; pass ledge with fine views of North Carolina side.

18.5   Swing around North Carolina slope of wooded Brier Knob (5,215 feet). No trail to summit. Return to crest, and descend very steeply.

19.3   Reach Starkey Gap (4,500 feet), formerly grassy, now wooded. Climb gradually along North Carolina slope.

20.1   Enter Sugar Tree Gap (4,435 feet). Note sugar maples here. Ascend along crest.

20.7   Pass through slight gap with good views of North Carolina.

20.9   Cross Chestnut Bald, with views on North Carolina slope.

21.1   Enter overgrown field.

21.2   Reach **Derrick Knob Shelter** on left. (Built-in bunks accommodate 12; spring nearby. Shelter is located where herder's cabin used to stand.) Keep left. Beyond shelter, enter woods.

21.4   Enter Sams Gap (4,840 feet). Take right fork. (Left is graded Greenbrier Ridge Trail, which leads 8.3 miles down to public road via Middle Prong Trail above Tremont Ranger Station. A good spring is 100 yards down and to left of Greenbrier Ridge Trail.) Continue along crest.

21.7   Swing around North Carolina side of Mt. Davis, formerly Greenbrier Knob.

23.2   Reach Cold Spring Knob (5,240 feet).

23.8   Pass Miry Ridge Trail on left, which leads 9.2 miles to Elkmont, former summer resort.

24.0   Reach Buckeye Gap (4,817 feet). Faint trail here on both sides; water may be found about 200 yards down North Carolina slope. Follow crest, alternately climbing and descending gradually through beech woods.

26.7   Reach **Silers Bald Shelter**. (Built-in bunks accommodate 12.) Just beyond shelter, trail to left leads 100 yards to spring. Beyond side trail to spring, bear left.

26.9   Cross crest of Silers Bald (5,607 feet). Silers Bald is named for family who pastured cattle on it in summer, driving them up Welch Ridge. Good view of Mt. LeConte on Tennessee side. To south is Welch Ridge; to east is good view of Clingmans Dome. High mountains are visible in all directions. Descend on switchbacks to east.

27.0   Enter beech woods.

27.1   Pass Welch Ridge Trail on North Carolina side (leads about 7.5 miles to High Rocks and 16 miles back to Fontana Lake). Continue on well-worn trail, passing through two small, grassy meadows from which good views of Silers Bald and other mountains can be seen.

27.9   Reach Jenkins Knob. Use care here. Keep well to left, entering woods about 100 feet before reaching summit of Jenkins Knob. Descend gradually.

28.4   Reach Double Spring Gap (5,507 feet) and **Double Spring Gap Shelter**. (Built-in bunks accommodate 12.) Name of gap indicates the existence of two unreliable springs, one on each side of state line. Better spring is on North Carolina side, 15 yards from actual crest; on Tennessee side, it is 35 yards from crest. Both springs flow into Tennessee River. From Double Spring Gap, ascend slightly.

29.0   Pass junction of Goshen Prong Trail on left (Tennessee) side; leads to Goshen Prong of Little River and ten miles to Elkmont.

30.6   Climb through burned North Carolina side of slope at head of Steel Trap Creek, reentering virgin forest.

30.8   Cross summit of Mt. Buckley (6,582 feet). Reach gap at northern base of Mt. Buckley, with fine view of East, or Main, Prong of Little River on Tennessee side. Mt. LeConte is very prominent.

30.9   Pass wide trail on right. This is Clingmans Dome Bypass Trail leading 1.0 mile to Forney Ridge Trail, from which it is 1.5 miles to Andrews Bald and 11.5 miles to Fontana Lake; also leads to Forney Ridge parking area. Andrews Bald is one of two balds in the park being preserved as open grassy meadows. Continue along crest.

31.3   Reach Clingmans Dome (6,643 feet), highest point on A.T. Rare mountain cranberry is abundant here. Side trail to right leads 50 yards to observation tower, which provides splendid view above balsam fir trees. From tower, hard-surfaced path leads downhill 0.5 mile to Forney Ridge parking area at end of Clingmans Dome Road, 7.6 miles from Newfound Gap. From Clingmans Dome, descend steeply into gap. Beyond, ascend. Reach summit of Mt. Love (6,446 feet), then descend gradually.

33.6   Reach Collins Gap (5,886 feet). Beyond, ascend steeply; fine views.

34.2   Reach summit of Mt. Collins (6,188 feet). Summit overgrown; 100 feet before reaching summit is partial view over North Carolina side. From summit, descend.

34.7   Sugarland Mountain Trail comes in on left. **Mt. Collins Shelter** is 0.5 mile down this trail. Built-in bunks accommodate 12; spring nearby.

35.1   Trail to right leads 35 yards to road and Fork Ridge Trail.

37.0   Reach Little Indian Gap. Ascend.

37.5   Reach Indian Gap. Old road crosses state line here. On Tennessee side, old road is known as Road Prong Trail; it leads 3.3 miles to Chimneys parking area on Newfound Gap Road.

38.0   Bear right. Old, obscure trail leading to summit of Mt. Mingus (5,802 feet) leads to left.

38.3   Reach crest of Mt. Mingus Ridge. Beyond, descend slope, with views of Mt. LeConte through balsam trees to left. Descend along Tennessee slope through beech and spruce forest.

38.7   Continue ahead where abandoned Thomas Ridge Trail to right leads through tunnel under road. Continue on Trail, paralleling road and rock retaining wall on right.

39.2   Reach parking area at crest of ridge in Newfound Gap. Cross parking area to Trail on opposite (east) side, which has magnificent panoramic view. Particularly noteworthy is the Balsam Range, "master" crosschain of Great Smokies.

Side Trails of Great Smoky Mountains National Park

Side trails in this chapter include all the trails that branch directly from the A.T. and most of those that diverge from them. The listing begins at the northeastern end of the park at Davenport Gap and proceeds southwest to Fontana Dam. This covers a large part, but not all, of the 900-mile network of trails in the Great Smoky Mountains National Park. Detailed descriptions of more than 500 trails in the park are given in the *Hiker's Guide to the Smokies* by Dick Murlless and Constance Stallings (Sierra Club, 1973). While this particular book is out of print, it can still be found in libraries.

Most of the side trails are standard four-foot graded paths; a few are narrower, graded foot trails; and others are substandard. They may be good or quite rough in places and might be overgrown in summer.

With the discontinuance of the CCC decades ago, inadequate appropriations and consequent lack of personnel have meant curtailing much of the Trail maintenance in the Smokies. Even some of the less-used "grade A" trails may be overgrown in summer.

Trails originating at the A.T. are numbered and referred to as leading north (into Tennessee) or south (into North Carolina), although they do not necessarily follow these compass directions. Where such trails do not originate at a point named in the guide, a distance is given from the nearest named point. The diverging trails are lettered as subdivisions of the side trails from which they branch; their beginnings are marked by distances from the A.T.

1. *Chestnut Branch Trail.* Leads south 2.0 miles to Big Creek Road near ranger station and campground.

2. *Lower Mt. Cammerer Trail.* Leaves A.T. 2.9 miles west of Davenport Gap; leads north 7.4 miles to public road at Cosby Campground on easy grade, going around north side of Mt. Cammerer (formerly White Rock), through young forest growth.

3. *Mt. Cammerer Trail.* Leaves A.T. five miles west of Davenport Gap; leads northeast 0.6 mile along crest to Mt. Cammerer firetower. Passes through rhododendron, laurel, azalea, and over bare rock.

4. *Low Gap Trail.* Crosses A.T. at Low Gap; leads north 2.5 miles to public road at Cosby Campground. Passes through beech, birch, pine,

and, toward lower end, some large virgin hemlock. Also leads south 2.5 miles along Low Gap Branch to Big Creek Trail, at Walnut Bottoms; then down Big Creek Trail 5.1 miles to Big Creek Primitive Campground near village of Mount Sterling. Section from Walnut Bottoms to campground is on gravel road.

5. *Camel Gap Trail.* Leaves A.T. at Camel Gap; leads 10.1 miles to Big Creek Primitive Campground near Mount Sterling village. There are good views of Big Creek watershed. The last 5.1 miles from Walnut Bottoms is on Big Creek Trail.

6. *Snake Den Ridge Trail.* Leaves A.T. 2.3 miles west of Camel Gap on east slope of Inadu Knob; leads north 5.3 miles to Cosby Campground. First mile is through spruce-type forest.

6-A. *Maddron Bald Trail.* Leaves No. 6 at 0.8 mile north of A.T., crosses Maddron Bald, and leads 7.2 miles to U.S. 321.

7. *Balsam Mountain Trail.* Leaves A.T. at Tri-Corner Knob; leads south 10.8 miles to Pin Oak Gap, where it intersects Balsam Mountain Road. Open to one-way motor travel from Heintooga to Round Bottom, May through October. Left on this road, Balsam Mountain Campground is 8.5 miles; to right, public road at Round Bottom on Straight Fork is five miles. Laurel Gap Shelter is seven miles from A.T. via this trail; accommodates 14; spring nearby.

7-A. *Gunter Fork Trail.* Leaves No. 7 at 5.6 miles south of A.T.; leads left five miles to Walnut Bottoms.

7-B. *Mt. Sterling Ridge Trail.* Leaves No. 7 at 6.5 miles south of A.T.; leads left 7.2 miles to N.C. 284 at Mt. Sterling Gap.

7-C. *Beech Gap Trail.* Leaves No. 7 at 8.5 miles south of A.T.; leads right 3.5 miles to public road at Round Bottom on Straight Fork.

8. *Hughes Ridge Trail.* Leaves A.T. at Pecks Corner; leads south 12 miles to public road at Smokemont Campground. Route mostly through northern hardwoods; exceptional views of the Bradley Fork virgin hardwood forest. A fine stand of flame azalea is at five miles.

8-A. *Bradley Fork Trail.* Leaves No. 8 at 2.2 miles south of A.T.; leads right 7.5 miles via Taywa Creek and Bradley Fork to public road at Smokemont.

8-B. *Enloe Creek Trail.* Leaves No. 8 at 4.7 miles south of A.T.; leads left 3.6 miles to Hyatt Ridge Trail.

8-C. *Chasteen Creek Trail.* Leaves No. 8 at five miles south of A.T.; leads right 5.5 miles via Chasteen Creek to public road at Smokemont.

9. *Dry Sluice Gap Trail (formerly Richland Mountain Trail)*. Leaves A.T. at Dry Sluice Gap; leads south 3.8 miles to Cabin Flats Trail via Bradley Fork Trail to public road at Smokemont.

9-A. *Grassy Branch Trail*. Leaves No. 9 at 1.8 miles south of A.T.; leads right 4.5 miles to Newfound Gap Road via Grassy Branch and Kephart Prong. Kephart Shelter is 3.8 miles from A.T. via this trail; accommodates 14; creek water.

10. *Boulevard Trail*. Leaves A.T. at crest of A.T. on shoulder of Mt. Kephart; leads north 5.3 miles to Mt. LeConte. This is ridgecrest trail through spruce and fir with exceptional views of Porters Creek watershed. From points near LeConte's High Top, trails lead to Myrtle Point and to Cliff Top, with spectacular views. Many of LeConte's ledges are covered with dwarf rhododendron and sand myrtle. A lodge on Mt. LeConte is open from late March to early November, where primitive accommodations are available. (Write LeConte Lodge, Gatlinburg, Tenn. 37738, for information.) A shelter is beside Boulevard Trail near LeConte's High Top. Built-in bunks accommodate 12. Spring is down Trillium Gap Trail below LeConte Lodge; see below.

10-A. *Jump-Off Trail*. Leaves No. 10 at 0.1 mile north of A.T.; leads right 0.8 mile to the Jump-Off, rock ledge offering spectacular view into valleys of Porters Creek watershed, almost 1,000 feet below. Route also crosses summit at Mt. Kephart (6,200 feet). To reach the Jump-Off, cross summit of Mt. Kephart, and follow worn footway.

10-B. *Trillium Gap Trail*. Leaves Mt. LeConte; leads 6.5 miles to Roaring Fork Motor-Nature Trail—open to one-way motor traffic from Cherokee Orchard down Roaring Fork, May through October. At 3.6 miles (Trillium Gap), turns left.

10-E. *Rainbow Falls Trail*. Leaves Mt. LeConte; leads 6.5 miles to public road at Cherokee Orchard. First section is down Rocky Spur, with excellent views of valleys to the north. Passes Rainbow Falls.

10-G. *Alum Cave Bluff Trail*. Leaves Mt. LeConte; leads 5.2 miles to Grassy Patch on Newfound Gap highway from Gatlinburg. Near start of trail, evidence of cloudburst that occurred in September 1951 may still be seen. At three miles, trail passes under Alum Cave Bluff; at 4.2 miles, through Arch Rock. From just below bluff, "needle's eye" can be seen in ridge off to right.

11. *Sweat Heifer Creek Trail*. Leaves A.T. one mile west of crest of A.T. on shoulder of Mt. Kephart; leads south 5.7 miles to Newfound Gap Road via Sweat Heifer Creek and Kephart Prong. Extends through severely burned-over area, now growing into fire cherry and northern

hardwoods. Good views of Oconaluftee Valley. Kephart Shelter is beside this trail 3.7 miles from A.T. Built-in bunks accommodate 14 persons; creek water.

12. *Road Prong Trail.* Leaves A.T. at Indian Gap; leads north 3.3 miles to Newfound Gap Road at Chimneys parking area. A historic trail, it is the original transmountain road. Constructed by Colonel Thomas with Cherokee Indians during Civil War for general war purposes and to obtain saltpeter from Alum Cave Bluff, in an unsuccessful attempt to supply Confederate armies then under siege in eastern Virginia. Abundance of rhododendron among virgin hemlock and hardwoods in this area. Crosses Road Prong several times without footbridge.

12-A. *Chimneys Tops Trail.* Leaves No. 12 at 3.4 miles north of Trail; leads left about 1.1 miles to top of Chimneys.

13. *Fork Ridge Trail.* Leaves A.T. 0.8 mile east of Mt. Collins; leads south 14.7 miles to public road at Deep Creek Campground via Fork Ridge and Deep Creek to Bryson Place, 8.6 miles from A.T. First mile is through virgin spruce and fir; to Deep Creek Gap, through northern hardwoods; and to Bryson Place, through virgin hardwoods.

14. *Sugarland Mountain Trail.* Leaves A.T. 0.4 mile east of Mt. Collins; leads north 12.1 miles to Little River Road at Fighting Creek Gap. Excellent views of Mt. LeConte and Sugarland and Little River valleys.

14-A. *Rough Creek Trail.* Leaves No. 14 about 4.8 miles from A.T. Leads left 5.0 miles to public road one mile south of Elkmont. Lower three miles is on gravel road.

14-B. *Huskey Gap Trail.* Crosses No. 14 at about 9.0 miles from A.T.; leads left 2.1 miles to Little River Trail south of Elkmont. Leads right 2.0 miles to Newfound Gap Road.

15. *Clingmans Dome Trail.* Leads 50 yards to tower and then on a paved path 0.5 mile downhill to Forney Ridge parking area at end of Clingmans Dome Road, 7.6 miles from Newfound Gap.

16. *Clingmans Dome Bypass Trail.* Leads 1.0 mile to Forney Ridge Trail, which begins at the end of Clingmans Dome Road (road closed in winter).

17. *Forney Ridge Trail.* Leaves Forney Ridge parking area and leads 11.5 miles to Fontana Lake. Marvelous views of Forney Creek and Noland Creek valleys. At 1.5 miles, crosses Andrews Bald, example of famous bald with its large mountain meadow. At lower end of meadow, turn sharp right. Unreliable spring is on lower end (southwest corner) of Andrews Bald.

17-A. *Forney Creek Trail.* Leaves No. 17 at 1.0 miles south of Forney Ridge parking area; leads right 10.8 miles via Forney Creek to Fontana Lake. Last 4.0 miles are on gravel road.

17-B. *Springhouse Branch Trail.* Crosses No. 17 6.6 miles south of A.T.; leads left 3.0 miles to gravel road on Nolan Creek and right 4.0 miles via Bee Gum Branch to Forney Creek Trail.

18. *Goshen Prong Trail.* Leaves A.T. 0.8 mile east of Double Spring Gap; leads north ten miles to public road, one mile south of Elkmont. The first 0.2 mile is through spruce; 1.2 miles is through rhododendron and hemlock; balance is through hardwoods. The last 2.3 miles are on the Little River Trail.

19. *Welch Ridge Trail.* Leaves A.T. 0.2 mile east of Silers Bald; leads south 7.5 miles on crest of Welch Ridge to High Rocks. Traverses second-growth hardwoods and offers views of adjacent valleys. Ends at Cold Spring Gap Trail.

19-A. *Hazel Creek Trail.* Leaves No. 19 1.5 miles south of A.T. and leads 14.0 miles via Hazel Creek and Lakeshore Trails to Fontana Lake.

19-B. *Jonas Creek Trail.* Leaves No. 19 2.0 miles south of A.T.; leads left 4.5 miles to Forney Creek Trail. Follows Yanu Ridge and Jonas Creek.

19-C. *Bear Creek Trail.* Leaves No. 19 at 6.4 miles south of A.T.; leads left 6.8 miles to Fontana Lake. Follows Jump-up Ridge and Bear and Forney creeks.

20. *Miry Ridge Trail.* Leaves A.T. 0.1 mile west of Buckeye Gap; leads north 8.2 miles to public road at Elkmont. Follows Miry Ridge and Dripping Springs Mountain to Jakes Gap and then down Jakes Creek Trail.

20-A. *Lynn Camp Prong Trail.* Leaves No. 20 at 2.5 miles north of A.T.; leads left 2.4 miles to Middle Prong Trail above Tremont Ranger Station. Lower end is on gravel road. Large laurel is seen on this trail.

20-B. *Blanket Mountain Trail.* Leaves No. 20 at Jakes Gap, 4.9 miles north of A.T.; leads ahead 0.8 mile to Blanket Mountain.

20-C. *Panther Creek Trail.* Leaves No. 20 at Jakes Gap 4.9 miles north of A.T.; leads left 2.2 miles to Middle Prong Trail above Tremont Ranger Station.

21. *Greenbrier Ridge Trail.* Leaves A.T. 0.2 mile east of Derrick Knob Shelter; leads north 8.3 miles to public road via Middle Prong Trail above Tremont Ranger Station. Route is through beech woods for 0.2 mile and then in cutover area.

22. *Jenkins Ridge Trail.* Leaves A.T. at eastern end of Spence Field; leads 6.0 miles to Pickens Gap on Lakeshore Trail.

23. *Bote Mountain Trail.* Leaves A.T. near center of Spence Field; leads north 7.2 miles to Laurel Creek Road. First 0.5 mile is through beech and birch forest; 0.5 mile, through laurel and hemlock; one mile, laurel slick; balance, on gravel road through pine and hardwoods.

23-A. *Anthony Creek Trail.* Leaves No. 23 at 1.7 miles north of A.T.; leads left through hardwood forest 3.2 miles to public road in eastern end of Cades Cove. Lower end is on gravel road.

23-B. *Lead Cove Trail.* Leaves No. 23 at 2.9 miles and leads 1.8 miles to Laurel Creek Road.

23-C. *Finley Cane Trail.* Leaves No. 23 at 5.4 miles and leads 2.7 miles to Laurel Creek Road.

23-D. *West Prong Trail.* Leaves No. 23 at 6.0 miles north of A.T.; leads right 2.7 miles to public road on Middle Prong Little River, above Tremont Ranger Station.

24. *Eagle Creek Trail.* Leaves A.T. near center of Spence Field; leads south 8.0 miles to Fontana Lake.

25. *Russell Field Trail.* Leaves A.T. at Russell Field; leads north 4.8 miles to public road in eastern end of Cades Cove. First 0.5 mile is across grassy bald; then 0.5 mile, through virgin hardwood forest; one mile, on pine ridge (Leadbetter Ridge); then down Right Prong of Anthony Creek, through beautiful forest of hemlock and rhododendron. Growth is so dense and moss-covered it gives tropical effect. Lower 1.3 miles is on Anthony Creek Trail, No. 23-A.

26. *Gregory Bald Trail.* Leaves A.T. at Doe Knob; leads west 7.2 miles to Parson Branch Road (open to one-way traffic from Cades Cove to U.S. 129 May through October). Route from Doe Knob to Sheep Pen Gap is portion of former A.T. in western Great Smokies, which was abandoned when A.T. was relocated to cross Little Tennessee River at Fontana Dam. Passes through Rich Gap at 2.0 miles from the A.T. At 2.9 miles from A.T., Gregory Bald (4,948 feet) has, in late June, an outstanding display of azalea. The bald comprises about 200 acres and has a fine panoramic view. Cherokee Indians called this bald "Tsistuyi," the "rabbit place," where the chief of the rabbits ruled. When settlers first came, they grazed sheep here. Great Smoky Mountains National Park maintains this and Andrews Bald as open areas by cutting new growth.

26-A. *Long Hungry Ridge Trail*. Leaves No. 26 at Rich Gap (also known as "Gant Lot," the mountaineers' name for where cattle were corralled to be "hardened up" or "gaunted...ga'nted" before being driven from the mountains); leads south eight miles via Twenty-mile Trail to N.C. 28, 3.7 miles from Deals Gap on U.S. 129. Follows Long Hungry Ridge, Rye Patch Branch, and Twenty-mile Creek. Lower 3.3 miles is on gravel road.

26-B. *Gregory Ridge Trail*. Leaves No. 26 at Rich Gap; leads north 4.9 miles to Forge Creek Road in western end of Cades Cove. Follows Gregory Ridge for about 2.2 miles and then descends and follows Ekaneetlee Branch and Forge Creek. On ridge, it passes through hardwoods and pine and, upon reaching branch, through some of largest poplars and hemlocks in park.

26-C. *Wolf Ridge Trail*. Leaves No. 26 at 3.1 miles from A.T.; leads left about 0.8 mile to Parson Bald, peak similar to Gregory Bald but smaller. Leads south 6.5 miles to Twenty-mile Trail about 0.5 mile from ranger station and N.C. 28.

27. *Twenty-mile Trail*. Leaves A.T. at Sassafras Gap, 0.5 mile north of Shuckstack firetower; leads right 5.0 miles to N.C. 28, 3.7 miles from Deals Gap on U.S. 129. Follows Proctor Branch and Twenty-mile Creek. Lower 3.3 miles is on gravel road.

28. *Lost Cove Trail*. Leaves A.T. at Sassafras Gap and leads left 3.5 miles to Eagle Creek and the Lakeshore Trail.

Important Addresses

Appalachian Trail Conference
P.O. Box 807
Washington and Jackson Streets
Harpers Ferry, W.Va. 25425
(304) 535-6331

ATC Regional Office
100 Otis Street
P.O. Box 2750
Asheville, N.C. 28802
(704) 254-3708

Carolina Mountain Club
P.O. Box 68
Asheville, N.C. 28802

Cherokee National Forest
Supervisor's Office
P.O. Box 2010
Cleveland, Tenn. 37320
(615) 476-9700

Cherokee National Forest
Nolichucky Ranger District
120 Austin Avenue
Greeneville, Tenn. 37743
(615) 638-4109

Cherokee National Forest
Watauga Ranger District
Route 9, Box 2235
Elizabethton, Tenn. 37643
(615) 542-2942

Cherokee National Forest
Unaka Ranger District
1205 North Main Street
Erwin, Tenn. 37650
(615) 743-4452

Great Smoky Mountains
National Park
Superintendent's Office
Route 2
Gatlinburg, Tenn. 37738
(615) 436-5615

Great Smoky Mountains
National Park
20-Mile Ranger Station
P.O. Box 66
Fontana, N.C. 28733
(704) 498-2327

Great Smoky Mountains
National Park
Big Creek Ranger Station
Newport, Tenn. 37821
(615) 486-5910

Great Smoky Mountains
National Park
Catalooche Ranger District
Route 2, Box 550
Waynesville, N.C. 28286

Nantahala Hiking Club
31 Carl Slagle Road
Franklin, N.C. 28734

Nantahala National Forest
Wayah Ranger District
8 Sloan Road
Franklin, N.C. 28734
(704) 524-6441

Nantahala National Forest
Cheoah Ranger District
Route 1, Box 16-A
Robbinsville, N.C. 28771
(704) 479-6431

Nantahala National Forest
Tusquitee Ranger District
201 Woodland Drive
Murphy, N.C. 28906
(704) 837-5152

Pisgah National Forest
Pisgah Ranger District
1001 Pisgah Highway
Pisgah Forest, N.C. 28768
(704) 877-3350

Pisgah National Forest
Toecane Ranger District
P.O. Box 128
Burnsville, N.C. 28714
(704) 682-6146

Pisgah National Forest
French Broad Ranger District
P.O. Box 128
Hot Springs, N.C. 28743
(704) 622-3202

Smoky Mountains Hiking Club
P.O. Box 1454
Knoxville, Tenn. 37901

Tennessee Eastman Hiking Club
P.O. Box 511
Kingsport, Tenn. 37662

TVA Map Sales
HB 1A, 1101 Market Street
Chattanooga, Tenn. 37402-2801
(615) 751-6277

National Forests in
North Carolina
P.O. Box 2750
Asheville, N.C. 28802-2750
(704) 257-4200

USGS Branch of Distribution
Box 25286
Federal Center
Denver, Colo. 80225
(303) 236-7477

Summary of Distances

North to South (read down)		South to North (read up)
0.0	U.S. 58, Damascus, Va.	287.9
3.5	Va.-Tenn. State Line	284.4
10.0	**Abingdon Gap Shelter**	277.9
11.1	McQueens Gap	276.8
11.5	McQueens Knob	276.4
14.8	Low Gap and U.S 421	273.1
18.2	**Double Springs Shelter,** Holston Mountain Trail	269.7
19.2	**Campsite**	268.7
21.7	Tenn. 91	266.2
24.9	Nick Grindstaff Monument	263.0
26.2	**Iron Mountain Shelter**	261.7
27.9	Turkeypen Gap	260.0
32.9	**Vandeventer Shelter**	255.0
37.3	Watauga Dam Road	250.6
38.2	Watauga Dam	249.7
39.2	**Watauga Lake Shelter**	248.7
40.7	Shook Branch Recreation Area	247.2
41.7	U.S. 321, Hampton, Tenn.	246.2
45.5	Big Pond Side Trail	242.4
46.5	**Campsites** on The Pond Flats	241.4
47.2	Side trail to U.S. 321	240.7
49.9	**Laurel Fork Shelter**	238.0
50.6	Laurel Falls	237.3
51.8	Dennis Cove, USFS 50	236.1
54.6	White Rocks Mountain Firetower	233.3
55.4	**Campsite**	232.5
57.6	**Moreland Gap Shelter**	230.3
59.0	**Campsite**	228.9
62.2	**Campsite**	225.7
62.7	Laurel Fork	225.2
63.4	**Campsite**	224.5

64.5	Walnut Mountain Road	223.4
66.7	**Sugar Branch Campsite**	221.2
67.7	Campbell Hollow Road	220.2
68.4	Buck Mountain Road	219.5
70.9	Bear Branch Road	217.0
71.2	U.S. 19E (to Elk Park, N.C./Roan Mountain, Tenn.)	216.7
71.7	**Apple House Shelter**	216.2
73.8	Doll Flats	214.1
76.2	Hump Mountain	211.7
77.1	Bradley Gap	210.8
77.7	Little Hump Mountain	210.2
79.5	**Yellow Mountain Gap Campsite**	208.4
	Overmountain Shelter side trail	
81.2	**Roan Highlands Shelter**, Low Gap	206.7
82.6	Grassy Ridge	205.3
84.2	Carvers Gap, Tenn. 143, N.C. 261	203.7
85.5	**Roan High Knob Shelter** side trail	202.4
86.1	Roan High Bluff	201.8
87.0	Ash Gap	200.9
88.8	Hughes Gap	199.1
90.1	Little Rock Knob	197.8
90.9	**Clyde Smith Shelter** side trail	197.0
92.8	Greasy Creek Gap	195.1
93.0	**Campsite**	194.9
96.9	Iron Mountain Gap, Tenn. 107, N.C. 226	191.0
98.1	Little Bald Knob	189.8
99.6	**Cherry Gap Shelter**	188.3
100.6	Low Gap	187.3
102.3	Unaka Mountain	185.6
103.3	USFS 230	184.6
103.9	Deep Gap	184.0
104.9	**Campsite**	183.0
105.2	Beauty Spot Gap	182.7
105.4	Beauty Spot	182.5
106.6	USFS 230	181.3
107.7	Indian Grave Gap	180.2
111.8	**Curley Maple Gap Shelter**	176.1
114.7	Nolichucky Expeditions	173.2
116.0	Nolichucky River, (Erwin, Tenn.)	171.9
119.3	Temple Hill Gap	168.6

121.7	**No Business Knob Shelter**	166.2
126.2	Spivey Gap, U.S. 19W	161.7
126.7	**Campsite**	161.2
127.8	High Rocks side trail	160.1
128.5	Whistling Gap	159.4
130.4	Little Bald	157.5
131.8	**Bald Mountain Shelter** side trail	156.1
132.7	**Big Stamp Campsite** side trail	155.2
132.9	Big Bald	155.0
135.7	Low Gap	152.2
137.0	Street Gap	150.9
138.9	Sams Gap, U.S. 23	149.0
140.6	High Rock	147.3
141.1	**Hogback Ridge Shelter**	146.8
142.2	Rice Gap	145.7
143.8	Frozen Knob	144.1
146.6	Boone Cove Road	141.3
147.1	Devil Fork Gap, N.C. 212	140.8
149.8	**Flint Mountain Shelter**	138.1
153.8	**Horse Creek Campground**	134.1
155.7	**Jerry Cabin Shelter**	132.2
159.1	Blackstack Cliffs side trail	128.8
161.1	Camp Creek Bald Firetower side trail	126.8
162.4	**Little Laurel Shelter**	125.5
165.7	Old Hayesville Road	122.2
167.3	Allen Gap, N.C. 208, Tenn. 70	120.6
171.0	**Spring Mountain Shelter**	116.9
172.7	Hurricane Gap	115.2
173.7	**Rich Mountain Firetower & Campsite** side trail	114.2
176.1	Tanyard Gap, U.S. 25 and 70	111.8
177.1	**Campsite**	110.8
178.7	Pump Gap	109.2
180.6	Lovers Leap Rock	107.3
182.0	Hot Springs, N.C. U.S. 25 and 70, N.C. 209	105.9
185.2	**Deer Park Mountain Shelter**	102.7
188.6	Garenflo Gap	99.3
192.3	Bluff Mountain	95.6
194.7	**Walnut Mountain Shelter**	93.2
196.0	Lemon Gap, N.C. 1182, Tenn. 107	91.9
196.5	**Roaring Fork Shelter**	91.4

201.4	Max Patch Mountain	86.5
202.2	N.C. 1182	85.7
204.9	Brown Gap	83.0
207.8	Deep Gap, **Groundhog Creek Shelter** side trail	80.1
209.8	**Campsite**	78.1
210.3	Snowbird Mountain side trail	77.6
211.8	Spanish Oak Gap	76.1
212.3	**Campsite**	75.7
212.7	**Painter Branch Campsite**	75.2
215.0	Waterville School Road	72.9
215.5	I-40 Underpass	72.4
215.8	Pigeon River	72.1
217.4	Davenport Gap, Tenn. 32, N.C. 284	70.5
218.3	**Davenport Gap Shelter**	69.6
221.6	Mt. Cammerer Tower side trail	66.3
225.4	**Cosby Knob Shelter**	62.5
226.0	Cosby Knob	61.9
229.3	Maddron Bald Trail	58.6
231.2	Side trail to Mt. Guyot	56.7
233.1	**Tri-Corner Knob Shelter**	54.8
234.1	Mt. Chapman	53.8
235.6	Mt. Sequoyah	52.3
238.3	**Pecks Corner Shelter**	49.6
239.6	Bradleys View	48.3
242.9	The Sawteeth	45.0
244.8	Charlies Bunion	43.1
245.7	**Icewater Spring Shelter**	42.2
246.0	Boulevard Trail	41.9
248.7	Newfound Gap, U.S. 440	39.2
250.4	Indian Gap	37.5
253.2	**Mt. Collins Shelter**	34.7
255.4	Mt. Love	32.5
256.6	Clingmans Dome	31.3
259.5	**Double Spring Gap Shelter**	28.4
261.0	Silers Bald	26.9
261.2	**Silers Bald Shelter**	26.7
263.9	Buckeye Gap	24.0
266.5	Sams Gap	21.4
266.7	**Derrick Knob Shelter**	21.2
267.8	Sugar Tree Gap	20.1

270.2	Mineral Gap	17.7
271.2	Thunderhead, East Peak	16.7
271.8	Rocky Top	16.1
273.0	**Spence Field Shelter**, Bote Mountain Trail	14.9
275.5	**Russell Field Shelter**	12.4
276.4	Little Abrams Gap	11.5
277.8	Devils Tater Patch	10.1
278.1	**Mollies Ridge Shelter**	9.8
279.0	Ekaneetlee Gap	8.9
280.4	Doe Knob	7.5
282.7	**Birch Spring Shelter**	5.2
283.9	Shuckstack Firetower side trail	4.0
287.9	Little Tennessee River, Fontana Dam, **Fontana Dam Shelter** (0.3 mile south)	0.0

Index

A

Abingdon, Va. 44-46
Abingdon Gap 47, 50
Abingdon Gap Shelter 45, 47, 50
Abingdon Road 47, 50
Albert Mountain 206
Allen Gap, N.C. 161-163, 167-168, 172-174, 176, 181
Alum Cave Bluff 224, 240-241
Alum Cave Bluff Trail 240
Andrews Bald 31, 236, 241, 243
Anthony Creek Trail 243
Appalachian Mountain Club 1
Appalachian Trail Conference ix, 2-4, 12-13
Appalachian Trailway News 3, 6
Apple House Shelter 82, 98-99, 108
Arch Rock 240
artificial respiration 18
Ash Gap 111-113
Asheville, N.C. 25, 141-144, 148-149, 155-156, 163, 173, 175, 183, 193, 210-211, 225
Avery, Myron H. 2

B

back or neck injuries 13
Backbone Rock 43, 47, 50
Bakersville, N.C. 98, 110, 116, 123
Bald Creek 41
Bald Mountain Campground 136
Bald Mountain Range 142, 186, 190
Bald Mountain Shelter 135, 144, 147, 151, 156
Bald Mountains 153, 155, 164, 171
Ball Ground 161, 165, 170
Balsam Corner 213, 219

Balsam Mountain 218
Balsam Mountain Campground 239
Balsam Mountain Trail 214, 218, 239
Bear Branch Road 81, 89
bears 201
Beartown Mountain 112-113
Bearwallow Creek 125, 132
Bearwallow Gap 161, 166, 169
Beauty Spot 123, 125, 127, 131
Beauty Spot Gap 124, 126-127, 131
Beaverdam Creek 43-44, 47, 51, 61
Beech Gap Trail 239
Beech Mountain 87, 90, 92, 101, 106
Beechnut Gap 229, 234
Big Abrams Gap 230, 233
Big Bald 25, 37, 41, 127, 131, 142-145, 147-151, 156, 163, 165, 170, 175
Big Bald Creek 147, 151
Big Butt 26, 29, 37, 143, 153, 161, 165, 170
Big Cove Gap 214, 218
Big Creek 211, 213, 219, 239
Big Creek Primitive Campground 239
Big Creek Ranger Station 193, 211-212, 220
Big Creek Road 166, 169, 238
Big Creek Trail 166, 169, 239
Big Firescald Knob 153, 166, 169
Big Flat 155-157, 159
Big Laurel Branch Wilderness 60, 64-65
Big Pigeon River 205, 208
Big Pine Mountain 81-82, 87, 91-92
Big Pond Trail 74, 79
Big Rock 170
Big Rock Spring 186, 190

Big Rock 165
Big Stamp 143, 145, 147-148, 150-151
Big Yellow Mountain 96, **105**
Birch Spring 224
Birch Spring Gap 231, 233
Birch Spring Shelter 231, 233
Bishop Hollow 89-90
Black Mountains 25, 97, 112-113, 131, 142, 166, 169, 183, 188, 200
Blackstack Cliff 161, 166, 169
Blanket Mountain 242
Blanket Mountain Trail 242
blazes 5
bleeding 14
blisters 14
Blood Mountain 206
Blood River 185, 191
Blue Ridge Divide 206
Blue Spring School 64-65
Bluff, N.C. 183, 185
Bluff Mountain 177, 179, 182-183, 185-186, 190-191
Boone Cove and Gap 155
Boone Cove Road 158
Bote Mountain 225
Bote Mountain Trail 225, 229, 234, 243
Boulevard Trail 215-217, 240
Bradley Fork 217, 239
Bradley Gap 96, 98, 101, 106
Bradleys View 215, 217
Braemar, Tenn. 70-72, 76, 81-82
Brier Knob 229, 234
Bright's Trace 97, 102, 105
Bristol, Tenn. 44-45, 52, 61
Brown Gap 25, 29, 192-195, 199
Browns Bridge 192, 211
Bryson City, N.C. 38, 204, 223
Bryson Place 241
Buck Mountain Road 76, 82, 85-86, 88, 90, 92-93
Buckeye Gap 103, 105, 207, 228, 235, 242

Buckeye Ridge 187, 189
Buffalo Mountain 128
Buladean, N.C. 110, 116-118, 120, 123-124
Burbank, Tenn. 110-111, 116
Burnsville, N.C. 135, 143
Buzzard Roost Ridge 181

C

Cades Cove 28, 223, 229-230, 233-234, 243-244
Cades Cove Road 243
Camel Gap 213, 219, 239
Camel Hump Knob 213, 219
Camp Creek Bald 26, 29, 37, 143, 153, 161-171
Campbell Hollow Road 88, 91
Canebrake Ridge 191
Carmen, N.C. 166, 169
Carolina Mountain Club 142, 144, 153, 183
Carter, Tenn. 61
Carter Gap 206
Carvers Gap 29, 41, 96, 98, 104, 109-111, 113-114
Cates Creek 196, 198
Catpen Gap 186, 190
Cedar Gap 81
Chapman Gap 214, 218
Charlies Bunion 207, 209-210, 215, 217
Chasteen Creek 239
Chasteen Trail 239
Cheoah Bald 207
Cherokee National Forest 38, 41-42, 47, 72, 109, 135, 153-154, 165, 170
Cherokee, Tenn. 208, 211-212, 223, 240
Cherry Creek Trail 194
Cherry Gap 122, 125, 132
Cherry Gap Shelter 116, 124-125, 132

Chestnut Bald 228, 234
Chestnut Branch Trail 212, 220, 238
Chestnut Log Gap 162, 166, 169
Chestoa, Tenn. 41, 123-124, 129,
    135, 141, 143
Chimneys 226, 237, 241
Chimneys Trail 241
Cliff Ridge 134-135, 137, 140
Cliff Top 240
Clinch Mountain 57
Clingmans Dome 201, 207, 216,
    222-223, 225-227, 231, 235-236,
    241
Cloudland 109-114
Clyde Smith Shelter 111, 116, 118,
    120, 124
Cold Spring Knob 228, 235
Cold Springs USFS Road 199
Coldspring Mountain 143, 153, 161,
    163, 165
Collins Gap 227, 236
Coon Den Falls 81, 83-84, 94
Copper Gap 214, 218
copperheads 8
Cosby, Tenn. 194, 212
Cosby Campground 212-213, 219-
    220, 238
Cosby Creek 213, 220
Cosby Knob 209, 211, 213, 220
Cosby Knob Shelter 220
Cosby Trail 220, 238
Cowee Valley 206
Crabtree Bald 195, 198
Crandull,Tenn. 44, 48, 50
Cross Mountain 26, 30, 43, 52, 54,
    57, 60, 67
Curley Maple Gap 122, 128, 130
Curley Maple Gap Shelter 124, 128,
    130, 135

D

Damascus, Va. 30, 37, 39, 41-47, 49,
    51-52
Davenport Gap 24-25, 37, 40, 153,
    192-193, 196-197, 209-212, 219-
    221, 226, 238
Davenport Gap Shelter 194, 197,
    212, 220
Davy Crockett Lake 153, 162
Deals Gap 202, 204, 223, 230-232,
    244
Deep Creek 241
Deep Creek Gap 241
Deep Creek Ranger Station 241
Deep Gap 122, 124, 126, 131, 176,
    181, 192, 196, 198-199
Deep Gap Creek 199
Deer Creek Gap 213, 219
Deer Park Mountain 185, 191
Deer Park Mountain Shelter 174,
    184-185, 191
deer ticks 19
Del Rio, Tenn. 183, 187, 193
Dennis Cove 70, 72, 74, 76, 81-83,
    94-95
Dennis Cove Road 68, 84
Denton Valley Road 47-48, 50
Derrick Knob 224
Derrick Knob Shelter 228, 235, 242
Devil Fork 158
Devil Fork Gap 25-26, 29, 37, 143,
    155-156, 161, 164, 171
Devils Creek 135, 138-140
Devils Creek Gap 134-135, 138-139
Devils Tater Patch 230, 233
Dick Creek 123
dislocation 14
Dixon Trail 167-168
Doe, Tenn. 61
Doe Knob 28, 38, 203, 207, 222, 230,
    233, 243
Doe River Valley 97, 101, 106
Doe Valley Road 61-62, 67

Doeville, Tenn. 63, 66
dogs 9, 39, 46, 53
Doll Flats 41, 88, 90, 96, 98, 101, 107
Double Spring Gap 48-49, 224, 227, 235-236, 242
Double Spring Gap Shelter 227, 235
Double Springs Road 52, 54-55
Double Springs Shelter 45, 54-55, 62
Dripping Springs Mountain 242
Dry Sluice Gap 215, 217, 240

E

Eagle Creek 229, 234
Eagle Creek Trail 229, 234, 243
Eagle Rocks 214, 218
Eagle Rocks Creek 214, 218
Ekaneetlee Branch 230, 244
Ekaneetlee Gap 230, 233
Elizabethton, Tenn. 34, 41, 44, 52, 57, 61-62, 70-71, 97
Elk Hollow Ridge 103, 105
Elk Park, N.C. 38, 41, 82-83, 97-99, 107
Elk River 88, 91
Elkmont 227-228, 235-236, 241-242
Elliott Hollow 63, 65-66
Engine Gap 103-104
English Mountain 213, 219
Enloe Creek Trail 239
Ephraim Place 127-128, 130
Ernestville, Tenn. 143, 155
Erwin, Tenn. 123-124, 127-128, 130, 135-136, 143-144, 155-156, 161, 163
exhaustion 14

F

Face Camp Branch 64-65
False Gap 215, 217-218
Feathercamp Ridge 44
Fighting Creek Gap 241
firearms x

fires 9
first aid 13
first-aid kit 22
Flag Pond 143, 148-149, 153, 155-156, 162
Flat Ridge 195, 199
Flattop Game Management Area 124
Flattop Mountain 134, 138-140
Flatwoods Road 58-59
Flint Creek 164, 170
Flint Gap 161, 164, 170
Flint Mill Gap 57-58
Flint Mountain 164
Flint Mountain Shelter 156, 162, 164, 170
Flint Rock 54-55, 57-59
Flint Spring Gap 234
Fodder Stack 215, 217
Fodderstack Mountain Trail 243
Fontana Dam 26, 28, 38, 40, 154, 202-204, 222- 224, 230-232, 243
Fontana Dam Shelter 232
Fontana Lake 223, 228-229, 231, 234-235, 241-243
Fontana Village, N.C. 203, 223-224
Forge Creek 244
Fork Ridge 241
Fork Ridge Trail 241
Forney Creek 241-242
Forney Ridge 222, 226-227, 236
Forney Ridge Trail 241
fractures 15
French Broad River 37, 40, 153, 172-175, 177-178, 182, 185, 191
frostbite 16
Frozen Knob 155, 158-159

G

Garenflo Gap 182-183, 185, 190-191
Gatlinburg, Tenn. 35, 38, 40, 194, 200, 202, 208, 210-212, 223-224, 240

getting lost 6
Glade Springs, Va. 44
Goshen Prong Trail 227, 236, 242
Gragg Gap 185, 191
Grandfather Mountain 86-87, 92-93, 101, 106
Granny Lewis Creek 137
Grassy Branch 240
Grassy Branch Trail 215, 217, 240
Grassy Fork 196, 198
Grassy Ridge 86, 88, 90, 96-99, 101-106, 118, 120
Gravel Knob 165, 170
Greasy Cove 34
Greasy Creek 118, 120
Greasy Creek Gap 115, 118, 120
Great Smoky Mountains National Park 200-202, 208, 210-211, 221-222, 238, 243
Green Ridge 161, 163
Green Ridge Knob 164-165, 171
Greenbrier Knob 228, 235
Greenbrier Pinnacle 210
Greenbrier Ridge Trail 228, 235, 242
Greeneville, Tenn. 161, 173-174
Greer Knob 231, 233
Greer Rock 144
Gregory Bald 31, 203, 233, 243-244
Gregory Bald Trail 233, 243
Gregory Ridge 244
Gregory Ridge Trail 244
Greystone 153, 162
Griffith Branch 71, 73, 79
Groundhog Creek Gap 195
Groundhog Creek Shelter 184, 194-195, 199
Gunna Creek 229, 234
Gunter Fork Trail 239
Guyot Spring 214, 219
Guyot Spur 214, 219

H

Hampton, Tenn. 68, 70-72, 74-76, 78, 81-82, 97
Hampton Creek 105, 109
Harmon Den 193, 199
Harmon Den Mountain 192, 199
heat cramps, exhaustion, stroke 17
heat weakness 18
Heaton Creek 103, 105
Hell Ridge 210, 213, 219-220
Hickey Fork Road 166, 169
Higgins Creek 143-144, 148-150
High Rock 157, 159
High Rocks 142, 145-146, 152, 227-228, 235, 242
High Top 240
Hogback Ridge Shelter 144, 156-157, 159, 162
Holston High Knob 42, 54-55, 57-58
Holston High Point 57
Holston Mountain 26, 30, 41-44, 46, 48-49, 52-55, 57-59, 69, 81
Holston River Valley 57
Horse Creek 101, 106
Horse Creek Campground 162, 165, 170
Horselog Ridge Trail 64-65
Horseridge Gap 74, 78
Hot Springs, N.C. 26, 29, 34, 36-37, 40, 153-154, 156, 161-162, 172-175, 177-178, 180, 182-185, 191
Hughes Gap 109-113, 115-117, 121
Hughes Ridge 214-215, 217-218
Hughes Ridge Trail 214-215, 218, 239
Hump Mountain 37, 92, 96, 99, 101-102, 105-107
Hungry Ridge Trail 244
Huntdale, N.C. 123-126, 131-132
Hurley Hollow 63, 66
Hurricane Gap 172-174, 176, 181
Hyatt Ridge 218
hypothermia 15

I

I-40 192-193, 195-199
I-81 44
Icewater Spring 211
Icewater Spring Shelter 215, 217
Inadu Knob 213, 219, 239
Indian Camp Creek 213
Indian Gap 36, 224-226, 236, 241
Indian Grave Gap 122-124, 127, 130
Iron Mountain 26, 30, 37, 39, 41-44,
    57, 60-61, 68-69, 73, 80-81, 110
Iron Mountain Gap 34, 40-41, 115-
    117, 119, 122-125, 127, 130, 133
Iron Mountain Shelter 61-63, 66
Iron Mountain Trail 61-62, 64-65, 67
Isaacs Cemetery 88, 90

J

Jacobs 45
Jacobs Creek Road 45
Jakes Creek 242
Jakes Gap 242
Jane Bald 26, 29, 86, 88, 90, 92, 96,
    103-104
Jefferson National Forest 42, 47, 50
Jenkins Knob 227, 235
Jenkins Ridge Trail 229, 234, 243
Jerry Cabin Shelter 162, 166, 169
John Taylor Hollow Gap 185, 191
Jonas Creek Trail 242
Jones Branch 88, 91, 122, 128-130
Jones Meadow 163, 166, 168-169
Josiah Trail 58-59
Jump-Off 210, 216-217, 240, 242
Jump-Up Ridge Trail 242

K

Kale Gap 182, 186, 190
Kan Lot 138-139
Kephart Prong 216, 240
Kephart Shelter 215-217, 240-241
Konnarock Crew 83, 96, 183
Koonford Bridge 76-77

L

Lamb Knob 185, 191
Laurel Creek 44
Laurel Creek Road 234
Laurel Falls 69, 75-77
Laurel Fork 41, 46, 69-72, 75-78, 82,
    86, 93, 95
Laurel Fork Gorge 26, 29, 36, 40, 68,
    72, 74, 78
Laurel Fork Shelter 71, 75, 77, 82
Laurel Gap Shelter 214, 218, 239
Laurel River 175
Laurel Top 215, 217-218
LeConte Lodge and Shelter 215-216
LeConte's High Top 240
Lemon Gap 153, 182-184, 187, 189,
    193-194
Lick Rock 155
lightning strikes 19
Little Abrams Gap 230, 233
Little Bald 142-143, 145-147, 151,
    229-230, 234
Little Bald Knob 41, 122-123, 125,
    132
Little Bottom Branch 185, 191
Little Bottom Branch Gap 185, 191
Little Deep Gap 58-59
Little Horse Creek 102, 106
Little Hump Mountain 86, 88, 90,
    92, 96, 102, 106
Little Laurel Shelter 162, 167-168,
    174

Little River Road 241
Little Rock Knob 41, 97, 102, 105, 115, 117, 119, 121
Little Shuckstack 231, 232
Little Tennessee River 24, 37-38, 154, 200, 203, 206, 222-223, 230-232, 243
Locust Knob 54-55, 230, 233
Locust Ridge Shelter 164
Long Hungry Ridge 244
Long Mountain 185, 191
Lost Cove 134
Lovers Leap 27, 172-174, 177, 179
Low Gap 43-45, 48-49, 52-53, 56-57, 103, 105, 122, 126, 132, 144, 148, 150, 213, 220, 238
Low Gap Branch 220, 239
Low Gap Campground 57
Lower Nidifer Branch 64-65
Luftee Knob 213, 219
Lyme disease 19

M

MacKaye, Benton 1, 36
Maddron Bald 213, 219
Maddron Bald Trail 213, 219, 239
Maple Springs Trail 47, 50
maps 200
Mars Hill 143
Marshall, N.C. 173, 183
Max Patch Mountain 25-26, 153, 182-183, 186-188, 190, 194, 207
Max Patch Road 182-183, 188, 192-195, 199
McCampbell Gap 230, 234
McCampbell Knob 230
McQueens Gap 44, 48, 50
McQueens Knob 45, 48, 49
Middle Prong Little River 228, 235, 243
Middle Spring Ridge 162, 165, 170
Mill Creek 81

Mill Ridge 172-173, 177, 179-180
Mine Flat 137, 140
Mineral Gap 229, 234
Miry Ridge 225, 227-228, 242
Miry Ridge Trail 228, 235, 242
Mollies Ridge 224
Mollies Ridge Shelter 230, 233
Morehead Gap Shelter 71
Moreland Gap 81, 83-84, 94
Moreland Gap Shelter 82, 84, 94, 98
Mountain City, Tenn. 44, 52, 61
Mt. Buckley 227, 236
Mt. Cammerer 208-210, 212-213, 220, 238
Mt. Cammerer Trail 212, 220, 238
Mt. Chapman 209-210, 214, 218
Mt. Collins 224-225, 227, 236, 241
Mt. Collins Shelter 226, 236
Mt. Craig 25
Mt. Davis 228, 235
Mt. Guyot 209-210, 213-214, 219
Mt. Kephart 209-210, 216-217, 225, 240
Mt. LeConte 36, 143, 210, 218, 226-227, 235-237, 240-241
Mt. Love 227, 236
Mt. Mingus 226, 237
Mt. Mitchell 25, 97, 142, 166, 169, 173, 182-183, 188
Mt. Rogers 101, 106, 110
Mt. Rogers National Recreation Area 42
Mt. Sequoyah 209, 214, 218
Mount Sterling 193-194, 198, 213, 219, 239
Mt. Sterling Gap 239
Mt. Sterling Gap Trail 239
Mud Gap 230, 233
Myrtle Point 240

N

N.C. 28 223, 231-232, 244
N.C. 208 156, 161, 172-173

N.C. 209 173, 178, 183, 185, 191
N.C. 212 155-156, 158, 161, 164, 171
N.C. 226 110, 115-116, 122-124
N.C. 261 96, 98, 109-110
N.C. 284 192-193, 196-197, 209-212,
    221, 239
N.C. 288 232
N.C. 1182 182-183, 187-189, 192-194,
    199
Nantahala National Forest 223, 231
Nantahala Outdoor Center 178-179
Nantahala River 205-207
Nantahala River Gorge 207
Newfound Gap 40, 208-209, 211-
    212, 216, 222-227, 233, 236-237,
    240-242
Newfound Mountains 192, 194-195,
    198
Newport, Tenn. 173, 183, 193-194,
    210-212
No Business Knob 41, 134-135, 137,
    139-140, 142, 146, 151
No Business Knob Shelter 124, 135,
    137, 140, 144
Noland Creek Valley 241
Nolichucky River 37, 41, 122-123,
    127-131, 134-137, 140
Nolichucky River Gorge 26
North Carolina Wildlife Manage-
    ment Area 198
North Toe River 97

O

Oconaluftee River 216
Oconaluftee Valley 241
Oglesby Branch 134, 138-139
Old Black 214, 219
Old Flint Mill Trail 58-59
Old Hayesville Road 167-168
Old Troublesome 214, 218
Overmountain Shelter 98, 102, 105
Overmountain Victory Trail 97

P

Paint Creek 162, 167-168
Paint Rock 173, 175
Painter Branch 194, 196, 198
Panther Creek Trail 242
parking 8
Parson Bald 203, 230, 244
Parson Bald Trail 244
Parson Branch Road 243
Pecks Corner 209, 211, 214, 217-218,
    239
Pecks Corner Shelter 214, 218
Perkins, Judge Arthur 2
pests 8
Peters Branch 64-65
Pigeon River 40, 153, 192-193, 196-
    197
Pigeon river 186, 190
Pigeon River Gorge 197
Pigeonroost, N.C. 125, 132
Pigeonroost Creek 125, 132
Piney Bald 122, 125, 132
Pinnacle Lead 214, 219
Pisgah National Forest 25, 37-38,
    42, 109, 135, 142, 144, 153-155,
    182, 192, 198
Pleasant Garden Recreation Area
    126, 131
Pond Mountain 26, 41, 68-69, 71-72,
    74, 76-77, 79
Poplar, N.C. 123, 126-127, 130-132
Poplar Creek 126, 131
Porters Creek 210, 240
Porters Gap 215, 217
Porters Mountain 209, 215, 217
Potato Top 70, 75-78
Pounding Mill Trail 167-168
Powell Knob 230, 233
Proctor Branch 244
publications 12
Pump Gap 172, 177, 179
Puncheon Fork Road 143, 148-149

R

Rainbow Falls 240
Rainbow Falls Trail 240
Rat Branch 76
Rat Branch Recreation Area 70, 73, 79
rattlesnakes 8
Red Ridge Gap 231, 233
Rice Gap 155-157, 159
Rich Gap 244
Rich Knob 52-55
Rich Mountain 26, 37, 153, 165, 170, 172-173, 176-177, 180-181
Richland Balsam 25
Richland Mountain Trail 215, 217, 240
Ripshin Ridge 115
Road Prong Trail 226, 236, 241
Roan High Bluff 109-110, 112-113, 118, 120
Roan High Knob 86, 88, 90, 92, 101-102, 105, 107, 109-110, 112-113
Roan High Knob Shelter 98, 111, 116
Roan Highlands Shelter 98, 103, 105, 111
Roan Mountain 25, 29, 36, 40-41, 57, 82-83, 96, 98-99, 102-103, 105, 109-111, 115-116, 119, 125, 127, 131-132
Roanoke, Va. 24-25
Roaring Fork 184, 189, 240
Roaring Fork Motor-Nature Trail 240
Roaring Fork Shelter 184, 187, 189, 194
Roaring Fork Valley 187, 189
Rock Creek Recreation Area 123-124, 127, 130
Rock Creek Road 123
Rocky Face Mountain 213, 220
Rocky Fork, Tenn. 143, 156, 161, 163-164, 170

Rocky Spur 240
Rocky Top 229, 234
Ross Knob 213, 220
Rough Creek Trail 241
Round Bald 86, 88, 90, 92, 96, 103-104
Round Bottom 239
Round Knob Campground Road 166, 169
Round Knob Spring 166, 169
Round Mountain 191
Roundtop Ridge 172
Roundtop Ridge Trail 180
Russell Field 224, 230, 233
Russell Field Shelter 230, 233
Rye Patch Branch 244

S

safety ix, x
Sams Gap 40-41, 142-145, 149, 153-157, 159, 228, 235
Sassafras Gap 231-232, 244
Saunders Shelter 45
Sawteeth Range 210, 217-218
Seng Ridge 167-168
Shady Gap 61
Shady Valley, Tenn. 41, 44-45, 52, 61-62
Shady Valley Road 54-55
Sheep Pen Gap 243
Shell Creek 86, 105, 110
shelters 201-202
Shelton Laurel Road 167-168
shock 15
Shook Branch Recreation Area 70, 73, 79
Shuckstack Mountain 222-223, 230-232, 244
Shuckstack Ridge 231-232
Shuckstack Trail 244
Shut In Creek 185
Siam Valley 61, 70

Silers Bald 201, 207, 222-224, 227-228, 235, 242
Silers Bald Shelter 228, 235
Silver Mine Trail 178-179
Silvermine Creek 172, 175, 179
Silvermine Creek Road 179
Silvermine Creek Valley 177
Skyway 226-227, 236-237
Slide Hollow 87, 92
Slipper Spur 147
Smokemont 239-240
Smokemont Campground 215, 217-218, 239
Smoky Mountains Hiking Club 144, 153, 200, 203
Snake Den Mountain 213, 219
Snake Den Mountain Trail 239
snake-venom poisoning 21
snakebites 20
Snowbird Mountain 153, 188, 192-198
South Holston Lake 45, 57-59
Spanish Oak Gap 58-59, 192, 196, 198
Spence Field 222, 224, 229, 234, 243
Spence Field Shelter 229, 234
Spivey Gap 34, 134-136, 138-139, 142-145, 152
sprains 15
Spring Creek 153, 178, 184
Spring Mountain 172, 176, 181
Spring Mountain Shelter 162, 174, 176, 181, 184
Springer Mountain 205-207
Spruce Pine 143
Squibb Creek Trail 165, 170
Standing Indian Mountain 206
Starkey Gap 229, 234
State Line Branch 153, 193-194, 196-197
State Line Trail 161
Steel Trap Creek 227, 236
Stony Creek 60
Stony Creek Valley 64-66

Straight Fork 239
Street Gap 142-143, 145, 148-149
Sugar Hollow 81-82, 87, 91
Sugar Tree Gap 228, 234
Sugarland 241
Sugarland Mountain Trail 241
Sugarloaf Gap 155, 158-159
Sugarloaf Knob 155, 158-159
sun stroke and sunburn 17-18
Sunup Knob 213, 220
Sweat Heifer Creek 240
Sweat Heifer Trail 216, 240
Swim Bald 207

T

Tanyard Gap 172-173, 175, 177, 180
Temple Hill 142, 146, 151
Temple Hill Gap 134, 137, 140
Temple Hill Knob 128, 140
Temple Ridge 134, 137, 140
Tenn. 32 192, 197, 209-210, 221
Tenn. 36 127, 130, 135
Tenn. 67 70
Tenn. 70 161-162, 167-168, 172-174, 176, 181
Tenn. 71 209, 222
Tenn. 73 239
Tenn. 91 44, 52, 54-55, 57-63, 65-67
Tenn. 107 110, 115-116, 122-123, 127, 130, 133, 174, 183, 187, 189, 193
Tenn. 133 43-44, 47-48, 50, 52
Tenn. 143 96, 98, 109-110, 116
Tenn. 352 143, 156, 158, 161
Tenn. 395 123-124, 127, 130
Tennessee Bluff 183, 186, 190
Tennessee Eastman Hiking Club 71
Tennessee-North Carolina state line 37, 50, 82, 96-98, 109-110, 116, 123, 135, 155-156, 161, 173, 183, 193
The Pond Flats 74, 78
The Register 3

Thomas Ridge 216
Thomas Ridge Trail 226, 237
Three Forks Wilderness Area 215, 217, 239
Thunderhead 201, 207, 222-223, 227-229, 231, 234
Tiger Creek 118, 120
Tobes Creek 192, 196-197
Toe River Valley 97, 127, 131
Trail Lands 4
Trailridge Mountain Camp 111, 116
Tremont Ranger Station 228, 235, 242-243
Tri-Corner Knob 209, 211, 214, 218-219, 239
Tri-Corner Knob Shelter 214, 218
Trillium Gap 240
Trillium Gap Trail 240
Tuckaleechee Cove 225
Tumbling Creek 144, 147, 151
Turkey Gap 192, 195, 198
Turkeypen Gap 63, 66
Twenty-mile Creek 244

U

U.S. 19 210, 223
U.S. 19E 25, 29, 36, 70, 81-84, 89, 96-99, 102, 105, 108, 135, 143
U.S. 19W 40, 122, 129, 134-135, 138-139, 141, 143-146, 152
U.S. 23 123, 135-136, 141-144, 148-149, 153, 155-157, 161
U.S. 25 172-174, 176-178, 180, 183, 185, 191, 193
U.S. 25W 156, 161
U.S. 58 43-44, 46, 51
U.S. 70 156, 161-162, 167, 172-174, 176-178, 180, 183, 185, 191, 193
U.S. 129 223, 231-232, 243-244
U.S. 321 40, 68-71, 73-79, 81-82
U.S. 421 43-45, 47-49, 52-53, 56, 59, 61

U.S. 441 211, 216, 223
Unaka 24-25, 46
Unaka Mountain 25, 41, 57, 81, 115, 119, 122-123, 126-127, 130-132, 140
Unaka mountain 34, 37
Unaka Springs 134, 136-137, 140-141
Unicoi, Tenn. 24, 29, 34, 41, 110, 116, 123, 126, 131
Upper Creek Trail 239
USFS 32 45
USFS 50 70, 76, 81, 83-84, 94-95
USFS 56 57-58
USFS 56A 57
USFS 69 44, 48, 50
USFS 132 127, 130
USFS 148 193
USFS 148A 193
USFS 230 123, 125-127, 130-132
USFS 467 174

V

Va. 91 44
Va. 716 43
Vandeventer Shelter 62, 64-65, 71
Vandeventer Trail 64-65

W

Walasi-yi Center 173
Walnut Bottoms, N.C. 213, 219-220, 239
Walnut Bottoms Trail 220
Walnut Mountain 76, 86, 92, 182-183, 186, 189-190
Walnut Mountain Road 81-82, 85-86, 92
Walnut Mountain Shelter 184, 186, 190

Watauga Dam 27, 29, 41, 61, 68, 70, 73, 80, 82
Watauga Dam Road 60, 61, 64-65, 70, 72-73, 80
Watauga Lake 41, 60, 64-65, 68, 70-72, 74, 76
Watauga Lake Shelter 62, 71, 73, 80
Watauga River 34
Watauga Valley 65
water ix, 6
Waterville, Tenn. 153, 192-194, 197, 211
Waterville School Road 192-193, 196-197
Wayah Bald 206
Waycaster Spring 75, 77
Welch Cove 203
Welch Ridge 227-228, 235, 242
Welch Ridge Trail 228, 235, 242
Wesser Bald 206
Whistling Gap 142, 144-146, 152
White Rock 210, 220, 238
White Rock Cliffs 166, 169

White Rocks Mountain 26, 41, 46, 71, 81-86, 88, 90, 92, 94, 98
Whiteoak Flats Trail 166-169
Whitetop Mountain 48-49
Wildcat Top 192, 195, 198
Wilder Mine 97
Wilder Mine Hollow 96-97, 99, 108
Wolf Laurel 147-148, 150
Wolf Laurel Road 150-151
Woolly Tops Lead 215, 217

Y

Yanu Ridge 242
Yellow Creek Gap 213, 219
Yellow Creek Mountain 38, 203
Yellow Creek Trail 213, 219, 239
Yellow Mountain 40, 88, 90, 92, 96, 105
Yellow Mountain Barn 98
Yellow Mountain Gap 96-98, 102, 105